"*Reckoning with History* traces the ways in which territ[ ] racial violence shaped American Christianity from[ ] Yoo's incisive exploration details how settler colonialism and slavery have distorted theological doctrines and ecclesial practices throughout the centuries. By centering the voices of Black, Indigenous, and dissenting Christians, this book challenges readers to confront the uncomfortable truths about how a colonial animus constrains the way contemporary Christians in the United States relate to the earth and to one other. Profound and timely, Yoo's narrative invites us to reckon with our colonial legacy so that, together, we might design a future that enables us to become the beloved community God desires."

—Ángel J. Gallardo, Assistant Professor of Church History,
Austin Presbyterian Theological Seminary

"Yoo offers an invaluable account of Christian hypocrisy during settlement and enslavement. He combines the professorial and the prophetic to challenge facile recollections of our common history. I pray this book inspires an honest assessment of what it means for the church to be a witness to God's reconciliation in Christ."

—Joseph Scrivner, Dean of Chapel, Stillman College

"*Reckoning with History* is a courageous book that outlines how majority sectors of the white church in the United States were deliberately invested in using Christianity to legitimize settler colonialism, war crimes, land theft, and slavery. Yoo issues an important call for Christians to honestly confront the dark legacy that underpins much of US history—and the church's complicity in it. Without forgetting the long history of resistance against the powerful forces that (de)formed US Christianity in the image of a colonial state, *Reckoning with History* challenges readers to embrace hard truths as an indispensable step toward fashioning a collective identity rooted in justice, humility, and love."

–João B. Chaves, Assistant Professor of the History of Religion
in the Américas, Baylor University, and author of
*The Global Mission of the Jim Crow South: Southern Baptist
Missionaries and the Shaping of Latin American Evangelicalism*

"Yoo's *Reckoning with History: Settler Colonialism, Slavery, and the Making of American Christianity* is a transformative exploration of the intertwined histories of faith, power, and oppression. With meticulous research and unflinching honesty, Yoo confronts the often-overlooked legacies of settler colonialism and slavery that have shaped American Christianity. His work challenges readers to move beyond sanitized narratives of religious history, offering instead a profound reckoning with the systems of exploitation and racial injustice that continue to influence Christian theology and practice today. What sets Yoo's scholarship apart is his ability to weave historical analysis with a call to action. He invites majority faith communities to grapple with the moral and ethical implications of their history, urging a collective commitment to repair, repentance, and reconciliation. His compelling prose and careful scholarship make this book an essential resource for theologians, clergy, and lay leaders seeking to understand the deeper roots of their faith traditions. *Reckoning with History* is not merely a book; it's a moral imperative. Yoo's work is a must-read for anyone committed to justice and truth."

–Damon P. Williams, Senior Pastor,
Providence Missionary Baptist Church, Atlanta

"At a time when too many American Christians believe too many smug and untruthful stories about their history and therefore call for Christian dominion, Yoo tells a truthful story and suggests that repentance might be more appropriate. He reveals the extent to which the white Christian churches have embodied some of the worst impulses in American history: They supported the settler colonialism that destroyed vast Indigenous cultures, and they defended or passively accepted two centuries of enslavement and a further century of racial subjugation. This is a powerful rejoinder to a triumphalist reading of Christian history. It should be read wherever Christians gather."

—E. Brooks Holifield, Charles Howard Candler Professor Emeritus
of American Church History, Emory University, and author of
Theology in America: Christian Thought from the Age of the Puritans to the Civil War

"In addition to providing much-needed pastoral guidance for the church's critical shift to the responsible repair of historic harms—and away from trendy and counterproductive institutional habits of privilege-shaming and guilt-mongering—*Reckoning with History* ultimately issues an invitation to practicing Christians in the United States to become the twenty-first century's extension of trans-ethnic decolonial cooperation among Christian people of the United States until this collective decolonial mission is complete.

I highly recommend Yoo's thoroughly researched and story-filled, clarifying and convicting, *Reckoning with History* for students of church history, social ethicists, and religious studies courses as well as faith formation ministries and church discussion groups."

—Jermaine Ross-Allam, Ministry Director,
Center for the Repair of Historic Harms,
Interim Unified Agency of the Presbyterian Church (U.S.A.)

Reckoning with History

Access free digital resources, which include a group study guide and companion session introduction videos from the author, at **www.wjkbooks.com/ReckoningWithHistory**.

Reckoning with History

*Settler Colonialism, Slavery, and the
Making of American Christianity*

WILLIAM YOO

WESTMINSTER
JOHN KNOX PRESS
LOUISVILLE · KENTUCKY

First edition
Published by Westminster John Knox Press
Louisville, Kentucky

25 26 27 28 29 30 31 32 33 34—10 9 8 7 6 5 4 3 2 1

Book design by Sharon Adams
Cover design by Mark Abrams

Library of Congress Cataloging-in-Publication Data

Names: Yoo, William, author.
Title: Reckoning with history : settler colonialism, slavery, and the
marking of American Christianity / William Yoo.
Description: First edition. | Louisville, Kentucky : Westminster John Knox
Press, [2025] | Includes bibliographical references and index.
Identifiers: LCCN 2024051354 (print) | LCCN 2024051355 (ebook) | ISBN
9780664265014 (paperback) | ISBN 9781646984145 (ebook)
Subjects: LCSH: United States--Church history. | Protestantism--United
States--History. | Settler colonialism--United States. | Settler
colonialism--Religious aspects--Protestant churches. | Slavery--United
States--History. | Slavery--Religious aspects--Protestant churches. |
Racism--Religious aspects--Protestant churches. | United States--Race
relations--History.
Classification: LCC BR515 .Y66 2025 (print) | LCC BR515 (ebook) | DDC
277.3--dc23/eng/20241213
LC record available at https://lccn.loc.gov/2024051354
LC ebook record available at https://lccn.loc.gov/2024051355

Most Westminster John Knox Press books are available at special quantity discounts when purchased in bulk by corporations, organizations, and special-interest groups. For more information, please e-mail SpecialSales@wjkbooks.com.

For my mother, Sook-ja Yoo,
my father, Kon-soo Yoo,
my mother-in-law, Jung-ja Choi,
and in memory of my father-in-law,
Bok-kyu Choi

Contents

Reckoning

List of Images

Chapter One

The Church with the Soul of a Nation

In 1849, Ebenezer Davies published an account of his recent travel in the United States. Davies was a British pastor in Guyana. His father-in-law, John Wray, founded Mission Chapel as a pastor with the London Missionary Society several years after his arrival in Guyana in 1808. Mission Chapel was the first church in Guyana to welcome enslaved persons, and the initial building was constructed in 1819. It was enlarged three years later to accommodate the growing number of worshipers, but it was destroyed by arson in 1823. A second building was completed in 1825. During Davies's ministry, Mission Chapel began plans in 1841 to erect a third building because of the continuing increase in church attendance.

Davies also rejoiced in the abolition of British slavery in the Caribbean and South America. In Guyana, only enslaved children under six years of age were initially declared free after the Slavery Abolition Act of 1833 took effect on August 1, 1834. Four years later, all enslaved persons in Guyana were emancipated. Davies surmised that his experience as the pastor "of a large congregation, of whom a great number were but a few years ago held in cruel bondage," would grant him "keener eyes and feelings more acute" toward slavery in the United States.[1]

Davies arrived by ship to New Orleans eager to attend worship services there, because he was "curious to know how people did really pray and preach, with slavery and slave-trading in their vilest forms around them."[2] Davies visited a myriad of congregations belonging to different Protestant denominations across the country, beginning in Louisiana and ending in New York. But the churches he frequented most were Baptist, Methodist, and Presbyterian. This fact about Davies's trip was not surprising. Baptists, Methodists, and Presbyterians were the three largest Protestant traditions in

1

the United States. In 1820, Baptists and Methodists each reported roughly 2,700 churches, and Presbyterians counted 1,700 churches. The only other tradition with over 1,000 churches was the Congregationalists (1,100), and the fifth and sixth largest traditions were Lutherans (800 churches) and Episcopalians (600 churches).[3] *The American Almanac* for 1850 compiled various denominational records and estimates to determine the following numbers: 1,230,069 Methodists, 952,693 Baptists, 435,377 Presbyterians, 227,196 Congregationalists, 163,000 Lutherans, and 67,550 Episcopalians.[4] In 1850, Methodists, Baptists, and Presbyterians accounted for 94 percent of all the churches within the eleven Southern states that would form the Confederacy eleven years later.[5]

Several components of American churches startled Davies. The first surprise occurred when Davies looked down at the floors of the sanctuaries he visited. As he approached First Presbyterian Church in New Orleans, Davies marveled at its architecture: "It is a beautiful building: seldom, if ever, had I seen a place of worship the exterior of which I liked so much." But once he stepped inside, he found the floor revolting because it was "stained all over with tobacco juice." Davies understood that spitting tobacco was a common practice in the United States, even among elite men from the upper class, but he was surprised that the "nasty habit" occurred during worship. Another British traveler, Frances Trollope, despised the ubiquity of chewing and spitting tobacco in public, and she also complained of this "most vile and universal habit" when observing it at a theatre in Washington, DC.[6]

The next surprise to Davies was more revolting than the tobacco spittle on the church floor. As worshipers entered the sanctuary, Davies saw all the Black people take their seats in the same section of the gallery. He watched for several minutes until "ultimately there were from forty to fifty of the sable race in that part of the gallery" and recounted, "Not one white was to be seen among the blacks, nor one black among the whites. There, then, was the 'Negro Pew!' It was the first time even my West Indian eyes ever beheld a distinction of colour maintained in the house of God!" When a white lay leader offered a prayer beseeching God to empower the congregation with "every grace and Christian virtue" and uphold their nation with "the great blessings of civil and religious liberty," Davies questioned how this worshiper reconciled the words he spoke aloud with the horrific sins of Black enslavement in his city and the terrors of racial oppression against people of color throughout his country.[7]

Davies visited a Baptist church in New Orleans the following Sunday and conversed with its pastor after worship. Davies explained how some English Baptist missionaries had advocated for abolition in the Caribbean and Guyana.

The pastor responded, "Slavery is a political institution. As a Christian minister, I have nothing to do with politics. My business is to preach the gospel, and try to save men's souls." And the pastor continued with a vigorous defense of enslavers and shared that he had no desire to fellowship with "uncharitable" Christians who questioned the faith of people in his church on account of their participation in slavery. Davies's frustration with the pastor intensified, especially as the day prior he had witnessed a slave auction, in which a multiracial woman named Elizabeth, "about eighteen years of age, evidently the daughter of a white man," was sold for $810, and he left the conversation with a better understanding of why some abolitionists called American churches "the bulwark of slavery."[8]

Several weeks later, Davies was invited to preach at Second Presbyterian Church in Cincinnati, Ohio. Davies selected the hymn "O'er the Gloomy Hills of Darkness" to precede his sermon. The Welsh Methodist William Williams of Pantycelyn composed the hymn, among the most well-known of his nearly 1,000 Welsh and English hymns. Many of Williams's English hymns were written at the request of Selina Hastings, countess of Huntingdon. Lady Huntingdon was a significant patron of Methodism in the United Kingdom. In addition to supporting Williams, she aided the ministries of Howel Harris, Charles Wesley, and George Whitefield. Lady Huntingdon's patronage was not limited to Methodism or Europe. She also invested in ministries among Indigenous and enslaved Black persons in North America. She met Samson Occom, a Mohegan pastor and the first ordained Indigenous Presbyterian minister in North America, when he visited England from 1766 to 1768, and thereafter financially supported his ministry. She was involved in the publication of Ukawsaw Gronniosaw's autobiography in 1772, the first such narrative from a formerly enslaved African printed in England, and she also helped make possible the publication of Phillis Wheatley's volume of poetry in Boston one year later, the first publication from an African American woman. Both Gronniosaw and Wheatley dedicated their works to Lady Huntingdon. Williams's hymn "O'er the Gloomy Hills of Darkness" includes a verse reflecting the missionary endeavors in North America that Lady Huntingdon and Williams himself championed:

> "Let the Indian, let the Negro,
> Let the rude Barbarian see
> That divine and glorious Conquest
> Once obtain'd on Calvary.
> Let the Gospel, &c.,
> Word resound from Pole to Pole."[9]

When the London Missionary Society, which included in its ranks Davies and his father-in-law, held its inaugural meeting in 1795, all who gathered at Lady Huntingdon's Spa Fields Chapel in London sang "O'er the Gloomy Hills of Darkness" as the opening hymn.[10] Therefore, it is not surprising that Davies chose this hymn for his first sermon in an American church.

But Davies was astonished and aggrieved when the congregation in Cincinnati arrived at the second verse. The words "Let the Indian, let the Negro" did not appear and instead were replaced with "Let the dark benighted pagan." Davies was furious that "the Indian" and "the Negro" had "vanished" and "a wretched alteration" appeared in their place. Davies immediately believed the change was "suspicious in design" and later learned that the revision existed in hymnals throughout the United States, except in those hymnals used in congregations of Welsh descent. Davies surmised, "Slaveholders, and the abettors of that horrid system which makes it a crime to teach a negro to read the Word of God, felt perhaps that they could not devoutly and consistently sing, 'Let the Indian, let the Negro.'"[11]

Settler Colonialism, Slavery, and the Making of American Christianity

This book confronts the histories of settler colonialism and slavery and illumines how these two devastating realities informed and ultimately deformed Protestant Christianity in the North American colonies and antebellum United States. Many years have passed since Ebenezer Davies decried the omissions of "the Indian" and "the Negro" in the white American rendition of a beloved Welsh hymn. Whereas Davies and others in the past spoke directly of "slavery," they did not address "settler colonialism" with this specific term. The concept of settler colonialism emerged in the 1960s as scholars engaged the histories of foreign intrusion in other territories and the processes by which these foreign groups exploited the resources of Indigenous populations and exerted political domination over them. Settler colonialism is one form of colonialism that emphasizes the seizure of Indigenous lands and displacement of Indigenous peoples by foreign settlers for the purposes of constructing their own ethnic, national, and religious societies.

I contend that settler colonialism and slavery shaped American Christianity in deep, haunting, distinctive, and enduring ways. Just as any trustworthy treatment of US history must grapple with the ideals, advances, compromises, and contradictions of democracy and freedom, the same holds true for understanding American Christianity. Yet I find that too many Christians in the United States today have incomplete, incoherent, and insufficient understandings of the history of settler colonialism, slavery, and American Christianity. Settler colonialism and slavery were among the greatest forces that have shaped American Christianity. I include in this book inspiring accounts of different Indigenous, Black, and white Christians who actively protested these racial oppressions.

But the larger story that unfolds in the pages of this book is the failure of white American Christianity. White Christians perpetrated horrible crimes against Indigenous and Black peoples. They justified their sins of land theft, enslavement, coercion, and violence with a vicious torrent of biblical texts and scriptural interpretations. They also remade American Christianity into a religion that bolstered their economic, political, and social interests. The reshaping of American Christianity did not happen all at once, but it occurred through a cumulative process of compromise, deception, defense, and conviction. White Christians crafted religious arguments to address the evolving circumstances of settler colonialism and slavery. The invention of racist theologies was often initially met with opposition from some Christians who questioned the morality and rationality of displacing Indigenous peoples and enslaving persons of African descent. But over time, the desire to accumulate more property and wealth quenched the qualms about forming a racially unjust nation, which were experienced by fewer and fewer white Christians. Racist theologies were vigorously defended and rigorously refined, and ultimately became normative convictions for white Christians in many churches.

Indigenous, Black, and concerned white Christians therefore reckoned with the deforming of American Christianity and constructed prophetic theologies of freedom, justice, and resistance. In doing so, they devoted their hearts, minds, and bodies to grasping the problems of racial oppression and worked toward reforms to solve these problems. In 1846, James McCune Smith, the first African American to earn a medical degree (from the University of Glasgow in Scotland) wrote his dear friend, Gerrit Smith, a white Presbyterian abolitionist. McCune Smith divulged his weariness even as he pressed on for Black liberation: "At times I am so weaned from hope, that I could lay me down and die, with the prayer, that the very memory of this existence should be blotted from my soul." The Black physician prayed to God "for renewed faith and hope and encouragement," but he also confessed that the obstacles to justice were deep and wide. White racism against people of color was rampant, so much so that "the heart of the whites must be changed, thoroughly, entirely, permanently changed." But McCune Smith did not prescribe antiracism as the sole remedy. Structural changes in education, employment, and housing were also necessary for racial equality in the United States.[12]

Gerrit Smith also wrestled with the perverse and pervasive ways that racial injustice infiltrated and influenced white Christianity. In 1858, Smith stated, "The Bible is really the best book in the world: though the present uses of it make it practically the worst."[13] He had previously argued in 1837 that the complicity and complacency of white Christians toward slavery illustrated that the defining feature of their faith was the "doctrine of expediency."[14] The white abolitionist was further dismayed when witnessing the rise, not the decline, of proslavery Christian doctrines and teachings over the previous two decades. White proslavery Christians had "misapprehended, misinterpreted, and perverted" the Bible such that "no other book—nay no number of books—does so much to darken the mind and shrivel the soul."[15]

Smith assessed the great revival movement sweeping across the nation—referring to what some of his contemporaries called the "Businessmen's Revival," because it had emerged from New York City's lower Manhattan in 1857—according to the following rubric: "There is a widespread revival of religion in our country. Of what religion time alone can surely tell. It is not Christianity, if it shall allow the rich to stand aloof from the poor, and the people of one complexion to refuse to associate with the people of another. It is not Christianity, if it is like the current religion."[16] The "very first lesson in the school of Christ" is to love one's neighbor, "rich or poor, white, red, or black," but one of the many devastating results of settler colonialism and slavery was the white Christian failure to enact this fundamental principle in the United States from the nation's founding to the Civil War.[17]

Roughly fifteen years before Ebenezer Davies's account, another English visitor also observed how white Americans had developed an antipathy toward talking and thinking about the obvious injustices against Indigenous and Black persons in their country. In 1834, Harriet Martineau began her travel throughout the United States. She had gained acclaim from her writings about economics in England and published in 1837 an account of her insights and observations from two years in the United States. Martineau emerged as one of the most prominent English intellectuals in the nineteenth century and is recognized today as the first woman sociologist.

Martineau participated in several public events in Massachusetts in which white residents honored the "Pilgrim Fathers" and celebrated how these ancestors colonized Indigenous territory that now formed their predominantly white commonwealth. In the town of Plymouth, Martineau attended the annual "Forefathers' Day" festival commemorating the initial arrival of the English ship *Mayflower* on Wampanoag land in 1620. As she approached Pilgrim Hall Museum, which was at this point in its tenth year of existence, the historical portrait that awaited visitors staggered Martineau: "Samosat, the Indian chief, is advancing, with English words of greeting, —'Welcome, Englishmen!' Elder Brewster, and the other fathers, with their apprehensive wives and wondering children, form an excellent group; and the *Mayflower* is seen moored in the distance."

The English sociologist found it curious that white Americans did not allow for even a moment to grapple with a history that resulted in the oppression of the very Indigenous nations and tribes that once inhabited all the lands across their nation. Instead, white Americans reveled in the revisionist histories they chose to tell themselves: "I felt as if in a dream, the whole time that I was wandering about with the rejoicing people, among the traces of the heroic men and women who came over into the perilous wilderness, in search of freedom and worship."[18]

Martineau had earlier witnessed a monument in the town of Deerfield marking the English military victory over a coalition of Indigenous tribes under the command of the Wampanoag sachem (chief) Metacom during a conflict known as King Philip's War (King Philip was the name that English colonists employed for Metacom) from 1675 to 1676. She regarded the rationale for this site as "far-fetched and dubious" because it marked the vicious and violent excesses of settler colonialism. Martineau interpreted "the story of King Philip" as "one of the most melancholy in the records of humanity" because the Indigenous leader rightly regarded his adversaries as "robbers" seeking to steal the lands and destroy the livelihoods of his people. She reflected, "Then occurs the question about the Indians,—'where are they?' and the answer leaves one less sympathy than one would wish to have with the present security of the settler."[19]

The orations delivered at civic gatherings such as Forefathers' Day also left Martineau "disgusted." The speakers, who were often local politicians, did not inspire their listeners toward responsible civic participation, especially in relation to Indigenous peoples, but instead spoke tawdry tales of half-truths and downright falsehoods. The first problem Martineau identified was speechmaking that fell prey to "the prostitution of moral sentiment" and "the clap-trap of praise and pathos." Yet the second ailment was no worse than the first: a misestimation of the American people. Martineau contended that the orators treated their listeners with even less regard than parents hold for their youngest children, because they perpetuated the notion that most white Americans could not engage complex ideas about their history, society, and nation.[20]

It was hard for white American Christians to ignore the sins of settler colonialism and slavery throughout the first several decades of the United States. In *The Indian World of George Washington: The First President, the First Americans, and the Birth of the Nation*, Colin G. Calloway rightly maintains that it is impossible to make sense of US history without understanding Indigenous peoples, persons of African descent, and the newly constituted federal government's grappling with them. In his first term as president, Washington met and dined with representatives from the Cherokee, Chickasaw, Muscogee (Creek), Mohawk, Oneida, and Seneca nations. Washington and other government officials invested significant effort and ink to conduct diplomatic relations with Indigenous leaders. Calloway therefore criticizes the glaring absence of Indigenous peoples in how Americans have remembered the past and assesses historical treatments of African Americans as lacking in depth. The historian contends, "From cradle to grave Washington inhabited a world built on the labor of African people and on the land of dispossessed Indian people."[21] The nation's first president interacted with enslaved Africans more frequently than with Indigenous peoples in his daily life, but the latter were always on Washington's mind, especially because Indigenous lands were central to his vision for the young nation's future. In subsequent years, settler colonialism and slavery would come to dominate civic discourse, as debates raged about the Missouri Compromise of 1820, the Indian Removal Act of 1830, and the Fugitive Slave Act of 1850, and Americans everywhere discussed the ramifications of several US Supreme Court decisions, such as what *Worcester v. Georgia* in 1832 signified for Cherokee sovereignty and what *Dred Scott v. Sandford* in 1857 meant for African American citizenship.

Like Davies, Martineau also criticized white Protestant clergy in the United States for their silence on slavery and racial injustice. Martineau too observed that "the Indian" and "the Negro" were nowhere to be found in congregational worship. She often encountered the boast that Protestant Christianity was flourishing in the United States, and that the reason for this growth was the "Voluntary Principle."[22] Unlike in her home country of England, there were no state-sponsored churches in the United States. Religious organizations were therefore voluntary associations, which meant they were responsible for financing their buildings and compensating their leaders without direct government assistance. One of the earliest church historians in the United States, the Swiss born and German American immigrant Philip Schaff, explained in Berlin to a German audience in 1854: "Another peculiarity in the ecclesiastical condition of North America, connected with the Protestant origin and character of the country, is the separation of church and state. . . . The church, indeed, everywhere enjoys the protection of the laws for its property, and the exercise of its functions; but it manages its own affairs independently, and has also to depend for its resources entirely on voluntary contributions."[23]

The voluntarism of American religious life astonished many European visitors, because it was wholly different from their contexts and cultures. Some could not fathom that churches were economically self-sufficient from the tithes and offerings of worshipers. Others doubted that educated men from the middle and upper classes of American society would seek to be clergy without the assurance of a decent salary apportioned through government funds. Martineau agreed that the voluntary principle was proving successful, with evidence of churches everywhere and ostensibly competent clergy in many of them. But one limitation was hesitant preaching, which strove to avoid making parishioners uncomfortable. White pastors were keenly aware of racial oppression, and they were attuned to the discourse among their congregants over the forced deportation of various Indigenous peoples and the westward expansion of slavery, but they refrained from preaching about the most pressing moral issues of their day, because they did not want to offend worshipers.

One component of American Protestantism that Martineau found admirable was that clergy were generally restrained in their pursuit of material gain. In her English context, Martineau observed that one of the abuses of established Christianity (meaning a state-sponsored Church of England) was that some ministers chased after "worldly pomp and state" in prestigious appointments with luxurious parsonages. It was therefore refreshing for Martineau to witness that "the clergy in America are not, as a body, seekers of wealth," which she attributed in large part to the reality that exorbitant salaries were available to only a few.

But Martineau also identified a significant weakness in American churches: Because clergy compensation took the form of "small salaries and large presents," it was difficult for pastors to preach freely and fully from their consciences and convictions: "The American clergy being absolved from the common clerical vices of ambition and cupidity, it remains to be seen whether they are free also from that of the idolatry of opinion."[24] As she considered the reluctance of most white clergy to publicly support the abolitionist movement and preach against slavery, Martineau understood that monetary greed was not the impetus behind this resounding silence. Rather, the scarcity of bold preaching was due to a desire to maintain one's modest livelihood working as a pastor. Yet Martineau did not absolve these pastors for their moral failings. She asserted that they were "the most backward and timid class in the society in which they live," because too many clergy compromised their holy vocations when refusing to raise "what may be disturbing questions before their people."[25] She connected this indictment with her larger criticism of white America: Whether in congregations, civic gatherings, or everyday conversations, there existed a troubling aversion, which sometimes evolved into an implacable hostility, toward addressing the pervasive sins of settler colonialism and slavery.

Reversing Sidney Mead's "The Nation with the Soul of a Church"

In 1975, Sidney E. Mead published a collection of essays in a book entitled *The Nation with the Soul of a Church*. Mead, a leading church historian who taught at several schools, including the University of Chicago Divinity School, Claremont Graduate School, and the University of Iowa, served as president of the American Society of Church History in 1953. Throughout Mead's career, he studied the interrelated dynamics of culture, politics, and religion in American history. Mead desired to know, "What is the religion of the American culture?" He affirmed the psychoanalyst Erik Erikson's observation that "self-identity is found in a sense of solidarity with the ideas and ideals of a historical community" and the theologian Paul Tillich's delineation of religion as an "ultimate concern" providing "the substance of culture" such that "culture is the totality of forms in which the basic concern of religion expresses itself."[26]

Mead therefore identified two distinct yet concurrent movements in US history. The first entailed how voluntarism fostered pluralism within Christianity and the rise of a wide variety of congregations and denominations in the absence of one dominant state-sponsored church. But Mead explained that there was nonetheless a broader and deeper American religion that developed alongside this panoply of many different churches, which he called "the religion of the Republic." In 1967, Robert N. Bellah advanced the notion of a powerful "civil religion in America" expressed "in a set of beliefs, symbols, and rituals" based on interpretations of this nation's founding.[27] Presidential inaugurations and Independence Day celebrations are liturgical acts honoring the ideals of democracy and liberty pronounced in the revered texts of the Constitution and Declaration of Independence. Mead's "religion of the Republic" likewise operated within and beyond Christianity.

At its best, national ideals inspired the American public toward a greater acceptance of cultural diversity and a more resilient solidarity of ultimate concern. In the case of American Christians, they were simultaneously "Christians and loyal citizens of the commonwealth in which they live; . . . the theology of their denomination is different from the theology that legitimates the constitutional and legal structure of their country."[28] Mead explained that American Christians adhered to both theologies and constantly engaged them as people who lived in two worlds—the world of their faith community and the world of their civic community—at the same time.

Mead borrowed the identifying marker of the United States as a "nation with the soul of a church" from the English philosopher G. K. Chesterton. Mead emphasized Chesterton's theological analogy between the United States and Christianity. Just as Jesus Christ was the incarnate Son of God, the United States was "actually incarnating" the principle of equality in the flesh of a nation. Chesterton heralded the United States as a unique nation because it was "conceived in liberty" and "dedicated to the proposition that all men are created equal" in its continuing commitment to a democratic government.[29] Mead contended that a nation could be understood through an examination of the animating memories and unifying aspirations within its people. Here Mead linked the democratic polity of the United States with the Protestant doctrine of the priesthood of all believers. The American uprising against the British monarchy and the early modern European Protestant departure from Roman Catholicism shared the conviction that the power to govern—colonies in the former and churches in the latter—belonged with the people in a representative democracy.[30]

Mead's interpretation of the United States as a nation with the soul of a church was multilayered. In addition to the common thread of representative democracy across national and Protestant church governances, Mead observed how Americans treated their country as if it was their church, measuring their identities by their nation's founding ideals and anchoring their hopes in professions of American exceptionalism. Mead noted that the absence of a state-sponsored religious tradition meant two things: the growth of many denominations in a pluralistic society in which no religious group could claim sole authority as "the church," and the nation functioning as "the church" in providing ultimate symbols, such as the flag, and essential principles, such as equality, for people to cherish, discuss, disagree about, and revere.

Mead traced a clear theological merging of Protestant Christianity with American exceptionalism and highlighted as an example of this phenomenon Lyman Beecher's sermon at the Forefathers' Day celebration in Plymouth in 1827, when the prominent white pastor preached, "Indeed, if it had been the design of heaven to establish a powerful nation, in the full enjoyment of civil and religious liberty, where all the energies of man might find scope and excitement, on purpose to show the world by experiment, of what man is capable . . . where could such an experiment have been made but in this country[?]"[31] Beecher was one of many American Christians who ascribed sacrality to their nation as divinely ordained to accomplish holy purposes. Harriet Martineau participated in this same civic holiday several years later, and one wonders what the English sociologist would have thought of Beecher's patriotic sermon, with its omission of Indigenous peoples and ongoing injustices of settler colonialism, if she was in attendance, and whether Beecher's address belonged among the treacly public orations that Martineau trenchantly criticized throughout her American journey.

Several European visitors commented on a nationalism among the American people that readily functioned as a civil religion. The French political theorist Alexis de Tocqueville remarked in 1835 on how patriotism in the United States was "a kind of devotion" that was augmented by ritual observances, ranging from national ceremonies to local elections, and enacted with unrivaled fervor. Like some religious adherents, many Americans held nationalist loyalties that Tocqueville surmised amounted to "a kind of religion": "It does not reason, but it acts from the impulse of faith and sentiment."[32] Tocqueville's colleague and traveling companion in the United States, Gustave de Beaumont, captured the intensity of American exceptionalism in a fictional novel, *Marie, or Slavery in the United States*, based on his visit. Beaumont recalled his interactions with a white Presbyterian pastor: "I heard him reiterate every day that General [Andrew] Jackson was the greatest man of the century, New York the most beautiful city in the world, the Capitol the most magnificent palace in the universe, the Americans the finest people on earth."[33]

In 1856, the English Wesleyan Methodist minister Frederick J. Jobson visited the United States and wrote one year later of his astonishment at how Americans regarded their first president. Jobson also described American patriotism with religious idioms: "The veneration for Washington in the States is unbounded. He is undoubtedly the national idol; his name, acts, and sayings still govern the Americans; and perhaps of all hero-worship among nations, there is none existing which is more signal or manifest than that of Washington among this people."[34] No contemporary politician was regarded as Washington, but Jobson considered it strange that every politician was interpreted in morally absolute and almost apocalyptic terms as belonging to either "the band of spotless patriots or the lowest class of scoundrels." One consequence of such extreme attributions was that many Americans seemed to Jobson "incapable of forming any moderate judgment of their public men," which resulted in a dearth of reasonable discussion on political issues.[35]

Like Davies and Martineau, these three European travelers also found that the perverse ubiquity of settler colonialism and slavery, which entailed white Americans perpetrating alarming and atrocious injustices against Indigenous and Black persons, illustrated the existence of obvious contradictions to the oft-celebrated ideals of American egalitarianism and liberty. But if the United States was a nation with the soul of a church, it was of the kind of church that did not acknowledge sin, confront wrongdoing, or practice repentance. Indigenous and Black persons were not just missing from the hymn that Davies chose for a worship service or the civic festivals that Martineau attended. The white Americans who conversed with Tocqueville, Beaumont, and Jobson refused to engage their questions about "the Indian" and "the Negro."

In what was likely an autobiographical description of what it was like talking to white Americans, Tocqueville explained: "A stranger may be well inclined to praise many of the institutions of their country, but he begs permission to blame some things in it, a permission that is inexorably refused." Tocqueville depicted this obstinate resistance among white Americans to discuss social injustices within their nation as an "irritable patriotism."[36] But to avoid the realities of settler colonialism and slavery in dialogues and hymns did not make them disappear.

Tocqueville lamented the enslavement of millions of Black persons and the displacement of myriad Indigenous nations. Although Protestantism was indeed institutionally flourishing, with several denominations experiencing increases in the numbers of their churches, colleges, seminaries, and missionary associations, Tocqueville maintained that some white American Christians failed to enact core principles of both their faith and their nation. The gospel of Christianity "declared that all men are equal in the sight of God" and the promise of democracy was that "all citizens are equal in the eye of the law." Yet Tocqueville stumbled upon obvious inconsistencies and outright immoralities. As he traversed "vast tracts of country formerly inhabited by powerful Indian nations who are now extinct" and witnessed the forced deportation of Choctaws from their homeland in Tennessee, Tocqueville felt deep pangs of remorse and believed "every European can perceive means that would rescue these unfortunate beings from the destruction otherwise inevitable."

As the abolitionist movement was making strides in the 1830s, it appeared to Tocqueville that white Christians were "the enemies of liberty" in their defense of slavery and resistance to Black liberation. Abolitionists therefore attacked white churches because "the high-minded and the noble advocate bondage."[37] Beaumont also highlighted the prevalence of racial prejudice among white Americans: "Never, since I had been in America, had I seen a white person take pity on a Negro; I had heard it constantly said that colored people were not worthy of commiseration, deserving nothing but contempt."[38] Jobson supported the various initiatives of white American Methodist missionaries among Indigenous peoples, but he could not ignore the greater sins of systematic Indigenous oppression at the hands of rapacious white settlers and the US government itself. Jobson stated, "But the cupidity of the American Government dispossessed them of the lands which, in mockery, had been 'guaranteed to them and to their children forever,' and drove them from their settled homes in the heart of the country to the uncultivated and uninhabited parts beyond the Mississippi."[39] Jobson was concerned for Indigenous peoples in the new territories allocated to them because he doubted the US government would secure their well-being when scores of white settlers eventually migrated westward. Although some white missionaries were steadfastly doing good, their ministries alone were not the remedy to address the ramifications of prior land dispossession and enduring anti-Indigenous discrimination, policy, and violence.[40]

Jobson recounted the terrible racial injustices he witnessed as demonstrations of evil unlike anything he had encountered in his life. On a train passing through Maryland and Virginia, Jobson saw enslaved Black persons sorrowfully laboring in fields with dejected countenances. In Baltimore, he preached at Sharp Street Church, the first African American Methodist congregation in the city, his first experience worshiping with a multitude of free and enslaved Black people. The few white persons in worship were other pastors who were also passing through the city en route to the Methodist Episcopal Church General Conference in Indianapolis. Jobson wryly opined, "Whites of the churches in America do not mingle and worship with the blacks, even when visited by an English minister, whom, perhaps, they flock in crowds to hear when he preaches in a church not set apart for the African race."[41]

As the service progressed, Jobson felt the power of the gospel expressed in prayer and song, and preached without restraint "from an overflowing heart" on the promises of liberty unleashed in Christ's anointing to proclaim good news to the poor. Jobson described what was happening as he spoke: "The whole mass of dark worshippers bowed and waved to and fro like a field of ripe corn before the wind; and, at length, clearing spaces around them, some of them leaped up from the ground and swung themselves round, literally 'dancing before the Lord.'"[42]

Yet Jobson later juxtaposed the awe-inspiring faith he felt at Sharp Street Church with the strong grip of proslavery theology in white American churches and the scourge of anti-Black racism across the nation. It was simultaneously inconceivable and evident to Jobson that so many white American Christians beheld God's justice and nonetheless either supported slavery or remained complicit in their inaction for Black liberation. Jobson sadly concluded that white American Christians exhibited unsurpassed "energy, expertness, and tact" in their economic development—they knew how to start a profitable business and build a large church—but their vile participation in slavery and vicious racial prejudices made them a people who were "disgracefully criminal" and "grossly inconsistent" as citizens of their country and followers of Christ.[43]

Mead's notion of the United States as a nation with the soul of a church is therefore disputable. Beaumont was just as critical as Jobson. One of Beaumont's milder judgments was that white American Christians held two contradictory passions: they loved money, and they loved God. For some clergy, their talk about banking systems and tariff laws was as serious as their religious meditations and sermons. Beaumont maintained, "I found this contrast all over the United States: these two opposed principles clash incessantly in American society; the one, a source of honesty, the other, of bad faith."[44]

Yet the bad faith of white American Christians in their cruel oppression of Indigenous and Black persons led Beaumont to more incisive opprobrium. The hypocrisy of white American Christians infuriated him. Mead portrayed white American Christians as simultaneously existing in two worlds. One was their specific community of faith. The other was a common larger society undergirded by the principles of democracy and freedom. Beaumont believed the ongoing injustices of settler colonialism and slavery corrupted both worlds. He acknowledged that unequal laws and arbitrary customs were found in a plethora of nations and societies across human history, but Beaumont simply judged the United States according to the claims and creeds of its people and found it a reprehensible republic that ruthlessly oppressed persons of African descent and remorselessly broke every promise it made to Indigenous peoples.[45]

I therefore implement a reversal of Mead's assertion and examine American Christianity as a church with the soul of a nation. The First Amendment in the US Constitution guaranteed religious freedom and set into motion a different trajectory for American Christianity in comparison to western Europe. Jane Louise Mesick, an historian of English travelogues about the United States, details how English visitors expressed the jarring contrast in their own words. When one visitor learned the generous annual salary of one Congregational minister in Hartford, Connecticut, he marveled that such an amount was possible without the government as the church's "nursing father" and surmised that some Americans "pay so much for religion because they want it."[46]

But the Christianity that many white Americans wanted came at a great moral cost. And European observers such as Martineau and Beaumont were not alone in questioning whether the price was too high. Black, Indigenous, and concerned white Christians in the United States protested the quiet acquiescence of some churches and willful malice of others in connection to the American sins of settler colonialism and slavery. They not only spoke out against evil; they worked for justice with prophetic conviction and holy rage.

To "Tremble for My Country": Competing for the Soul of a Church and a Nation

In 1774, one year after Phillis Wheatley published her book of poems, she penned a letter to the Mohegan pastor Samson Occom. Wheatley and Occom were friends who exchanged letters. They likely first met in Boston when the famed English revivalist George Whitefield was preaching there in 1764.

Occom had accepted Whitefield's invitation to accompany him on his preaching tour across New England. Occom subsequently corresponded with both Phillis and her enslaver, Susanna Wheatley, and stayed at the Wheatley home when visiting Boston.[47] Phillis Wheatley was kidnapped as a child from Senegambia and transported to the docks of Boston Harbor in 1761. Her exact age when she arrived is unknown, and the closest estimate is in one account from 1834 that suggests Wheatley was "about seven years old, at this time, from the circumstance of shedding her front teeth."[48] Her African name is also lost to history. After enduring roughly four months experiencing the terrors of the Middle Passage on the slave ship *Phillis*, the enslaved child emerged naked to be sold. Only 75 of the 96 enslaved Africans survived the voyage, a mortality rate that was higher than most transatlantic slave voyages but not uncommon.[49] A prominent white couple, John and Susanna Wheatley, purchased the child. John, a wealthy merchant, renamed her after the slave ship that had brought her to them, and Phillis was to be trained as "a faithful domestic" worker serving Susanna directly.[50]

But Phillis also wrote brilliant poetry and utilized her newfound celebrity in 1773 to obtain her freedom. She despised slavery and began her letter to Occom expressing gratitude for his support of abolition: "I have this day received your obliging kind epistle, and am greatly satisfied with your reasons respecting the Negroes, and think highly reasonable what you offer in vindication of their natural rights."[51]

The main thrust of Wheatley's letter entailed condemnation of Black enslavement and criticism of the hypocrisy of the emerging revolution in the North American colonies. Slavery was an affront against God's creative order. "In every human breast," Wheatley wrote, "God has implanted a principle, which we call love of freedom; it is impatient of oppression, and pants for deliverance."[52] All people, regardless of skin color, possessed a capacity for liberty and capabilities to flourish in any circumstance.

Wheatley herself was evidence that persons of African descent could thrive in a predominantly white society if given equal access to education and employment. The Black mathematician Benjamin Banneker expressed a similar sentiment to Thomas Jefferson in 1791. In his letter, Banneker appealed to "the rights of human nature" and "the obligations of Christianity" in explaining that Black persons were not only created in the same divine image as white persons but also had commensurate intellectual abilities. As a free person of color, Banneker was proud to "cheerfully acknowledge that I am of the African race," while also lamenting "the unjustifiable cruelty and barbarism" that reduced enslaved Africans to brutes and chattels.[53]

Wheatley adapted popular revolutionary rhetoric, in which white colonists compared their plight under excessive British taxation to the ancient Israelites in Egyptian captivity from the book of Exodus, and instead identified white enslavers as "modern Egyptians." Without efforts to rid the colonies of slavery, the revolutionary cause was not as righteous as the patriots professed. And the patriots were neither as holy nor as heroic as they thought themselves to be. Wheatley ended her letter emphasizing the immoral incongruity of a revolutionary movement that did not pursue Black liberation. "This I desire not for their hurt," wrote Wheatley about the patriots, "but to convince them of the strange absurdity of their conduct whose words and actions are so diametrically opposite." The Black poet then employed an acerbic irony in juxtaposing the revolutionary "cry for liberty" alongside the continual desire of white persons to exercise "oppressive power" over enslaved Africans, which were contradictory impulses that did not "require the penetration of a philosopher to determine."[54]

Although there is no trace of Occom's letter that prompted Wheatley's fierce reply, Occom's antislavery convictions are palpable in one of his sermons from 1787. Occom preached from Luke 10:26–27, which recounts the parable of the Good Samaritan and captures Christ's twofold summary of the divine law in love toward God and neighbor. The sermon began with the definition of a "true neighbour": "When he sees his neighbour in distress, he is as ready to help him as he is willing to be helpt when in the same circumstance, he is ready to feed the hungry as he is willing to be fed when hungry himself."[55] Occom denounced proslavery Christianity as antithetical to the gospel. He understood that some enslavers and enablers of slavery employed Christian justifications for their iniquities and countered: "You that are slavekeepers, do you love God, and do you love your neighbour, your neighbour Negroe as yourself, are you willing to be slaves yourselves, and your children to be slaves too?" Enslaved Africans were fellow neighbors and the clear scriptural mandate therefore called for Black liberation. Occom surmised Christian enslavers were "not neighbours to anyone" and "consequently they are not lovers of God," which illustrated that a person's self-identification as a Christian did not necessarily make them so.[56]

In addition to the impossibility of proslavery Christianity, Occom also engaged settler colonialism and nationalism. During the American Revolution, Occom remained politically neutral. He advised the Oneidas in 1775 to refrain from participating in a war that was not theirs to fight. Occom advanced a twofold argument. He first articulated a theology of pacifism grounded in Christ as the divine "peacemaker" who heralded an end to all war and bloodshed. Christians were instructed to unite "as one family in peace," obeying the "new command" from Jesus in John 13:34 to love one another. Occom then offered his interpretation of the war, expressing sympathy for the rebelling colonists, before imploring the Oneidas to avoid meddling in the "quarrels among the white people."[57]

One historian maintains that Occom "made the most powerful case for Native American sojourning neutrality."[58] Occom delivered his sermon on neighbor-love in 1787, two weeks before the delegates of the Constitutional Convention gathered in Philadelphia, and the Mohegan preacher understood the importance of relations between the new American republic and various Indigenous nations. The parable at hand illustrated an extension of love across two persons of different nationalities: "And this love the Samaritan showed to a stranger and to a man who was quite of another nation, yea of a nation who despised him." Occom acknowledged the inherent instincts of nationalism and did not believe the Bible prohibited the "very natural" inclination "for every nation to have a national love." Yet the ethic of neighbor-love persisted as Christians were instructed to love all persons rather than solely those who shared their national and racial identities. In the postrevolutionary context of the United States, Occom dreamed of a racially just world in which "English, Indians and Negroes and so forth" honored one another and lived together in peace.[59]

In 1781, Thomas Jefferson wrote a book, *Notes on the State of Virginia*, that took the form of answers to a series of queries that the French politician François Barbé-Marbois presented to leaders of each of the thirteen North American colonies. Jefferson revised the work in 1782 and first published it three years later in Paris, when he resided there as the US minister to France. Jefferson's *Notes* found a wide transatlantic circulation, especially after an edition in London in 1787, and it emerged as one of the earliest and most significant treatments of culture, politics, religion, and society in the newly formed United States. Jefferson also composed the initial draft of the US Declaration of Independence, which was then revised in committee by John Adams, Benjamin Franklin, Robert Livingston, and Roger Sherman, but Jefferson alone was later credited with the most famous sentence in the document: "We hold these truths to be self-evident, that all men are created equal, that they are endowed by their Creator with certain unalienable Rights, that among these are Life, Liberty, and the pursuit of Happiness."[60]

Yet Jefferson disagreed with Wheatley, Banneker, and Occom about the racial destinies of Indigenous and Black persons in their nation. He wrote more highly about Indigenous peoples than persons of African descent in *Notes*. Jefferson refuted the question of gradual Black emancipation, such as a proposal that

pushed to liberate enslaved persons at the age of twenty-one, with several rationales. One was the "deep rooted prejudices entertained by the whites," which
would obliterate any possibility of Black flourishing in the country. Another was
Black racial inferiority, which was evident when measuring the three races that
comprised much of the United States. Jefferson wrote least about white people
because he either took for granted their racial superiority or understood that his
readership did. In Jefferson's estimation, Indigenous peoples had less contact
than Black persons with white communities, but nevertheless the intellectual
capacities and creations of the former exceeded the latter. Indigenous peoples
"astonish you with strokes of the most sublime oratory; such as prove their reason and sentiment strong, their imagination glowing and elevated."[61] Persons
of African descent, despite their greater proximity to white people, languished
in comparison. Jefferson averred, "But never yet could I find that a black had
uttered a thought above the level of plain narration; never saw even an elemen-
tary trait of painting or sculpture."[62] Jefferson contended that even persons of
African descent generally preferred "the fine mixtures of red and white" skin
over the "immovable veil of black" skin on their own bodies.[63]

Jefferson had doubts about publishing *Notes* because he anticipated criticism. To use a contemporary idiom to describe Jefferson's concern, the Virginian politician feared the "cancel culture" of his day. But he worried about
his commentary about the immoralities of slavery, not his blatant anti-Black
racism. A month after the initial publication of *Notes*, Jefferson responded to a
French editor seeking permission to reprint excerpts from the work. He agreed
to the request with conditions: "The strictures on slavery and on the constitution of Virginia are not of that kind, and they are the parts which I do not wish
to have made public, at least till I know whether their publication would do
most harm or good."[64] In *Notes*, Jefferson delineated the barbarism of slavery
and its devastating effects on both enslaved Africans and white enslavers. He
acknowledged, "The whole commerce between master and slave is a perpetual exercise of the most boisterous passions, the most unremitting despotism
on the one part, and degrading submissions on the other."[65]

White children of enslavers were reared to be tyrants because they grew up
watching and learning how to exert the coercive power required to sustain the
ongoing enslavement of Black people. Jefferson explained that the maintenance
of slavery necessitated systemic oppression abounding in intensive surveillance
and incessant violence, because no human of any race, even the Black race that
Jefferson considered inferior, willingly acceded to enslavement. The wheels of
slavery fostered economic growth in the United States, but it "destroyed" the
morality of enslavers and violated the God-given rights of the enslaved. Jefferson therefore confessed, "Indeed I tremble for my country when I reflect that

God is just: that his justice cannot sleep forever."[66] Jefferson panned Wheatley's poetry as "below the dignity of criticism," but even he could not deny Wheatley's condemnation of American enslavers and enablers of slavery: "The Almighty has no attribute which can take side with us in such a contest."[67]

Francis Le Jau was one of the earliest missionaries with the Society for the Propagation of the Gospel in Foreign Parts (SPG) in South Carolina. The Church of England founded the SPG in 1701, and the organization commissioned Anglican clergy across British colonies in North America and the Caribbean. Le Jau was a French Huguenot who first migrated to England after the revocation of the Edict of Nantes in 1685 (the revocation restored the favored position of the Catholic Church and made Protestants less welcome in France) and then to South Carolina in 1706. As he resided among English settlers, Indigenous peoples, and enslaved Africans, Le Jau often trembled for the colony, where he sought to love God and neighbor. There were ample opportunities for the missionary to administer divine grace, but Le Jau continually questioned the efficacy of his ministry, because he was caught in the larger web of colonial racial capitalism.

From his first months in South Carolina, he observed how the economics of colonization trumped his ministry of evangelization. He felt that he was facing insurmountable odds because "Mammon has hitherto got too many worshippers," as seemingly every white colonist desired to make enormous profits in transatlantic trade.[68] Le Jau quickly understood that the accumulation of profit derived from the exploitation and enslavement of Indigenous and Black persons. He admired the Indigenous individuals and families he met and confessed that they made him ashamed of his European identity: "The Indians I have conversed with do make us ashamed by their life, conversation, and sense of religion quite different from ours; ours consists in words and appearances, theirs in reality."[69] Too many white colonists acted unjustly toward Indigenous peoples and committed a multitude of sins ranging from trickery in barter exchanges to violence and enslavement. Le Jau despised how some white traders instigated conflicts between Indigenous nations to obtain and enslave Native prisoners of war whom they then trafficked and sold.

White colonists tried to prevent Le Jau from preaching to enslaved Africans and Natives as well as free Indigenous persons. Some of the resistance was explicit, as more than a few white colonists did not feel remorse for their "evidently evil" actions. But some of the backlash was subtle. "I am not blamed openly, for all honest people stand with me," Le Jau reported, "but it seems by their whispers and conduct, they would not have me urge of contributing to the salvation, instruction, and human usage of slaves and free Indians."[70] The insidious and pervasive ways in which white colonists dehumanized people of color as commodities troubled Le Jau, and these injustices prompted doubts about whether the seeds of anything good could be planted in the wicked soils of English colonization.

Why We Must Reckon with History

Some Christians dared to defy the unjust systems undergirding first the English colonial enterprise in North America and then the United States. Indigenous and Black Christians challenged the immoral structures of economic exploitation, land dispossession, and enslavement, as well as the white people who were oppressing them. In 1794, in the first copyrighted African American pamphlet, Absalom Jones, the first ordained African American Episcopal priest, and Richard Allen, the first bishop of the African Methodist Episcopal Church, reckoned with the injustices of slavery. The impetus for their pamphlet was to defend free African Americans in Philadelphia from accusations of plundering white homes when many people fled the city during a yellow fever epidemic in 1793. Jones and Allen countered that Black residents risked their lives to assist in caring for the sick and burying the dead. The Black pastors accepted a personal invitation from Benjamin Rush, a white physician and abolitionist, to join him on the medical front lines to "procure medicine duly prepared" and "administer them" to patients. Jones and Allen professed, "This has been no small satisfaction to us; for, we think, that when a physician was not attainable, we have been the instruments, in the hand of God, for saving the lives of some hundreds of our suffering fellow mortals."[71]

But they quickly turned their attention to the moral maladies of slavery and its deadly consequences. Both men were formerly enslaved and had experienced firsthand how slavery divided enslaved families, dampened enslaved minds, depressed enslaved spirits, and defiled Black hearts with a vicious hate for their white oppressors. Jones and Allen acknowledged the significant racial wealth gap between white and free Black residents, but they explained that the reasons for this chasm were discriminatory laws and white antipathy toward African Americans.

Because Black enslavement was at the root of all these evils, Jones and Allen implored white Americans to also reckon with "how hateful [in the Exodus narrative] slavery is in the eyes of that God" who wreaked havoc on Pharoah and his people for enslaving the ancient Israelites. They directly appealed to the parental affections, patriotic allegiances, and religious convictions of their white readers: "If you love your children, if you love your country, if you love the God of love, clear your hands from slaves, burden not your children or country with them."[72] Jones and Allen also encouraged their Black readers to take after the example of Christ and forgive white persons because they understood all too well how racial anger could consume a Black person with soul-crushing bitterness.

In 1823, the Cherokee preacher David Brown also beseeched his white American listeners in Salem, Massachusetts, to reckon with their history. The crowd had assembled to hear Brown talk about white Christian missionary endeavors among Indigenous peoples. The atmosphere was more electric than usual as the audience awaited with bated breath to hear from an Indigenous Christian speaker. Yet Brown did not immediately launch into the conventional plea for mission support. The historian Joel W. Martin explains about Brown: "Before talking about missionaries and his kinsmen and kinswomen in the present, he wanted his audience to encounter some bitter truths about the past from a Native American perspective."[73] Brown invited his listeners to journey with him back to North America before European contact, to remember that Indigenous peoples "were in a more tranquil and prosperous state previous to their acquaintance with Europeans."

The Cherokee preacher named the problem of overly romanticized depictions of Native America as an idyllic paradise: "Far from me, however, to insinuate that the native population were free from vice, immorality, and occasionally destructive wars; for they are also the descendants of sinful apostate man." But Brown also stated that European intrusions resulted in the "direful catastrophes" of disease, dispossession, and death for Indigenous peoples.[74] He confronted his white audience with the fullness of history and challenged them to behold his righteous indignation and work toward repairing the ongoing outcomes of settler colonialism. One way to right these wrongs was to aid "Christian missions to the Indians," which many of his listeners were likely ready to do.

Brown did not stop there, though. Another way to specifically support "the Cherokee, Choctaw, Chickasaw, and Creek nations, whose council fires still burn on the eastern side of the Mississippi," was to ensure the US government protect their lands from encroaching white settlers and the southeastern politicians who wanted these territories for their respective states.[75] Brown endorsed the ministry of evangelization, but he also recognized its limitations. The only way to stop the wheels that put the oppressive systems of settler colonialism and slavery into motion was political action.

To Reckon with a History We Never Learned

The structure of this book consists of two main parts. The first part, chapters 2–4, examines settler colonialism; the second part, chapters 5–7, focuses on slavery. In the final chapter, chapter 8, I draw lessons from this history to offer insights on ministries of racial justice in American churches today. I believe this book will startle more than a few readers, because it presents a little-told (or untold) history that is horrible, tragic, and traumatic.

I lament how little I learned about Indigenous peoples, settler colonialism, African Americans, and slavery in my educational training, first for congregational leadership as a pastor and then for academic instruction as a professor. What explains the deficiencies in my education and our collective misunderstanding of American Christian history? One reason is the contested place of church history in theological education. In E. Brooks Holifield's presidential address to the American Society of Church History in 2003, the historian traces the disputations that prevented ready acceptance of church history in college, university, and seminary curricula. Holifield points out that "it took a long time for the history of Christianity to secure a place in American classrooms," because focused and sustained historical study was considered dangerous for student formation, especially in relation to their faith commitments.[76] In the 1820s, several faculty members from Andover Theological Seminary, one of the earliest Protestant seminaries, resisted the hiring of a colleague specializing in history. One professor told the school's trustees that the study of history should be "altogether subordinate," and another openly expressed his concerns about the perils of too early (and perhaps too much) exposure to the complexities of the Christian past.[77] In 2005, Samuel Hugh Moffett captured the enduring discomfort with church history in recalling a story from the 1950s that "floated around the divinity school quadrangle" at Yale. Roland Bainton, a professor of church history, bumped into one of his faculty colleagues after chapel one day, and the colleague asked, "Roley, how can you know so much about church history and still be a Christian?"[78]

Although church history has secured its place as among the requisite disciplines in theological education, the attending fears and fragilities remain. In 1891, the biblical studies professor Charles Augustus Briggs delivered an address at his school, Union Theological Seminary in New York, imploring his students and colleagues to pursue deeper and fuller understandings of the Bible. Briggs opposed the regnant "theory of [biblical] inerrancy" because it fostered deficient and dishonest interpretations in seeking to "explain away" obvious textual errors.[79] If Christians truly desired to get serious about their faith, they needed to stop regarding the Bible as a vulnerable infant. Briggs surveyed the landscape of American Christianity and surmised, "The Bible has been treated as if it were a baby, to be wrapped in swaddling-clothes, nursed, and carefully guarded, lest it should be injured by heretics and skeptics."[80]

I share Briggs's conviction on biblical studies but apply it in this book to church history. Too many historical approaches treat both the American past and students of that past like babies. We therefore receive incomplete narratives that tell only some of the story and imbibe an incoherent concoction of partial truths that either elides the ugliest sins or isolates a few inspirational heroes. We grow up and we grow old, but our insufficient understanding of history leaves us in a perpetual state of Christian infanthood. We don't know how to reckon with a history we never learned.

Reckoning with history is not an easy task. But reckon we must, if we desire a more faithful understanding of American Christianity and seek a more perfect American union. We must confront the sins of settler colonialism and slavery and comprehend how these sins shaped American Christianity. In 1711, a white woman from a South Carolina plantation approached the Anglican minister Francis Le Jau with a question that staggered him. She asked if the enslaved persons she owned could go to heaven, and if so, whether she would have to see them there.[81] We do not know Le Jau's reply, but John Fletcher, a white Christian man from Louisiana, published a defense of slavery in 1852 offering an answer. Fletcher believed the Christian heaven was a place of persisting racial inequalities and was therefore confident that the eternity awaiting white enslavers would not be uncomfortable for them.[82] After several years of working among Indigenous peoples, the white Baptist pastor Isaac McCoy could scarcely tolerate the unbridled and unrepentant racism of so many of his fellow white American Christians. In 1827, McCoy denounced the broken treaties and cruel injustices of Indigenous land dispossession as "a poor commendation indeed of a Christian nation" and four years later challenged Americans to prove their patriotic self-identification as "the most favored people that have ever inhabited the earth" through their individual actions and government policies toward Indigenous peoples.[83]

There were several competing natures in the soul of white Christian America. One spewed hateful theologies and racist ideas, such as weaponizing Roman Catholic papal bulls from 1493 on European "discovery" and interpreting the Noahic curse of Ham in Genesis 9 to claim divine permission to steal Indigenous lands and enslave African persons. Another appealed to the Bible as a source of liberation that offered pathways of equality, justice, and mutuality for a multiracial nation.

But the most dominant nature evinced neither conviction nor courage. Instead, the heartbeat of American Christianity pounded with a yearning for compromise. It is not enough to reckon with the worst and most vicious racist doctrines. We must also study the incremental corruptions and quotidian concessions that white American Christians made to make room for settler colonialism and slavery in their consciences, churches, and country. And we must learn from those who were inspired to remake a better nation. But too often these heroes are applied as a balm to soothe our consciences and minimize the consequences of history. If we want to envision and enact a deeply hopeful future together, we need a deeply honest understanding of our past.

Settler Colonialism

Chapter Two

"What Right Have I to Go Live in the Heathens' Country?"

The Deceptions of Land Acquisition and Indigenous Evangelization in Early Modern European Colonialism

In 1622, Robert Cushman returned home to England after visiting the Plymouth colony in Massachusetts with a burning desire to mobilize further support for the fledgling and precarious colonial enterprise. Cushman shared the religious convictions and economic aspirations of the colonists in Plymouth and had previously worshiped with them in the Netherlands, before they all reunited on Wampanoag land that bore the name of Patuxet. The word "Wampanoag" refers to "the land of the east, the place where the sun rises, and to the original people of this place."[1] The Wampanoags had lived in Patuxet and throughout southeastern Massachusetts for over 10,000 years before the arrival of the *Mayflower* in 1620.

In 1603, Cushman was fined and imprisoned for posting "libels" on the doors of several churches in Canterbury. Cushman had written, "Lord have mercy upon us," to express his condemnation of the Church of England for its theological compromises that he saw as corruptions of the faith.[2] Cushman migrated to the Dutch city of Leiden in 1611 to join a small but growing community of fellow English believers who had separated from the Church of England. After several years with the separatist community in Leiden, Cushman emerged as one of the leaders of a new project: colonization in North America. He helped to negotiate arrangements with Sir Edwin Sandys, an English politician who was also a powerful director within the Virginia Company of London, for a group among the church in Leiden to initiate a new colony. Sandys did not like the English separatists, but he was willing to overlook their religious dissension because he desperately needed people to live, farm, and trade in North America.[3] Cushman too understood that colonization required forging a wider array of alliances than congregational ministry.

Soon after Cushman reached Plymouth, he learned that the colonists were struggling. They were ready to worship God in a new land, but they were otherwise unprepared, with inadequate knowledge in agriculture, horticulture, and hunting. The colonists were armed with a lot of faith, but not many of the necessary life skills to survive in North America. Their previous residence of Leiden was in a foreign country, but the Dutch city was in Europe and therefore had some contextual similarities that facilitated relocation for the English separatists.

When Cushman shared with Plymouth's governor, William Bradford, that the colony's investors were angry that the *Mayflower* returned without "valuable cargo," Bradford grew incensed and told Cushman that half of the colonists had died in their first year there. The grieving community was nevertheless resilient and making progress. The governor surmised that in time there was "hope of recovery" for financial investments, but "no recompense" for those buried in the North American soil. Cushman expressed sympathy, but he also divulged instructions that his ship (named *Fortune*) be stocked with a bounty of North American goods, such as pelts of beaver, before departure to England.[4]

Although Cushman secured sufficient cargo to satisfy Plymouth's investors, he understood that many in England had doubts about colonization itself. In addition to economic questions about transatlantic profits, moral quandaries abounded in England. One challenge concerned the safety of the English abroad, especially on settler expeditions with families of women and children alongside men. Some colonial efforts preceding the *Mayflower* resulted in high mortalities, such as the mysterious disappearance of over one hundred settlers on Roanoke Island between 1587 and 1590, and reports from the colony in Jamestown included violent episodes of fighting against hostile Indigenous peoples.

Another dilemma revolved around the ethics of Indigenous conquest and land dispossession. The English employed the oppressive devastation of Indigenous communities that accompanied Spanish colonization in the Americas, which the public learned about through translations of the works of Bartolomé de las Casas and other Spanish critics, as evidence of England's moral superiority over Spain and vindication of Protestant departures from Roman Catholicism. But criticism of Spanish colonization prompted questions in England about English imperial ambitions in the Americas. If it was obviously wrong for Spain to seize Indigenous lands and displace Indigenous peoples, why would England want to do likewise?

Cushman would return to writing as his primary means of public expression. But this time he authored more than a brief message to post on church doors. He addressed the questions of colonization in a tract entitled "Reasons and Considerations Touching the Lawfulness of Removing out of England into the Parts of America." He acknowledged the ethical debate that stifled support for colonies such as his beloved Plymouth: "But some will say, what right have I to go live in the heathens' country?"[5] Cushman offered answers that he hoped would not only ease English consciences but also present a distinctively Protestant approach to settler colonialism that would stir English hearts and open English purses.

Cushman began his tract highlighting the Protestant emphasis on scriptural authority as the means of divine revelation. He contrasted the biblical past, when the "God of old did call and summon our fathers by predictions, dreams, visions, and certain illuminations to go from their countries, places, and habitations," to his contemporary age and the difference in how people of faith discerned God's direction. Cushman observed that God "speaks in another manner" because of the provision of the Bible. "But now the ordinary examples and precepts of the Scriptures, reasonably and rightly understood and applied," Cushman maintained, "must be the voice and word that must call us, press us, and direct us in every action."[6] Unlike the Spanish, English Protestants did not need papal ordinances to guide their colonial enterprise in the Americas. Instead, they trusted in their scriptural interpretations. And Cushman argued that there was ample evidence in the Bible to make the case for settler colonialism.

Cushman was certain that Jesus Christ's command in Matthew 28:16–20 to evangelize throughout the world, known as the Great Commission, supported English colonization. The English began traveling to the Americas shortly after Christopher Columbus returned from the Caribbean to Spain in 1493, but mainly for trade and not settlement. In 1497, the Italian seafarer John Cabot led the English ship *Matthew* to Newfoundland and claimed it for King Henry VII.

Cabot also brought back an impressive haul of fish. More important, his report on the abundance of Atlantic cod set into motion an expansive transatlantic economy. Cod soon joined herring as among the most desired fish in early modern Europe. One economic historian notes that "for the fishing industry the voyage of John Cabot in 1497 was of more direct importance than that of Columbus," leading to the presence of more than two hundred English and French ships in Newfoundland by 1578.[7]

But it was not until the late sixteenth century that the English tried to establish settlements in North America. As English colonization was growing, Cushman contended that settlement, rather than trade, was the most effective approach to Indigenous evangelization. It was not enough to "pray for the conversion of the heathens" from afar. Fulfilling the Great Commission required direct and sustained contact with Indigenous peoples. Cushman presented two possibilities: "Now it seemeth unto me that we ought also to endeavor and use the means to convert them, and the means cannot be used unless we go to them or they come to us." But Cushman added that only one of the options was viable. Indigenous peoples could not come to the English because "our land is full." So, the English must live among the Indigenous in North America, since "their land is empty."[8]

In making his case for settler colonialism as the means for Indigenous evangelization, Cushman delved into two other thorny issues, overpopulation in Europe and land ownership in the Americas, that long preceded him and persisted for centuries after the publication of his tract. In 1944 Eric Williams, a political science professor at Howard University, published a groundbreaking book, *Capitalism and Slavery*, that illumined the primacy of economic motivations driving early modern European colonialism. Williams would leave his university post a few years later to return to his homeland, Trinidad and Tobago, to advocate for its independence from British rule. In 1962 he became that nation's first prime minister.

In *Capitalism and Slavery*, Williams harkened back to the work of the eighteenth-century Scottish economist Adam Smith, who postulated that the prosperity of a new colony could be measured by one simple factor: "plenty of good land."[9] During Cushman's visit to Plymouth in 1621, he accompanied one of the colony's leaders and a future governor, Edward Winslow, on a trip across several miles in southeastern Massachusetts, known to the Wampanoag as Pokanoket, and journeyed along a network of trails connecting scores of Wampanoag communities. They viewed men catching fish and women carrying baskets of produce as well as cultivated cornfields and sections of forest cleared of underbrush through intentional burning.[10]

Cushman saw plenty of good land for English colonization, but his tract omitted that the land he surveyed was teeming with life. Instead, Cushman now averred that Indigenous land was like the pre-Adamic creation described in the first chapter of Genesis. It was "a vast and empty chaos." He also portrayed Indigenous land as "spacious and void." His desolate depiction of North America provided the theological grounds for settler colonialism: "As the ancient patriarchs therefore removed from straiter places into more roomy, where the land lay idle and waste, and none used it, though there dwelt inhabitants by them, (as Genesis 13:6, 11, 12 and 34:21, and 41:20), so is it lawful now to take a land which none useth, and make use of it."[11] Cushman employed two deliberate and interconnected interpretive moves. His first move was the deployment of biblical exegesis delineating the lawful conditions for land ownership. His second move declared that the land in North America was unused, because the colonists had divine permission to occupy and own only land that "lay idle and waste."

This chapter treats how deception emerged as one of the most dominant modes of Christian doctrine and practice in early modern European colonialism. Cushman was neither the first nor the last Christian to engage in this vein of dishonest and dreadful colonial chicanery. He and others found the scriptural texts they needed to invent racist theologies that justified Indigenous land dispossession. Early modern European Christians also utilized the religious rhetoric of evangelism to argue that their intention to convert Indigenous peoples warranted their sins of coercion, exploitation, and violence toward Indigenous peoples. European colonists reasoned that the mission of saving Indigenous souls required seizing their land. But there were also a few Christians who dared to speak gospel truths and risked everything to cut through all the lies.

"Christ Did Not Die for Gold": Bartolomé de las Casas against the (New) World

In 1550, two men met in Valladolid, a city in northern Spain, for a debate that both hoped would end the swirling controversy regarding the ethics of colonization and Indigenous rights in the Americas. One man, Juan Ginés de Sepúlveda, was a learned scholar who devoted his life to rigorous academic inquiry at several colleges in Spain and Italy. Sepúlveda acquired expertise in the disciplines of canon law, philosophy, and theology, and he published several treatises defending the Catholic faith from emerging Protestant critiques. But the chief reason for his place in this debate was his work supporting Spanish conquest in the Americas, most notably in *Democrates secundus*, composed around 1544, in which the humanist scholar reasoned that Spanish violence perpetrated against Indigenous peoples in the Americas was just and necessary to establish colonies on their land and to evangelize them.

The other man, Bartolomé de las Casas, spent almost his entire life in the Americas, and received an entirely different education than his debate counterpart. Las Casas was first a colonist, who exerted rule over Indigenous persons assigned to him in an *encomienda*, the oppressive Spanish colonial labor system that forced Indigenous persons to offer tribute in gold, silver, and other natural resources and mandated that las Casas and other *encomenderos* provide Christian instruction to their workers. Though the Spanish crown carefully and continuously noted that the *encomienda* system did not permit Indigenous enslavement, las Casas and others in the Americas understood that the differences between slavery and *encomienda* existed only in theory and not in practice.

After ten years as an *encomendero*, las Casas could no longer participate in what he knew in his soul was a cruel and unjust colonial structure. He gave up his *encomienda* and instead remained in the Americas as a Dominican friar. Las Casas returned to Spain on several occasions to advocate for Indigenous rights and criticize what his country and church were doing. In 1515, he implored King Ferdinand, who was near death, to halt the terrible injustices, which he had initiated as the ruler who funded Christopher Columbus's voyage in 1492, before it was too late. Las Casas explained to the king, his fellow clerics, and anyone else within earshot that Spanish colonization had devolved into a system in which *encomenderos* "had no thought that those natives were made of flesh and blood" and instead "put them to work in the mines and at other projects the Indians could only accomplish as slave labor."[12] Las Casas insisted that Indigenous evangelization was nothing but a "lame and false excuse of converting them to our Holy Catholic Faith" because there was no evidence of Christian ministry in the Americas.[13] It was therefore not surprising that las Casas was Sepúlveda's debate opponent.

Sepúlveda and las Casas vehemently disagreed, and each endeavored to dismantle the other's arguments, but the two men were never in the same room together during their debate in Valladolid. Sepúlveda spoke first in the chapel of the Colegio de San Gregorio before a panel of judges comprising fourteen government officials, priests, and theologians. Without las Casas in attendance, Sepúlveda delivered a lecture for roughly two to three hours answering the question at hand concerning the morality of colonial violence. More specifically, the two men addressed whether Spanish colonists should continue initiating "war on those Indians" before "preaching the faith to them so that, once they have been subjugated, they may more easily and conveniently be instructed in and enlightened by the teachings of the gospel."[14]

Sepúlveda expounded a fourfold argument defending Spanish colonialism. One rationale was that the colonial subjugation of Indigenous peoples in the Americas was just punishment for their sins of blasphemy in their religious practices, which Sepúlveda and other Spaniards referred to as idol worship, and violations of natural law, citing Spanish reports of human sacrifices among some Indigenous communities. Another rationale was that the punitive wars accompanying Spanish colonialism protected the weak and innocent within Indigenous communities in the long run because the Christian rule of the Spaniards was both ethically and religiously superior to precolonial Indigenous lifeways. A third reason detailed how conquest through warfare was the most efficient conduit to evangelization because it was the fastest method to expose Indigenous multitudes in the Americas to Christianity. Sepúlveda appealed to church history and scriptural regulations, such as the endorsement from Pope Gregory I in support of Christian militarism against people of other faiths and instructions in Deuteronomy 20 that granted the ancient Israelites permission to wage war against people of different religions, to buttress his point that armed conquest enabled the Spanish to convert Indigenous peoples after they were defeated.[15]

The final reason was probably the most controversial. Sepúlveda employed the Greek philosopher Aristotle's notion of natural slavery and surmised the Indigenous peoples whom the Spanish encountered in the Americas were inherently inferior and thusly among those who Aristotle taught were *natura servi* ("slaves by nature"). In *Democratus secundus*, Sepúlveda utilized the contrast between the "intelligence, ingenuity, magnanimity, temperance, humanity, and religion" of the Spaniards to what he viewed as the uncivilized societies and dull minds of Indigenous peoples as evidence to justify colonialism.[16]

When Sepúlveda finished speaking, the judges summoned las Casas. Though las Casas did not hear his opponent's address, he was familiar with Sepúlveda's arguments, because the two men were engaged in a longstanding and bitter dispute for roughly a decade. And the larger debate across Spain and the Americas about colonial policy had been raging for several decades. When Columbus made landfall in 1492, he recorded his impressions of the Taínos who met him on an island in the Bahamas. They called the island Guanahaní, which the Spanish later named San Salvador and the English designated as Watlings Island. The Taínos were "naked as their mothers bore them" and many had different colors of paint on their faces and bodies.

More importantly to Columbus, he observed that the Taínos did not possess intricate weaponry because he only saw "small spears" made of wood. They did not have iron, which Columbus surmised when several Taíno men cut themselves upon touching his sword. He also learned that the Taínos had fought off Indigenous warriors from other islands who attempted to capture them, but Columbus was confident that the Taínos could not withstand European military force. He concluded about the Taínos, "They ought to make good and skilled servants, for they repeat very quickly whatever we say to them. I think they can easily be made Christians, for they seem to have no religion."[17]

But Columbus's main objective was trade—the Italian mariner convinced King Ferdinand and Queen Isabella to fund his search for a new sea route to Asia—and he returned to Spain with seven captured Taínos and something equal in worth to (if not of greater worth than) Asian spices: he brought back gold and a promising report than there was plenty more in the Americas. Yet las Casas lambasted the devastating consequences of Columbus's voyage. Unlike Sepúlveda, las Casas did not testify to magnanimity among the Spanish in the Americas: "Each Spaniard had an itch for gold and a narrow conscience."[18]

Las Casas grieved the unfolding tragedy of Spanish colonialism. Spanish colonists willfully oppressed and wantonly killed Indigenous peoples in their pursuit of riches. Across the Americas there was a gross dehumanization of Indigenous peoples, who were regarded only for their labor as the means of production. It was evident to las Casas that "Christ did not die for gold," but he believed that the resounding message of Indigenous evangelization mediated through Spanish colonialism was this abhorrent gospel.[19]

Las Casas clearly had a lot to say about Spanish colonialism. Sepúlveda laid out his argument before the judges in a few hours, whereas las Casas spoke to them for five or six days. Las Casas claimed to have read every word of the 500-page manuscript that he had prepared for the debate. Sepúlveda argued that the judges grew weary from listening to las Casas and asked him to stop before he had finished. The judges dismissed after hearing from las Casas and deliberated on their own for several months before returning for a final session in 1551.

Ultimately, they did not render a decision. Las Casas felt that the majority of the judges privately sided with him but hesitated publicly because of their concerns about colonial unrest in Peru and fears of greater hostilities toward reform. Sepúlveda believed there was a generational divide, with the older judges agreeing with him and the younger ones supporting las Casas.[20] Nonetheless the debate at Valladolid made evident the limits of Indigenous evangelization within the Spanish colonial structure. Las Casas reinforced an argument he made in a treatise from 1534 entitled "The Only Way of Attracting All Peoples to the True Religion." He did not refute that one of the results from colonial subjugation was increased Indigenous exposure to Christianity. But Indigenous peoples were forced to listen to Spanish preaching and pressured to convert in the *encomienda* system. Las Casas found that Indigenous peoples conveyed "diverse expressions of natural intelligence" and were therefore good candidates for Christian instruction, but he also insisted that genuine evangelism could not manifest in these oppressive conditions.

Las Casas explained, "The one and only way of teaching all humanity the true religion was established by divine providence for the whole world and for all times—through rational persuasion of the intellect and the gentle attraction or incitement of the will."[21] He also understood that missionaries like him were most effective when hearers saw "the Christian life shine in our conduct." "To advance the gospel by the power of arms is not Christian example," las Casas contended, "but a pretext for stealing the property of others and subjugating their provinces."[22] Spanish conquest repelled Indigenous evangelization, and las Casas thought it was impossible to reconcile colonialism and Christianity.

The contradiction between colonialism and Christianity was often acknowledged but rarely challenged. The main reason is because Europeans involved in early modern colonialism, ranging from the Spanish in the sixteenth century to the English in the seventeenth century, comprehended that Indigenous evangelization alone was not sufficient motivation to sustain an expensive transatlantic enterprise. Sepúlveda admitted that Spaniards went to the Americas principally for economic reasons and would not risk their lives or invest their funds solely for missionary purposes. It was the extraction of valuable resources, and not gospel proclamation, that lay at the heart of colonialism.

But Sepúlveda did not, and could not, concede the moral ground to las Casas. The stakes were too high. Sepúlveda's personal reputation was not all that hung in the balance. The international standing of his country, Spain, and the religious authority of his church tradition, Roman Catholicism, were also on trial. Sepúlveda, like many supporters of colonialism in the Americas, did not highlight financial gain as prominently or as vociferously as he did his other rationales, even though it was a foundational justification. Sepúlveda and others understood that some compromises were necessary, but las Casas was enraged at the deceptions and self-delusions that his detractors employed and embodied.

If Sepúlveda was right about the economic centrality of Spanish colonialism, then las Casas believed the logically sound and obviously true corollary was for his opponent to plainly state that his approach to Indigenous evangelism was corrupted to make room for greed and violence. Las Casas demanded that Sepúlveda honestly confess that lust for gold and silver was more important to Spanish colonists than love of God and neighbor.[23] But Sepúlveda refused to make this concession, because he was concerned that Spain's international foes and religious rivals, such as English Protestants, would point to the hypocrisy and sinfulness of Spanish colonization as evidence of Spain's moral failings and the result of doctrinal errors within Roman Catholicism.

Maybe Christ Died for Land: The Virginia Company, Jamestown, and an English Settlement on Tsenacommacah

When Robert Cushman penned his promotional tract on English colonialism in 1622, his English readership was familiar with Spanish accounts of their exploits in the Americas, as well as the moral and religious controversies that ensued. Las Casas's best-known publication, *Brevísima relación de la destrucción de las Indias*, first published in 1552, was translated into English as early as 1583. Different translations were also printed in 1620 and 1656. Las Casas's work has been translated under various English titles, such as "A Short Account of the Destruction of the Indies," but the title in 1656 conveyed a polemic tone against both Spain and Catholicism: "The Tears of the Indians: Being an Historical and True Account of the Cruel Massacres and Slaughters of Above Twenty Millions of Innocent People Committed by the Spaniards in the Islands of Hispaniola, Cuba, Jamaica, Etc."[24] An English translation of the Spanish Jesuit missionary José de Acosta's *Historia natural y moral de las Indias* from 1590 appeared in 1604 as "The Natural and Moral Historie of the East and West Indies."[25]

One section of Acosta's book treated the Spanish notion that the Caribbean islands Columbus reached on his voyages were the wealthy region of Ophir mentioned in the books of Kings and Chronicles in the Hebrew Bible. Some Spaniards instead believed that Peru was Ophir. Acosta observed, "They base this on the fact that Scripture tells us how fine gold and very precious stones were brought from Ophir, and very precious wood, all of which abound in Peru according to these writers."[26] Acosta was skeptical about all claims linking the Americas with Ophir, but he also recognized how the theories revealed the significance of gold, silver, and other resources within Spanish colonialism.

Acosta also admitted in a different work, *De procuranda Indorum salute*, that "the exploitation of metal mines" was "the objective sought by the Spaniards with their great sea voyages." He added that mining was "the reason why merchants barter, judges sit, and even, often enough, priests preach the gospel."[27] As English Protestants read Spanish Catholic criticisms of their colonial enterprise, they were convinced that they could, and would, do better in the Americas.

In 1556, the English pastor John Ponet wrote *A Shorte Treatise of Politike Power*, in which he advocated for just resistance to tyrannical monarchs. Ponet, the bishop of Winchester from 1551 to 1553, left both his position and the country after the ascension of the Roman Catholic Mary Tudor to the English throne. In addition to providing several biblical examples of righteous opposition to wicked rulers, Ponet detailed Spanish oppressions against Indigenous peoples in the Americas as evidence against Mary's Catholicism.[28]

Despite English efforts to enact a morally superior colonial system, their early attempts and impressions bore some similarities to the Spanish. In 1588, Thomas Hariot, an English mathematician and scientist, published a report of his experiences with Sir Walter Raleigh's second expedition to Roanoke Island from 1585 to 1586. Raleigh directed three expeditions to North America in the 1580s but did not participate in the voyages himself. He recruited Hariot for his scientific expertise and hoped Hariot would be able to precisely identify the natural resources of wherever the expedition made landfall. Raleigh's first expedition returned from Roanoke Island to England with a bag of pearls and two Algonquian-speaking Roanoke men, Manteo and Wanchese. Hariot spent time with Manteo and Wanchese, and they all learned the other's language before all three men traveled to Roanoke Island.[29]

Hariot praised the Roanokes as kind, inquisitive, and open to interactions with the English. They were "clothed with loose mantles made of deer skins" around their waists and otherwise naked. Like Columbus, Hariot observed that the Indigenous persons he met did not have iron tools or weapons. Hariot was also confident that the Roanokes could be easily converted to Christianity; they were a people "not to be feared" but instead "they shall have cause both to fear and love us, that shall inhabit with them."[30] Hariot interpreted Roanoke religion as a belief in "many gods which they call Mantóac" and creation narratives that resembled Christianity, with the notable exception that they professed the first human was a woman. The English scientist showed his Bible to the Roanokes and was glad for their openness to his religion, but Hariot tried in vain to convince them that the book itself was not a sacred object as some embraced it close to their chests and kissed it with their mouths.[31]

The problems that besieged Hariot's journey were due to the English guests, not the Roanoke hosts. Violent skirmishes arose because some of the English first attacked and killed the Roanokes, and the Roanokes retaliated. One account traces the hostility to confusion about one missing silver cup, which the English accused the Roanoke of stealing. When a small party of English soldiers could not retrieve the cup from the Roanokes, they angrily burned a Roanoke village and destroyed its crops.[32] Hariot left the English colony in 1586, but when another ship returned to Roanoke Island in 1590, there was no sign of any colonists. Their fates are unknown, but one hypothesis is that many were killed in warfare against the Roanokes, and the few English survivors lived among the Roanokes. If this is the case, Hariot's report provides strong evidence that the English colonists were at fault. He disclosed that some of the colonists had greedy intentions and quick tempers. Hariot also later wrote of the Roanokes, "To confess a truth: I cannot remember, that ever I saw a better or quieter people than they."[33]

The lost colony on Roanoke Island did not deter further English colonization in North America. The Virginia Company of London was founded in 1606 when Sir Thomas Gates and a small group of investors secured a charter from King James I to establish settlements along the eastern seaboard of North America. The charter gave the Virginia Company a royal "license" to "make habitation, plantation, and to deduce a colony of sundry of our people into that part of America, commonly called Virginia, and other parts and territories in America."[34]

The primary motivations for the charter were twofold: to fortify England's imperial power in transatlantic trade, and to create a greater English presence in North America to thwart the expansion of Spanish colonialism northward. The charter indicated that the designated Indigenous lands in North America, roughly from South Carolina to Maine, were "not now actually possessed by any Christian prince or people." Because the Indigenous inhabitants lived "in darkness and miserable ignorance of the true knowledge and worship of God," the charter emphasized conversion of "the infidels and savages" as a driving impetus for colonization.[35] Evangelism was given first place on the charter and preceded the many stipulations for trade and settlement. But the attention devoted to trade and settlement, spanning approximately 3,400 words, far exceeded the short section on evangelism, comprising 98 words.

The charter illumines several components of early modern European expansion into Africa, Asia, and the Americas. Colonialism is at once both straightforward and complex. Colonialism entails foreign intrusion, but it also manifests in different forms, such as trade and settlement, and unfolds through multiple processes over time. Edward W. Said connects colonialism with imperialism, defining imperialism as "the practice, the theory, and the attitudes of a dominating metropolitan center ruling a distant territory" and colonialism as "a consequence of imperialism" through the "implanting of settlements on distant territory."[36] D. K. Fieldhouse understands colonialism as the domination and exploitation of a subject people "by the foreign society and its agents who occupied the dependency to serve their own interests, not that of the subject people."[37]

Several scholars also underscore the differences between colonialism and settler colonialism. Walter L. Hixson maintains that "what primarily distinguishes settler colonialism from colonialism proper is that the settlers came not to exploit the indigenous population for economic gain, but rather to remove them from colonial space."[38] Patrick Wolfe explains that settler colonialism is not an event but rather a cumulatively destructive force, because it necessitates the ongoing "elimination of the native" for foreign settlers to construct their own societies on colonized territories.[39] Deborah Bird Rose's obvious yet profound observation about Australian history illustrates the inherently hostile intention of settler colonialism: Aboriginal and Torres Strait Islander peoples "got in the way just by staying at home."[40]

In 1606, the Virginia Company concentrated on several forms of colonialism, ranging from commercial and extractive to land dispossession and settlement, but their charter accentuated how Christian missionary endeavors would ensure that their colonial enterprise would bestow blessings to the Indigenous peoples they encountered and bring greater glory to God. One year later, approximately one hundred Englishmen (some were teenage boys, and all were male) established the first settlement in Virginia, which they named after the king who granted them the charter: Jamestown.

An interrogation of the Virginia Company begins with understanding the definitions of the two words "Virginia" and "company." As Sir Walter Raleigh prepared for his expedition in 1584, he soon thereafter named his North American destination "Virginia," after Elizabeth I, the queen who supported him. There is scant evidence of Raleigh's internal deliberations about his naming process. For example, we do not know if Raleigh considered employing the queen's proper name instead of the famous moniker honoring her decision to never marry ("Virgin Queen"). But the English ultimately found that this designation of Virginia proved useful in promoting their interpretations of Indigenous territory as a "virgin land."

As the Jamestown colony began, one of its strongest initial impressions was that the Indigenous inhabitants, Algonquian-speaking people belonging to a confederacy of at least six different tribes (that have been collectively named the Powhatans, after one of its leaders), were unlike the gentle and kind Roanokes.[41] The Powhatans were neither angry nor vicious, but they were wary of the English visitors and did not warmly greet them. The English quickly realized the Powhatans were not naive, which was how Columbus depicted the Taínos and Hariot the Roanokes, but a formidable people with their own political systems and societal structures. In 1612, one of Jamestown's leaders, Captain John Smith, divulged that the Powhatans were a "very barbarous" people who lived differently than the English but nonetheless had a functioning "monarchical government" that was in good order and "would be counted very civil."[42]

The Powhatan name for Virginia, Tsenacommacah, meant "densely populated land," and signified that the English colonists landed in territory that was the very opposite of a "virgin land." Yet the English insisted that Tsenacommacah was a barren land in dire need of their presence. Samuel Purchas, a prominent Anglican cleric who studied at St. John's College in Cambridge and the University of Oxford, published several accounts of English colonization across Africa, Asia, and the Americas. In 1614, Purchas described North America in sexual terms as a feminine land longing for a strong masculine lover to properly care for and satisfy it. Powhatan territory was "virgin soil not yet polluted with Spaniard lust" and therefore "justly called Virginia." Purchas did not hesitate to portray the Jamestown colony as a worthy suitor who would "make thee of a ruder virgin, not a wanton minion; but, an honest and Christian wife."[43] The colonists quickly learned that it was easy to write lovely words about settler colonialism from England, but hard to accomplish it in North America.

The first two years of the Jamestown colony ranged from difficult to disastrous. Roughly 60 percent of the colonists died within the first year, mostly from starvation and disease, but also from violent skirmishes with the Powhatans. They struggled to find food and drinking water. When some of the colonists grew ill and died after imbibing water from a nearby river, others surmised that the contaminated water (which in their recollection was "full of slime and filth") resulted in "the destruction of many of our men."[44] One historian points to the inadequate capacities of the colonists. Of the first settlers, 30 to 40 percent came from the English gentry, and these gentlemen had no manual skills for building, farming, fishing, and hunting. A compounding problem was that the gentlemen brought along their personal attendants, and these men also knew little about constructing forts in the wilderness.[45]

The few men with the requisite abilities proved challenging to manage, because their main interests were to procure immediate individual wealth rather than collaboratively to work toward establishing a long-term settlement. Captain John Smith and others at Jamestown reluctantly turned to the Powhatans for help and bartered their European goods for corn and other crops. Smith and his colleagues also had to frequently apologize to the Powhatan leaders when some Englishmen stole from Powhatan food stores and attacked them without provocation. Investors and supporters of English colonialism were bitterly disappointed upon receiving early reports from Jamestown for two reasons. First, the absence of Indigenous evangelization, as well as the lack of piety among the colonists, bothered them. Second, and more importantly, the colony was a financial catastrophe, with little evidence of future profits.

In 1609, with the fate of Jamestown in peril, Sir Thomas Smythe, the new treasurer of the Virginia Company, and his fellow investors in London acted decisively to address the colony's problems. These next steps are best understood through the lens of the word "company." For all the talk about making Indigenous persons Christian converts, the catalyst of English colonization was transatlantic commerce. Above all, the Virginia Company was a business venture that was created for the same reason as any other company: to make money. In the 1580s, the English writer Richard Hakluyt visited France and reported the exorbitant profits derived from the fur trade. One ship returned from North America and sold beaver, otter, and sable furs for profits of 1,400 to 1,500 percent. Another French merchant told Hakluyt that his four-month expedition to the coast of Nova Scotia resulted in an exchange of European goods worth 40 livres (4 pounds) for cargo valued at 440 crowns (130 pounds).[46]

The historian Karen Ordahl Kupperman provides a meticulous exposition on the economic features of Jamestown. Colonialism was expensive; the English therefore created joint-stock companies to finance projects that were too costly for an individual or a small group: "Joint-stock companies were not like modern corporations with continuing capital funds; usually they operated as umbrella organizations that allowed members to subscribe to more limited joint-stocks under the company's aegis."[47] Joint-stock companies created Jamestown and Massachusetts Bay as well as Shakespeare's Globe Theatre, but the funding behind Jamestown was distinctive. In 1609, the Virginia Company attracted a huge number of investors with a lower stock price (12 pounds and 10 shillings per share) as well as a promise of land in Virginia and a monetary return for every investor when the stock was divided in 1616. The stock price was still substantial (equivalent to approximately $3,600 US in 2023), but it was less than other companies and ultimately drew in over six hundred individual investors and fifty London guilds as corporate subscribers.[48]

The Virginia Company also recognized the need to counter the bad press about Jamestown to recruit new investors and future colonists. The company therefore commissioned influential preachers in London pulpits to deliver sermons that it subsequently published as pamphlets. The hope was that these sermons would simultaneously allay existing concerns and reinforce the international and religious stakes of the colonial enterprise. In 1609, William Crashaw, Robert Gray, and William Symonds were among the clergy who took up the cause. Symonds preached from Genesis 12 and connected the divine call for Abraham to leave his homeland and settle in another country to English colonization. The Jamestown colony was therefore a fulfillment of God's command to "replenish the earth." But Symonds also emphasized Indigenous evangelization and instructed that the colonists "must have a longing and a liking to spread the gospel abroad."

He also addressed moral criticisms of land dispossession: "The country, they say, is possessed by owners, that rule and govern it in their own right: then with what conscience, and equity can we offer to thrust them, by violence, out of their inheritances?" Symonds offered several answers. One entailed a scriptural appeal to the military conquests of Joshua, David, and Solomon against foreign countries practicing other religions. Another acknowledged the virtues of realism over the fantasies of idealism. Symonds derided the pacifism of Anabaptists and their unrelenting disapproval of compromise, but he also maintained that English colonization could be less violent and more peaceable than the systematic "bloody invasion" of the Spanish in the Americas. In the preface to the published sermon, Symonds contrasted the blessing of English Protestantism with the curse of Spanish Catholicism. Unlike the Spanish "papists" who relied on "the Great Whore" (presumably Satan) for their colonial conquest, the English were inspired by Elizabeth I, "a pure virgin," and her royal relative, James I, who took the mantle as "planter of the gospel in places most remote." Their colonial destiny in North America was surely to "present this land a pure virgin to Christ."[49]

Gray and Crashaw also engaged the questions of land dispossession, but both preachers also touched on the commercial nature of English colonization more than Symonds. Later colonists in Massachusetts marshaled one of Gray's defenses of settler colonialism. Gray gently suggested that the Indigenous peoples in North America did not own their lands but had only a "general residence there," because "they range and wander up and down the country, without any law or government." The English colonists therefore had a valid claim to take the lands as their own to cultivate for civil and godly ends.

But Gray more strongly expressed his aspirations for peaceful coexistence between the English and Indigenous in Virginia. Gray also warned about the dangers of avarice and exploitation in transatlantic commerce. He conceded that the economics of trade often required "deceit and fraud" as every participant sought to maximize one's profits in barters and exchanges.[50] Crashaw worried less about English exploitation of Indigenous peoples. He agreed that "a Christian may take nothing from a heathen against his will" and advocated for "fair and lawful" economic transactions. But Crashaw insisted that the English were always the more generous partner, because they offered the benefits of civility and religion in addition to material commodities. Indigenous peoples received European clothing to "cover their bodies from the shame of the world" and English Protestantism to "cover their souls from the wrath of God."

Of the three preachers, Crashaw was the only one to directly address the Virginia Company's investment campaign. Crashaw provided two assurances. The first was the promise that God honors faithfulness. If the colonial enterprise resulted in the spiritual conversions of many Indigenous souls, then worldly gains would surely follow. The second was probably less convincing. Crashaw pointed to the scriptural teaching in Matthew 10:42, in which Christ celebrates the person who gives a cup of cold water in his name, and the London preacher proposed that supporting the spiritual mission of the colonial enterprise was its own reward, even if financial profits lagged.[51]

"Where Religion and Profit Jump Together": Building an English City on an Indigenous Hill

Nearly thirty years after the Wampanoag sachem Massasoit Ousamequin first encountered the English colonists from the *Mayflower* at Patuxet, Massasoit was aggrieved when several Wampanoag hunters were arrested for trespassing on land near Bridgewater, Massachusetts. When he met with the English soldier Myles Standish to discuss the matter in 1649, they were both over sixty years of age. Standish was among the Plymouth colony leaders with whom Massasoit had negotiated a peace treaty in 1621. Despite the treaty, Standish demonstrated his martial capacities often in the next two decades through his aggressive and effective military campaigns against the Wampanoags and other Indigenous nations. Standish retired from active duty and purchased a fourteen-square-mile tract of land from Massasoit to start a small plantation of his own.

But Massasoit and Standish understood the terms of purchase differently. The Wampanoag sachem maintained that he and his men had continual access to the tract for hunting, whereas the retired English military officer insisted that they did not, because the land was now his private property. Massasoit retorted, "What is this thing you call property? It cannot be the earth. For the earth is our mother, nourishing all her children, bears, birds, fish, and all men. The woods, the streams, everything on it belongs to everybody and is for the use of all."[52] The intercultural conflict over land sovereignty had raged since 1621. The historian James Axtell explains how the English colonists sought to transport their European ideas about real estate to Indigenous territories: "Forests were not public property but belonged to the nobility, who regarded them as private game preserves."[53] But the Wampanoags understood the forest as a common space for shared use, and they (and many other Indigenous nations) utilized their generational wisdom, passed down for centuries prior to European arrival, to employ sustainable hunting practices that ensured balance. They killed animals to fill their stomachs and clothe their bodies, but they were careful to preserve their lifeways and did not slaughter more than they needed in any given season. After Standish arrested the Wampanoag hunters, Massasoit expressed his fury at Standish specifically and English settler colonialism more broadly when he asked the following question about land: "How can one man say it belongs to him only?"[54]

In 1605, the English merchant and reporter James Rosier accompanied Captain George Weymouth on an expedition to the coast of Maine. Rosier published an account of the voyage in the same year with hopes to establish a settlement with financial support from the wealthy Catholic nobleman Thomas Arundell. Rosier and Weymouth made landfall on Wabanaki territory, which the Indigenous nation called Dawnland.[55] The English visitors erected a Christian cross on the shore. Christopher Columbus initiated this colonial practice in the Americas and Rosier noted that the important act of planting the cross was "never omitted by any Christian travelers."[56]

The religious symbol came to bear different meanings for European colonists and Indigenous peoples. For the former, it was a sign of discovery and conquest. For the latter, it was a harbinger of conflict and doom. Wabanaki land was breathtakingly beautiful. Rosier marveled at the rivers, streams, sands, and mountains. There were "more good harbors for ships" than in all of England and a dazzling abundance of natural resources, ranging from wildlife to vegetation. Rosier described Dawnland as though he was in the garden of Eden: "Yet this place of itself from God and nature affordeth as much diversity of good commodities, as any reasonable man can wish, for present habitation and planting."[57] The Wabanakis who met Rosier were amiable and greeted him and his companions with "kind civility." Weymouth directed the kidnapping of five Wabanaki men, who were transported to England on the return voyage for future reconnaissance. Rosier did not express remorse for the Wabanaki captives, but he grappled with the moral contradictions of colonization. He conceded the necessity of "private profit" as a motivation for settler colonialism, but Rosier asserted that the "sole intent" of their expedition was Indigenous evangelization, with "true zeal of promulgating God's holy Church, by planting Christianity."[58] English investors funded additional voyages to Wabanaki territory over the next several years and started transatlantic networks for trade, but Rosier's dream of a settlement did not come to fruition.

Colonial efforts that Weymouth and Rosier initiated among the Wabanakis nonetheless had devastating consequences for Indigenous nations throughout North America. Rosier's account of the Wabanakis resembled Columbus's impressions of Taínos in content as well as misinterpretation. Both travelers believed that they made landfall on idyllic paradises and gave sole attribution to their Christian God. One historian of Columbus criticizes the explorer's observations and how they have reverberated into the present for missing the main reason why the Indigenous lifeways he encountered were so good: The Taínos had lived there for many generations—actively learning from experience and making necessary revisions—and "achieved a means of living in a balanced and fruitful harmony with their natural surroundings that any society might well have envied."[59] Another historian contends that the Western Hemisphere prior to Columbus's arrival and subsequent European contact was "a thriving, stunningly diverse place, a tumult of languages, trade, and culture, a region where tens of millions of people loved and hated and worshiped as people do everywhere."[60]

Yet Rosier failed to state the obvious: Dawnland was a flourishing territory because of the Wabanakis. After 1605, the Wabanakis in Maine as well as the Wampanoags in Massachusetts had their worlds turned upside down because of an invisible enemy. Deadly pathogens traveled from Europe to North America and caused the spread of various infectious diseases and epidemics among Indigenous peoples. Indigenous geography never comprised "virgin lands" as the imposing English settlers described them, but historians have referred to the epidemiological phenomena in the Americas after 1492 as "virgin soil" epidemics and pandemics because of the introduction of infectious diseases to previously unexposed Indigenous peoples.

In western South America, smallpox epidemics in 1524, 1525, 1532, 1533, 1535, 1558, and 1565, as well as fatal outbreaks of diphtheria, influenza, measles, and typhus, annihilated the Tawantinsuyu (also known as the Inca Empire) population, resulting in a cumulative mortality rate of 90 percent. Smallpox is thought to have originated from the germs of either a camel or a gerbil "jumping" to humans in Africa, Asia, and Europe. Smallpox killed many Africans, Asians, and Europeans, but these populations also acquired immunity from antibodies over time. Neither camels nor gerbils, nor humans transmitting smallpox viral strains and variants, were in the Americas prior to European contact.[61]

After the English colonists aboard the *Mayflower* arrived in 1620, they learned that a devastating epidemic preceded them from 1616 to 1619. It was one of the worst epidemics in the history of North America, killing as many as nine-tenths of the Indigenous population in coastal New England. Wampanoags and other Indigenous communities engaged with Dutch, English, and French traders, and historians identify these encounters as the cause of the epidemic. One contemporary study of seventeenth-century accounts proposes that the disease was viral hepatitis.[62] Though the precise disease remains uncertain, the tragic results are evident. In 1637, one English colonist, Thomas Morton, vividly recalled the "plague" that struck the Wampanoags from 1616 to 1619 and its aftermath. The Wampanoags "died in heaps as they lay in their houses," and asymptomatic persons unknowingly carried the diseases with them to other communities. With no one left to bury the dead, human carcasses were strewn everywhere, and crows descended to pick at the dead flesh. When Morton remembered "the bones and skulls upon the several places of their habitations," he described the scene as a "newfound Golgotha" (the site outside Jerusalem where Jesus was crucified).[63]

The Wampanoags were a suffering and grieving community when the English colonists arrived to establish Plymouth. They were also in severe bewilderment because they did not know the causes of the new diseases infecting them and how to medically treat the infirmed. The colonists did not have access to the epidemiological resources we have today, but they had experienced the spread of smallpox and other infectious diseases in Europe. Yet their most resounding determination about the epidemics that befell the Wampanoags, first in 1616 to 1619 and then again in 1633, was to point to divine providence. Unlike the turbulent beginnings of Jamestown, in which that settlement encountered a fierce and strong Powhatan confederacy, the colonists at Plymouth and elsewhere in Massachusetts interpreted epidemics as signs of God's favor upon their colonial efforts. The spread of infectious diseases among Indigenous peoples was the handiwork of God for the purpose of "sweeping away great multitudes of the Natives by the smallpox a little before we went thither, that he might make room for us there."[64] This cruel interpretation is both morally repugnant and at odds with their own religious claims about colonization, because there were fewer "Indian souls" to save. But the heartless response of the colonists is also clarifying. Their true intent was land acquisition, not Indigenous evangelization.

The contradictory motivations of evangelism and settler colonialism are also evident in the founding of the Massachusetts Bay Company and the deliberations of one of its leaders, John Winthrop. This joint-stock company received a charter in 1629 from King Charles I, and Winthrop was drawn to establishing a new colony in Massachusetts for at least two reasons. The king's escalating hostility toward Winthrop's Puritan religious community compelled Winthrop to seek a new home outside of England. English colonization, though still in its early stages, had proven profitable by 1629, especially with the growth of tobacco agriculture in Virginia and fur trade commerce in New England, and the Massachusetts Bay Company was one of several new business entities entering into the lucrative transatlantic colonial marketplace. One report from the Plymouth colony in 1624 acknowledged the manifold difficulties of colonization, including the persistent temptation to engage in immoral pursuits of wealth, but it also suggested that New England would emerge as a place "where religion and profit jump together."[65] Winthrop, a wealthy lawyer and landowner in Suffolk, was convinced that leading this venture was an answer to his prayers. It was an opportunity to construct an economically flourishing settlement where he and his fellow Puritans would also be free from religious persecution and the pressure to compromise their beliefs.

In 1630, Winthrop led a fleet of eleven ships and roughly seven hundred colonists from England to North America. The ships departed over several successive months, and Winthrop, as the colony's governor, was aboard the flagship (named *Arbella*) that was the first to set sail. It was on the *Arbella* that Winthrop preached a sermon conveying an image of New England as "a city upon a hill" that became his best-known contribution to American civil religion. In his sermon, Winthrop reminded the passengers that they would be able to succeed in their undertaking only by working together in a spirit of Christian love and unity. He declared, "There are two rules whereby we are to walk one towards another: justice and mercy."[66] The colonists had a sacred mission: "For we must consider that we shall be as a city upon a hill. The eyes of all people are upon us . . . that the Lord our God may bless us in the land whither we go to

The Seal of the Province of Massachusetts Bay

possess it."[67] Although the Massachusetts Bay Company's stated intention was Indigenous evangelization—the center of its seal displayed an almost fully nude Indigenous man saying, "Come over and help us"—there is no mention of the Wampanoags or other Indigenous peoples in Winthrop's sermon. Winthrop spoke of their territories only as land that the colonists must possess to build their English city on an Indigenous hill.

Winthrop and other Puritan leaders in the Massachusetts Bay colony further developed the proposal that Robert Gray offered in 1609 regarding how Indigenous peoples who did not properly use their lands forfeited their ownership rights. Whereas Gray speculated with caution, Winthrop turned this argument into a robust and conclusive systematic theology of land. Winthrop delineated two different rights concerning land: a natural right and a civil right. The former existed "when men held the earth in common" with every person "sowing and feeding where he pleased." But the civil right of ownership superseded the natural right of common use when individuals enclosed parcels of land to raise cattle and farm crops. Winthrop traced the rise of the civil right to the book of Genesis and included as proof the biblical account of Abraham needing to purchase Hittite land from Ephron in Genesis 23 to bury his wife, Sarah. The Indigenous nations in seventeenth-century Massachusetts failed to cultivate their territories according to Winthrop's legal and scriptural analyses; therefore the English colonists could exercise a civil right to own the land: "And for the Natives in New England they enclose no land neither have any settled habitation nor any tame cattle to improve the land by, and so have no other but a natural right to those countries."[68]

Winthrop added several caveats. He cautioned against taking all the land, even though it was legal to do so. Since there was "more than enough" land for the colonists and Indigenous peoples, he recommended that the former leave some land for the latter as a prudent diplomatic strategy.[69] Winthrop and other colonial leaders also permitted the pretense of Indigenous land ownership when that made it easier to acquire land. Because Indigenous peoples did not comprehend Christian theology or European law, English colonists let them pretend as if they owned their lands, if they were willing to sell them.

Another colonist, Roger Williams, despised these Puritan machinations and derided the legal and theological underpinnings as irrational, dishonest, and dishonoring the name of Christ. Indigenous peoples clearly had rightful possession of their lands. They did not set aside parcels of land for individual ownership, but they knew the precise bounds of their territories and "they hunted all the country over, and for the expedition of their hunting voyages, they burnt up all the underwood in the country, once or twice a year."[70] Williams made this point about clearing the forest for more efficient hunting as evidence that Indigenous peoples also knew how to "improve the land" just as the ancient patriarch Abraham did and the English were doing.

Williams was unhappy about a lot of things in the Massachusetts Bay colony and unafraid to speak his mind. In addition to his criticisms of land dispossession, Williams advocated for religious freedom. All Englishmen (sixteen years of age and above) were required to take an oath of loyalty to the colony's governor and other officials, which concluded with the words "so help me God." Williams believed it was wrong to compel men who were not church members to say the oath. One biographer of Williams elucidates his position: "Let the magistrate deal with citizens as members of a civil society only, Williams pleaded, and let the church keep itself unspotted from the world."[71] The combination of his controversial viewpoints on Indigenous land rights and oathtaking threatened foundational pillars that upheld the colony; Williams was therefore banished in 1635 for propagating false and dangerous opinions.

Another biographer of Williams maintains that the specific crimes against him fluctuated. Some colonists insisted that Williams was expelled for civil reasons, not religious heterodoxy. Though the governor, John Winthrop, did not include Williams's criticisms of Puritan land acquisition practices on the formal listing of charges, other colonists stressed that this advocacy of Indigenous rights was in fact the primary reason for his banishment.[72] Williams understood that land was crucial for the futures of both the English and the Indigenous in North America. He did not oppose all land transactions between the two parties, but Williams wanted the English to fairly purchase parcels of North American territory from Indigenous peoples. After his expulsion, Williams went to Rhode Island and bought land there from the Narragansetts who owned it. At the time, Winthrop's assessment that there was more than enough land for English colonies and Indigenous communities held true. But in subsequent years both Winthrop and Williams witnessed in part the cumulatively destructive force of settler colonialism, though they did not experience its culmination. There is never enough land, because the colonists and their descendants always want more.

Williams spent several years among the Narragansetts and in 1643 published a book, *A Key into the Language of America*, detailing his interactions with them and providing an extensive glossary of words from the Algonquian language they spoke. It became immediately popular, as many copies were sold to English readers in London who were curious about the native inhabitants of North America, and it is recognized today as an early example of cultural anthropology and the first study of a North American Indigenous language written in English.[73] Williams posited that Indigenous communities were more hospitable than English colonies: "It is a strange truth that a man shall generally find more free entertainment and refreshing amongst these Barbarians, then among thousands that call themselves Christians."

Williams also appealed to Acts 17:26 when comparing Europeans and Indigenous peoples in North America, emphasizing that there were no natural differences between the two, as they shared the same humanity as equally created by the God who made all races of one blood. He then cited Ephesians 2 to indicate that all by nature were also "children of wrath" in need of God's salvation through Jesus Christ.[74] Williams was certainly aware of the escalating disparagement from some clergy in England about the absence of evangelism in the colonies. In 1641, seventy-six English and Scottish ministers published a petition criticizing the dearth of Indigenous converts in New England and Virginia. Instead of preaching the gospel in North America, the colonists appeared to be chasing only after financial profit, "to possess the land of those infidels, or of gain by commerce."[75] But Williams himself did not preach among Indigenous communities.

This decision to intentionally refrain from Indigenous evangelization, despite his close contact with the Narragansetts and his position as probably the most capable English speaker of Algonquian, was an uncommon conviction and perhaps his most controversial one. But he explained in 1645 that the oppressive conditions of English settler colonialism made it impossible for him (or any English Christian) to convey the genuine message of Christianity in all its fullness and goodness to Indigenous peoples. Like las Casas, Williams too believed that the only way of attracting people to Christianity was in freedom and without coercion. Williams desired for Indigenous peoples to learn about Christianity without the obfuscations and corruptions of colonialism.[76] He confessed that he did not have a clear answer for what then English colonists should do in North America, but Williams asked that his readers trust in God's sovereignty and timing.

Williams therefore exposed the deceptive underpinnings that supported the claims of Robert Cushman, John Winthrop, and other defenders of English settler colonialism. In 1622, Cushman helped to formulate an early modern English legal doctrine, *vacuum domicilium*, that defined Indigenous territories in North America as vacant because the Indigenous peoples were roaming over rather than cultivating the land. The English therefore had the rights "to go live in the heathens' country" and own Indigenous territories.[77] Yet Williams revealed what other colonists also knew: The Wampanoags, Narragansetts, and other Indigenous nations had clearly demarcated boundaries of what constituted their land and the land of others. One colonist, William Wood, admitted this in 1634, when writing, "The country as it is in relation to the Indians is divided as it were into shires, every several division being swayed by a several king."[78] Just as England was divided into distinct shires, or counties, such as Cheshire and Yorkshire, so too was the Indigenous continent of North America. Williams also challenged Cushman's appeal to the Great Commission and the conversion of the "heathens" to defend settler colonialism. Indigenous evangelization was on the lips of many proponents of English colonization, but this endeavor was not in the hearts of many colonists in North America. And Williams concluded that one of the many destructive consequences of settler colonialism was the impossibility of genuine Christian ministry among Indigenous peoples.

France, Spain, and England all made religious claims to justify their colonial oppressions in the Americas. Students in primary and secondary education have since learned that the French were in pursuit of "fur, fish, and the faith" whereas the Spanish desired "God, gold, and glory." The alliterations make it easy to remember these colonial intentions, but the lessons misrepresent history because they imply that the three components were equal in terms of motivation. I also learned these lessons in my own education, but I cannot recall a commensurate threefold alliteration to summarize English colonization. I imagine that "land, liberty, and the Lord" would convey a similar distortion that dilutes a reckoning with history.

Another oversimplification can be found in some contemporary treatments of the doctrine of discovery. Patrick Wolfe explains that a series of Roman Catholic papal bulls in the fifteenth century, most notably *Inter caetera* and *Eximiae devotionis*, which divided territories to Portugal and Spain for colonization and evangelization in 1493, are "misleadingly referred to, in the singular, as the doctrine of discovery": "Though a thoroughgoing diminution of native entitlement was axiomatic to discovery, the discourse was primarily addressed to relations between European sovereigns rather than to relations between Europeans and natives."[79] These papal bulls, and legal theories such as *vacuum domicilium*, provided legal and theological permissions for Europeans to colonize Indigenous territories around the world, but they alone do not adequately illumine the making, shaping, bending, and breaking of Christianity in Indigenous North America. In recent years, many Christian traditions, ranging from Roman Catholicism to various mainline Protestant denominations, have repudiated the doctrines that enabled discovery, but I fear that some Christians have mistakenly presumed that these solitary denunciations are sufficient confessions for the totality of settler colonialism and its ongoing consequences. To reckon with history is to confront the sinful actions and incremental compromises as well as the righteous protests and incisive criticisms that resulted from the insatiable hunger for land.

Chapter Three

"If the People of the United States Will Imitate the Ruler Who Coveted Naboth's Vineyard"

The Theological Roots of Indigenous Displacement and the Emergence of the United States as a Colonial Power

In 1798, Jeremiah Evarts left his family's farm in Vermont to attend college in New Haven, Connecticut. The eighteen-year-old white man enrolled at Yale College because he enjoyed reading books and writing more than tilling fields and agriculture. The college freshman's parents, James and Sarah Evarts, were from Guilford, Connecticut, an agrarian town east of New Haven, and moved to Vermont before Jeremiah was born. James and Sarah joined other emigrants from Connecticut in pursuit of better economic opportunities in Vermont. An increase in Connecticut's population and a decrease in available land across the state propelled many young couples to seek new homes and farms northward. James and Sarah Evarts first settled in Sunderland, Vermont, but the area was too mountainous for agrarian families; so the couple relocated to Georgia, Vermont, in 1787. The town of Georgia was along the shores of Lake Champlain, and the Evarts family worked hard to establish a successful farm there. They were not exceedingly wealthy, but James Evarts was confident that with proper care and attention his family's farm would continue to generate healthy profits for his children and grandchildren.

James desired for his eldest son, Jeremiah, to manage the homestead, but Jeremiah had passions that were leading him toward a different vocation. When Jeremiah was five years of age, he returned home from school and implored his father to buy him a new book. James asked, "What! Is your book worn out?" Jeremiah answered, "Oh no, sir; but I have read all the sense out of it."[1] After graduating from Yale, Jeremiah did not follow in his father's footsteps. Instead, he devoted his life to protecting Cherokee land in the state that shared the name of the town where he grew up, Georgia.

Jeremiah Evarts flourished at Yale, and his experience there was an archetype of the transformative opportunities that elite higher education provided for young white men in the middle and upper classes. In addition to his intellectual growth from the academic learning within Yale's classrooms, Evarts took advantage of access to political and social engagements in New Haven. The Connecticut General Assembly met alternately in Hartford and New Haven when Evarts was at Yale, and he attended debates and dined with state representatives, including the governor and lieutenant governor, when the General Assembly did its work in New Haven. One classmate of Evarts remembered him as "prominent for his sagacity, his manly and industrious habits, his generous regard of his companions, his wisdom and scholarship, in the whole of his collegiate course."[2] Evarts also attended revival meetings. Yale's president, Timothy Dwight, a theologian and Congregational minister, urged the students to be diligent in their studies and faithful in their piety. Dwight did not want every student to be a pastor, but he did want them all to be observant Christians. In 1802, the college president preached a sermon entitled "The Youth of Nain" from Luke 7:11–17. In this passage, Christ visits a funeral in the town of Nain and performs the miracle of resurrecting the grieving widow's deceased son. Many of Dwight's students, including Evarts, testified to either converting or recommitting to Christianity after this sermon and the subsequent revival meetings on campus.[3]

Evarts became a lawyer and married Mehitabel Sherman Barnes, the daughter of one of Connecticut's leading politicians, Roger Sherman, who was a judge in the state's Superior Court, US senator, and signatory of the Declaration of Independence. After practicing the law for several years in New Haven, Evarts yearned to do work that was more closely connected to Christianity. He first accepted an invitation to be the editor of a religious periodical in Massachusetts and then to join the executive leadership of the American Board of Commissioners for Foreign Missions (ABCFM), a new organization founded by recent graduates of Williams College in 1810. The ABCFM developed into a formidable church-related association that supported hundreds of Congregational, Dutch Reformed, Presbyterian, and other Protestant missionaries across Asia, Africa, and Indigenous nations in North America. In 1812, the ABCFM sent its first missionaries to several Asian countries, including Adoniram and Ann Hasseltine Judson to India. By 1840 the organization had commissioned 694 missionaries.[4] For Evarts, the mission work among the Cherokee Nation in the southeastern United States captivated his heart and mind. And he experienced another transformation that was as deep as his religious conversion at Yale. Evarts determined that the political controversies surrounding the expulsion of the Cherokees from their territory in Georgia not only imperiled tens of thousands of Cherokees but also represented a pivotal moment that tested the justice and humanity of his nation.

In 1829, Evarts appealed to 1 Kings 21 when writing, "If the people of the United States will imitate the ruler who coveted Naboth's vineyard, the world will assuredly place them by the side of Naboth's oppressor. Impartial history will not ask them, whether they feel gratified and honored by such an association."[5] Evarts was aware that many white Christians associated their nation with ancient Israel and saw themselves as God's chosen people, but he searched the Scriptures and found that the United States, in its unjust dealings with the Cherokees, was in closer accordance with the wicked rulership of Ahab and Jezebel. In 1 Kings 21, Naboth refuses to sell his vineyard to King Ahab because it is an inheritance from his ancestors. Ahab's wife, Jezebel, then conspires with local officials to have Naboth stoned to death for spurious charges, so that Ahab can take possession of the vineyard he covets. The prophet Elijah then fiercely condemns Ahab and Jezebel for perpetrating such blatant evils against God and humankind.

Evarts utilized a pertinent scriptural passage that was haunting in its condemnation of land dispossession, but he inhabited a world in which white Americans, including many Christians, ruthlessly seized Indigenous territories. Some white Christians simply ignored Evarts's religiously motivated activism, whereas others refuted Evarts and other Indigenous rights activists by wielding their own scriptural texts and racist theologies.

This chapter focuses on the theological roots of Indigenous displacement and the emergence of the United States as a colonial power in the years and decades following national independence. Jeremiah Evarts did not stand alone in the fight against Cherokee expulsion. An inspiring coalition of Indigenous and white women and men participated in this righteous struggle. But white Christianity in North America had a long record of loud sermons and quiet compromises to justify the most appalling sins of settler colonialism, and therefore the proponents of Cherokee expulsion were equipped with all the lessons of history that they needed to win. White Christians intruded upon Indigenous lands, disrupted Indigenous lifeways, and then imposed culturally informed religious doctrines about land use and private property as irrefutable universal truths that supported Indigenous displacement.

"All for Land and Elbow-Room Enough in the World": To Acknowledge the Fullness of History as a Nation and a Church

In *Neither Settler nor Native: The Making and Unmaking of Permanent Minorities*, Mahmood Mamdani compares the words of President Barack Obama and the Rev. Dr. Martin Luther King Jr. on American settler colonialism and

Indigenous history. In 2009, six days after delivering his first inaugural address, Obama said the following in an interview at the White House: "My job to the Muslim world is to communicate that the Americans are not your enemy. We sometimes make mistakes. We have not been perfect. But if you look at the track record, as you say, America was not born as a colonial power."[6] In 1964, King reflected, "Our nation was born in genocide when it embraced the doctrine that the original American, the Indian, was an inferior race." King went further and maintained that the United States deliberately displaced and oppressed Indigenous nations: "We are perhaps the only nation which tried as a matter of national policy to wipe out its indigenous population. Moreover, we elevated that tragic experience into a noble crusade. Indeed, even today we have not permitted ourselves to reject or feel remorse for this shameful episode."[7]

Mamdani contends that King was closer to the truth than Obama but also recognizes why most Americans prefer Obama's rendering of the past: "The innocence of Obama's statement is the innocence of America, the lie the population tells itself over and over again."[8] Mamdani supports King's assessment and delineates how "white settlers and their governments systematically drained North American territories of their Indian inhabitants" through violence, forced migration, legal coercion, and economic exploitation.[9]

In January 2013, several days after Obama's second inaugural address, Randall Kennedy, a law professor at Harvard Law School, published an article in *Time* magazine challenging Obama in his second presidential term to be more honest about the limits of American exceptionalism. Kennedy disagreed with Obama's critics, who charged the nation's first Black president with insufficiently embracing the idea of American exceptionalism. Instead, Kennedy found that Obama sometimes engaged in an unhealthy patriotism that "revels in national idolatry": "And so, in line with previous Presidents, Obama lauds the pioneers who 'blazed' a westward trail but never mentions the systematic acts of ethnic cleaning by which the U.S. wrestled lands from Indian nations. He praises the Founding Fathers, making no mention of the slaves who fled them or of the fact that many more blacks and Indians fought on the side of King George than with George Washington."[10] Though Kennedy was right about the past, it is likely that Obama accurately understood the temper of the nation he was leading. Some Americans wanted to learn from the fullness of history, but many more simply did not have the appetite for such a reckoning.

One way that some Americans, including Christians, have sought to address one of their nation's founding sins is the practice of land acknowledgment. But others are increasingly questioning the purposes of this practice. In their article from 2021, Theresa Stewart-Ambo and K. Wayne Yang observe that

Indigenous land acknowledgments are more common in Canada than the United States, where they are also called territorial acknowledgments, and that the practice gained momentum following the 2015 final report of the Truth and Reconciliation Commission of Canada. Stewart-Ambo and Yang write, "Although without the same context of federal accountability (yet), land acknowledgments in the United States are increasingly practiced by individuals, institutions, and organizations as a gesture toward creating equitable and inclusive environments."[11]

Stewart-Ambo and Yang also compare Indigenous versus non-Indigenous land acknowledgments. They note that Indigenous acknowledgments are not new but rather continuations of ancient practices that illustrate deep relationships to land and ancestors as well as commitments to honor all the living beings that inhabit the land. Contemporary acknowledgments from Indigenous peoples also highlight colonial disruptions. Menominee scholar Rowland Keshena Robinson explains that his territorial acknowledgment recognizes "ancient relations of friendship, kinship, and alliance" and "the relatively obvious fact (as far as we as Indigenous Peoples and Nations see it) that the land was stolen from us by the expansion of white settler sovereign power."[12] But non-Indigenous acknowledgment practices sometimes reveal contradictory impulses that involve honoring Indigenous peoples and nations as the original inhabitants of a territory, but obscuring the unjust colonial histories of land dispossession. Perhaps the most egregious abuses of this practice are found in acknowledgments that thank Indigenous peoples for their stewardship of land that they no longer reside on and fail to mention why they are not presently there.

In 1975, Francis Jennings explicated both the clear motivations and complex processes of American settler colonialism. Jennings refuted the notion of North America as a "virgin land" that some English colonists and supporters of colonialism in England promoted to justify white ownership of Indigenous lands. Though Indigenous peoples did not follow English practices of separating their territories into enclosed parcels for private use, they clearly cultivated their lands to reflect their ideologies of civilization and community. Jennings contended that the English colonists "did not settle a virgin land" but instead "invaded and displaced a resident population." The historian added, "This is so simple a fact that it seems self-evident."[13] The obvious reason for perpetuating a Christian theology of land ownership that simultaneously conformed to English customs of private property and condemned Indigenous understandings of communal use, although the latter more closely resembled the first Christian community after Pentecost in Acts 2:42–47, was because it was a religious means to achieve the ends of settler colonialism.

Increase Mather, a prominent seventeenth-century Puritan pastor in Boston and sixth president of Harvard College, was prone to delivering incisive sermons that scornfully rebuked hearers for their sins, especially those iniquities that he thought illustrated religious decline and a falling away from the supposed pure faith of the first generation of English colonists. Later historians employed the term "jeremiads" (after the prophet Jeremiah in the Hebrew Bible) for this genre of sermons. In the aftermath of a brutal war against the Wampanoags, Mather preached a jeremiad in 1676 outlining the sins that required repentance. Mather believed that God was displeased with the colonists due to their insufficient attention to church attendance and an excessive focus on physical appearance. The preacher despised men flaunting elaborate periwigs and women adorning hair extensions, jewelry, and other "whorish fashions" in public.[14] But Mather included a sin that unintentionally (at least by Mather's intentions) revealed that seizing Indigenous territory was the true aim of English colonization, when he declared, "*Land! Land!* Hath been the idol of many in *New-England*: Whereas the first planters here that they might keep themselves together were satisfied with one acre for each person, as his propriety, and after that with twenty acres for a family, how have men since coveted after the earth, that many hundreds, nay thousands of acres, have been engrossed by one man."[15] Mather's memory of colonial beginnings overstated the self-proclaimed economic modesty of Puritans—the Plymouth colony governor William Bradford's brief experiment in the 1620s of communal farming failed because the colonists desired privatization, and the desire for private property surged as early as the 1630s—but his jeremiad nonetheless identified that the desire to possess land belonging to others was the unjust motivation driving American settler colonialism.

Mather was upset that people who "profess themselves Christians have forsaken churches and ordinances, and all for land and elbow-room enough in the world," but he did not mean to address a foundational sin or to prompt structural reform.[16] Mather did not question whether his ancestors rightly obtained Indigenous land. Instead, he diagnosed the sin as coveting "elbow-room" and urged his hearers to care less about purchasing extravagant clothing and additional land and devote more of their time and energy toward individual acts of piety and congregational worship.

Jennings traced the strategies that English colonists and white Americans used to displace Indigenous peoples. Armed conquest was certainly one, but it was not the preferred pathway, because it also resulted in white casualties of war. A bevy of various white officials, politicians, and pastors therefore employed methods such as making treaties with illegitimate tribal leaders, offering land grants to white settlers within or near Indigenous territories to harass Indigenous peoples and encroach on their lands, and levying legal fines to compel Indigenous peoples into debts that could be repaid only through land appropriations.[17] Another approach within white-Indigenous relations was for the former to simply disregard agreements or unilaterally revise treaties to meet changing circumstances, ranging from increases in local white populations to discoveries of valuable natural resources.

One rationale for Obama's claim that the United States was not born as a colonial power focuses on foreign relations with countries beyond North America. The United States was involved in the transatlantic slave trade until 1808 and exerted its force diplomatically and militarily in the Americas by the middle of the nineteenth century and across the world by the end of the same century, but the nation did not participate in Western imperialism with the same depth and intensity of European nations at its founding in the late eighteenth century.

But the notion that the United States did not begin as a colonial power quickly crumbles with even a cursory glance at its unjust engagements with Indigenous nations in North America. In *Hollow Justice: A History of Indigenous Claims in the United States*, Lumbee scholar David E. Wilkins cites a study of the Indian Claims Commission that finds that the United States acquired approximately 443 million acres of Indigenous land from 1789 to 1840 "for some 31.3 million in cash and 53.8 million acres for Indian settlement further west" and that "this cost to the government of about ten cents per acre compared favorably to the value of [$]1.25 per acre that was the minimum purchase price for lands of the public domain."[18] In 1820, Jedidiah Morse, a Congregational pastor and geographer (and father of Samuel F. B. Morse, the inventor of the American telegraph), was commissioned to visit numerous Indigenous nations and submit a report of his findings to the US Secretary of War John C. Calhoun. Morse identified the problem of fraudulent agreements that were not negotiated with the "real" and "acknowledged" tribal leaders. But Morse also divulged that even the legal transactions greatly favored white Americans, and he hinted at the coercive and exploitative measures involved: "More than two hundred millions of acres of some of the best lands in our country, have been purchased, after our manner, and at our own prices, of the Indians. . . . With this statement before him, founded on official documents, will any man hazard his reputation as an honest, fair, and just man, by saying, 'We have no funds to give for civilizing the Indians?'"[19] Morse did not overtly criticize the federal government, but he also believed that it was plainly evident that his nation had wronged Indigenous peoples.

"Now God Doth Offer You That Opportunity": Transatlantic Trade, English Settler Colonialism, and the Remaking of an Indigenous Continent

The roots of white American oppression against Indigenous peoples are found in the threefold aims of English colonization: trade, settlement, and Indigenous evangelization. The historian Jill Lepore encapsulates the manifold issues and multiple layers of European intrusion into the Americas with the following questions: "Are all peoples one? And if they are, by what right can one people take the land of another or their labor or, even, their lives?" Lepore then contends that "any historical reckoning with these questions begins with counting and measuring" and therefore provides important facts: Between 1500 and 1800, roughly two and a half million Europeans migrated to the Americas and as many as fifty million Indigenous persons died. Europeans extracted enormous wealth from the natural resources of the Americas, which included minerals, timbers, animal furs, and lands. The Americas comprised over twenty million square miles, whereas Europe was spread across four million square miles.[20]

In 1630, Francis Higginson, a Puritan pastor in the Massachusetts Bay colony, wrote about the "commodities" in "New England's plantation," in a promotional tract. Higginson declared, "The abundance of sea fish is almost beyond believing, and sure I should scarce have believed it except I had seen it with my own eyes." He marveled at the diversity of fish, such as bass, cod, herring, and mackerel, and added that there were also ample numbers of crabs and oysters. Higginson transitioned from the waters to the forests of New England and reported that there were timbers from an array of trees, such as birch, cedar, pine, and spruce, to build both houses and ships, as well as many animals to hunt for their furs and skins. The pastor was confident that "a poor servant here that is to possess but 50 acres of land, may afford to give more wood for timber and fire as good as the world yields, than many noblemen in England can afford to do." And he ended his tract with an appeal to Christianity and Romans 8:31. In addition to a favorable accounting of natural resources, Higginson pointed to the presence of "plenty of preaching and diligent catechizing" in the colony as divine assurance: "And thus we doubt not but God will be with us, and if God be with us, who can be against us?"[21]

The primary focus of Higginson's tract was trade, and the secondary one was settlement. There was hardly any mention of Indigenous evangelization. Higginson criticized Indigenous peoples as lazy and stupid, due to their preservation of natural resources. He charged, "The Indians are not able to make use of the one fourth part of the land."[22] Higginson and other English colonists at first struggled to understand Indigenous lifeways in Massachusetts. They saw that Indigenous peoples lived among vast natural resources, yet did not extract as much as possible from the waters and forests. The English settlers did not grasp that Indigenous peoples had cultivated their land for thousands of years and employed generational wisdom to make for themselves a sustainable world of sufficiency rather than excess.

One historian explains, "But the way Indians had chosen to inhabit that world posed a paradox almost from the start for Europeans accustomed to other ways of interacting with the environment. Many European visitors were struck by what seemed to them the poverty of Indians who lived in the midst of a landscape endowed so astonishingly with abundance."[23] Some English colonists attributed the abundance of natural resources in North America to their Christian God as well as their own prayers. Higginson was closer to the truth when he assessed Indigenous peoples. But the abundance of fish, timber, and other natural "commodities" he witnessed was the direct result of Indigenous wisdom, not indolence. Indigenous peoples were responsible stewards who extracted and killed only what they needed for two purposes. They practiced mutuality with animals as fellow creatures and engaged in interconnected relations of reciprocity that sought to honor the earth and all its inhabitants, ranging from plants to trees and animals to humans. In doing so, they also ensured that future generations would also have more than enough to flourish.

Yet in Massachusetts and throughout North America, English colonists and white Americans disrupted and ultimately destroyed these Indigenous lifeways. Between 1652 and 1658, one trading post in Springfield, Massachusetts, accumulated roughly nine thousand beaver pelts and hundreds of fox, mink, moose, raccoon, and other animal skins. In 1654 alone, this trading post exported 3,723 pounds of beaver to England.[24] In 1723, the French Jesuit missionary Sebastian Rasles observed that the Abenakis in Maine were reduced to a diet of corn, beans, and pumpkins because "the game of their country," such as deer and elks, had all either been killed or fled.[25] The environmental historian Carolyn Merchant expounds how European colonization and subsequent American expansion in North America also negatively altered a multitude of ecosystems. In New England, the severe reduction in the beaver population had a domino effect of devastating consequences for other wildlife. There were fewer black ducks, ring-necked ducks, and hooded mergansers in Maine with the decrease in beaver ponds where they bred. The decline in beaver dams resulted in flooding that displaced muskrats and otters. Raccoons ate frogs and snakes from beaver flowages and had less to eat when these ponds first became marshes and then meadows. Merchant contends that "the colonial ecological revolution completed in northern New England by the late seventeenth century was the first phase of a process of deconstructing the environment and reconstructing human consciousness."[26]

Very few English colonists questioned the changes they instigated, because the result was a shifting abundance in their favor. The waters and forests were no longer teeming with animals and trees, but the colonists themselves were making profits and expanding settlements. In 1637, one colonist, Thomas Morton, wondered aloud whether the Indigenous knew something that the English did not. Whereas his people were consumed by the pursuit of more material wealth, Morton saw how Indigenous peoples exercised true freedom by wanting little.[27]

Indigenous peoples resisted the ways in which the English and other European colonists were remaking their worlds. Initially, many Indigenous nations did not consider these new visitors as a grave threat to their existence. In the northeastern region of North America, European traders had established a transatlantic network by the time the first waves of English colonists arrived in Massachusetts in the 1620s and early 1630s. Indigenous peoples varied in their feelings toward this foreign intrusion, but many also willingly participated in exchanges of European goods for their natural resources.

But English colonization soon differed from Dutch and French enterprises. The latter two countries were not nearly as invested in settlements. In 1627, only 107 French persons resided in Canada, and only 18 of this number desired to be long-term settlers (the remainder came as employees of trading companies). The French population increased only to 356 persons in 1640.[28] The English population in North America greatly exceeded the French in the same time span. From 1629 to 1642, roughly 20,000 English colonists arrived to settle in New England.[29] In the Massachusetts Bay colony alone, the English population increased from 4,000 in 1634 to 6,000 in 1635 and then to 11,000 in 1638.[30] In Virginia, the English population rose from 6,000 in 1624 to 55,000 in 1680.[31]

Indigenous peoples were therefore facing nearly insurmountable odds. They were overwhelmed in at least two ways. They were trying to oppose escalating encroachment from a seemingly endless influx of white foreigners who arrived on their shores in ship after ship, while also suffering from epidemics caused by the viruses that the colonists brought with them. In 1642, the Narragansett sachem Miantonomi sought an alliance with the Montauks in Long Island, New York, to deter the English. Miantonomi observed, "For you know our fathers had plenty of deer and skins, our plains were full of deer, as also our woods, and of turkeys, and our coves full of fish and fowl. But these English have gotten our land, they with scythes cut down the grass, and with axes fell the trees; their cows and horses eat the grass, and their hogs spoil our clam banks."[32] The Narragansett sachem understood what was at stake in the struggle against the white foreigners. He implored the Montauks to join him; otherwise "we shall all be starved."[33] The precious world that Miantonomi had inherited from his ancestors and strove to maintain as a leader of his community was in peril.

Miantonomi's criticism of English colonization was directed toward settlement rather than trade because of the dangers the former wrought upon Indigenous peoples. Prior to the seventeenth century, the English were primarily interested in North America for mercantile reasons, such as trade with Indigenous peoples, the search for gold and silver, and the discovery of a westward waterway route to Asia through North America (known as the Northwest Passage). As English settlements emerged and expanded, even white traders divulged to their Indigenous clientele that the settlers were a serious threat to them. In the Carolinas, a trader named John Ellis warned the Catawbas about English settlers in the area and told them that the colonists "had no right to the lands by them possessed and that even his Majesty had no right to those lands."[34] When the colony's governor learned of Ellis's comments, he announced that he would arrest anyone making similar remarks in the future.

The historian Barbara Arneil explains that the motivations of traders differed from settlers. Traders did not necessarily deal fairly with Indigenous peoples, and often engaged in deceitful practices to increase profits, but they also "had no vested interest in either displacing the Amerindians from their lands or converting them to Christianity."[35] In daring to speak out against the injustices of English settler colonialism, Ellis was not entirely altruistic. His own livelihood as a trader depended on working with Catawbas. Traders generally preferred Indigenous peoples over European colonists as business partners, because the former were more skilled in delivering the desired natural resources and easier to exploit in transactions. Despite Ellis's ulterior agenda, the trader was right in identifying English settler colonialism as a menace to Indigenous North America.

Pastors and theologians in England viewed the Indigenous continent as a solution to the problem of overpopulation in their nation. In 1624, Richard Eburne, vicar of the parish church of Henstridge in Somerset, published a treatise entitled "A Plain Pathway to Plantations" in support of settler colonialism. As a pastor, Eburne was attuned to the conversations that arose among his parishioners and understood that colonization was a lively topic of debate. He acknowledged that the primary focus of colonization was in its potential to serve as a release valve for domestic problems. Migration to North America would alleviate the challenges accompanying an increasing population in

England, which included diminishing economic prospects, escalating crime, and growing concerns about civil disorder and higher taxes. The broader English public therefore regarded the "main end" of colonization as "to move our people of England to plant themselves abroad and free themselves of that penury and peril of want wherein they live at home."[36]

Eburne agreed that there were economic and societal benefits to migration, but he argued that English settler colonialism needed a higher aim: "That one proper and principal end of plantations is, or should be, the enlargement of Christ's church on earth and the publishing of his gospel to the sons of men."[37] Yet despite Eburne's stated intent to provide a theological "doctrine of plantations," he devoted much of his treatise to overpopulation at home and far less to Indigenous evangelization abroad. Eburne contended that healthy and able-bodied people among the lower classes should emigrate to North America. He appealed to scriptural examples of migrants, such as "Abraham and Sarah, Isaac and Rebecca, Jacob, and many other famous, godly, and holy patriarchs and persons," and pointed to divine providence in the expansion of English settler colonialism.[38] Colonization was no longer confined to a few merchants and traders. Instead, there were now possibilities for thousands of people to gain access to economic mobility through land ownership. Eburne observed, "Now God doth offer you that opportunity, with choice of place, to rid yourselves from your present misery and distress. . . . Be not too much in love with that country wherein you were born, that country which, bearing you, yet cannot breed you, but seemeth and is indeed weary of you."[39]

The parish vicar further expounded on national pride to elucidate his doctrine of plantations. Because "Englishmen above many others are worst able to live with a little," the expansion of colonization from trade to settlement was a sign of divine favor upon their nation. Eburne recognized that many persons in England preferred migration to relatively known contexts in other parts of Europe to the entirely unknown wilds of North America, but he contended that Indigenous territory was the more faithful destination. In Deuteronomy, the ancient Israelites relocated to Canaan, an inhabited land with "great and goodly cities" that they did not build themselves. In Indigenous North America, God granted England an opportunity to exceed even ancient Israel: "God prepareth them a place, a land, wherein they may build them cities, towns, and houses to dwell in; where they may sow land and plant them vineyards and orchards too, to yield them fruits of increase, as the Psalmist writeth (Ps. 107:39)."[40] Eburne insinuated that to oppose colonization was to reject the open arms of God desiring to carry a suffering people to a promised land where they could build their own homes and cities.

There were several problems with the reports, sermons, and treatises promoting English colonization. One lesser predicament concerned the ways in which pastors and theologians such as Eburne and Higginson oversold the promises and undersold the perils of settler colonialism. There was an abundance of natural resources in North America, but humans also needed to exercise resilience and learn the proper skills for trade and settlement. In 1628, the English naval captain Christopher Levett lambasted both his country's promotional literature and some of the colonists' unpreparedness for life in Indigenous North America. Levett wrote, "I will not do therein as some have done, to my knowledge speak more than is true: I will not tell you that you may smell the cornfields before you see the land, neither must men think that corn doth grow naturally (or on trees), nor will the deer come when they are called . . . nor the fish leap into the kettle."[41] Levett employed a sardonic wit to illustrate that farming, fishing, and hunting in North America were not as easy as some pastors suggested—Atlantic cod did not leap into kettles—but he also did not fully explain the larger challenges of Indigenous resistance to the presence of the English.

A greater predicament was that English settler colonialism was inherently a dirty business that required armed conflict and bloodshed. The antipathy and violence that transpired between English colonists and Indigenous peoples in the seventeenth century continued after the thirteen colonies won their independence from British rule and formed the United States. Indigenous peoples were neither as friendly nor as docile as Eburne and other pastors described them. Eburne readily dismissed Indigenous resistance and presented only two outcomes for white-Indigenous relations. Indigenous peoples would "submit themselves tractably to live" under white dominion or flee from their lands in fear of the English.[42] In 1622, the renowned English poet and dean of St. Paul's Cathedral in London John Donne preached a sermon about the "Virginia plantation" that effusively praised it as a glorious missionary enterprise that fulfilled Christ's promise in Acts 1:8. Just like the disciples at Pentecost, the colonists in Virginia were recipients of an outpouring of the Holy Spirit so that they could be witnesses of the gospel and save Indigenous souls in the "uttermost part of the earth."[43] But white colonists in Virginia and Massachusetts did not treat the Powhatans, Pequots, Wampanoags, and other Indigenous peoples as objects of conversion. Indigenous peoples were instead obstacles to colonization. Eburne was right about English desires to build new homes and cities, but he was wrong about the ease of this colonial project and entirely missed that many colonists despised the Indigenous persons who stood in their way and how this revulsion developed into a wider hatred of all Indigenous peoples in North America.

"We Had Sufficient Light from the Word of God for Our Proceedings": Wanton Violence, War Crimes, and the Remaking of Christianity in North America

In 1621, George Thorpe, one of the Virginia colony's leaders, wrote a letter to Sir Edwin Sandys in London that indicated how unpopular Thorpe's designs for harmonious relations with the Powhatans and Indigenous evangelization through mission schools were among the colonists. Thorpe sadly admitted, "There is scarce any man amongst us that doth so much as afford [the Powhatans] a good thought in his heart and most men with their mouths give them nothing but maledictions and bitter execrations."[44] He added that the discord among the Powhatans and colonists was the result of the latter party: "If there be wrong on any side it is on ours who are not so charitable to them as Christians ought to be, they being (especially the better sort of them) of a peaceable and virtuous disposition."[45] But Thorpe also overestimated the forbearance of the Powhatans after repeated English intrusions and attacks. In 1622, after a colonist murdered one of the Powhatan chief's advisers, the Powhatans killed Thorpe and 346 other English colonists in retaliatory attacks against numerous English settlements across Virginia.[46]

The English colonists responded to this massacre in 1622 with both military force and diplomatic chicanery. Additional ships arrived with more fighting men and ammunition. The historian Edmund S. Morgan details the English tactics that resulted in their victory over the Powhatans by 1625: "Since the Indians were better woodsmen than the English and virtually impossible to track down, the method was to feign peaceful intentions, let them settle down and plant their corn wherever they chose, and then, just before harvest, fall upon them, killing as many as possible and burning the corn."[47] The colonists also made treaties with the Powhatans that they never intended to keep but instead were aimed at "lulling the Indians into security, the better to surprise them."[48] One English negotiator poisoned the drinks that he offered to the Powhatans after signing a treaty, which killed roughly two hundred of them immediately and the English slaughtered another fifty staggering Powhatans weakened from the poison.

When the Virginia Company of London learned of these insidious schemes, its directors instructed the colony's leaders to act more honorably and justly in their military campaign. The directors wanted the colony to triumph, but they were also acutely aware of the moral and religious claims they made to promote colonization. Sir Francis Wyatt, the colony's governor, penned a letter that acknowledged uneasy questions abroad about their machinations in Virginia but dismissed them as naive accusations from uninformed people who did not grasp the harsh conditions on the ground.[49] Settler colonialism was a treacherous endeavor, and the governor even sent his wife, Lady Margaret Wyatt, back to England one year before he ended his term and returned home himself in 1625. But one of the legacies that Sir Francis Wyatt left behind was a playbook for how to defeat, displace, and dispossess Indigenous peoples. And the Virginia colony's actions in the 1620s also illustrated both the limits and distortions of white Christianity as English colonists, including clergy, first tolerated and then defended the taking of an Indigenous continent through aggression and deceit.

Scriptural justifications for wanton violence and war crimes perpetrated against Indigenous peoples illustrate the deliberate remaking of Christianity in North America. In 1636, English colonists in Massachusetts and Connecticut waged war against the Pequots. Pequots, who resided on territory in Connecticut along the Thames River and starting in 1622 engaged in fur trade with the Dutch, by 1630 emerged as the dominant Indigenous power in the area. But English intrusions into Connecticut disrupted both Pequot trade with the Dutch and Pequot control of strategic coastlines. Between 1634 and 1636, Indigenous peoples killed two English traders—John Stone in 1634 and John Oldham in 1636—seeking to expand their own networks from Massachusetts into Connecticut. Though the circumstances surrounding their deaths were uncertain, and some English colonists believed that Narragansetts rather than Pequots murdered Oldham, the Massachusetts Bay colony marshaled a band of militants to attack the Pequots. During this war, an English army in 1637 attacked a Pequot village near the Mystic River and killed between four hundred and seven hundred women, children, and elderly men. As Pequot and English men engaged in combat against one another, Captain John Mason and Captain John Underhill ordered their English forces to burn the exposed and vulnerable village and slaughter everyone seeking to escape the fire.

The historian Alfred A. Cave argues that this vicious act entailed a war crime: "No military necessity requires that noncombatants fleeing a burning village be shot or impaled. The massacre at Fort Mystic was an act of terrorism intended to break Pequot morale."[50] Mason and Underhill anticipated some disapproval of their leadership and therefore both captains provided religious rationales for their actions. Mason declared that the massacre of the Pequots was mandated by God to humble and punish those "savages" who dared to oppose Christians. The Pequots were "the enemies of [God's] people" and God made them "as a fiery oven" to "judge among the heathen, filling the place with dead bodies."[51] Underhill demonstrated more restraint than Mason and acknowledged that some of their troops were tormented by their participation in the murder of so many women and children, but Underhill ultimately found vindication in the Bible: "Sometimes the Scripture declareth women and children must perish with their parents; sometimes the case alters: but we will not dispute it now. We had sufficient light from the word of God for our proceedings."[52]

Yet Underhill also noted that the English army's unsparing tactics horrified their Narragansett and Mohegan allies. Some Narragansett and Mohegan men joined the English military to weaken the Pequots' stronghold within their region, but Underhill remembered how they disapprovingly "cried *mach it, mach it*; that is, it is naught, it is naught, because it is too furious, and slays too many men" when beholding the carnage at Fort Mystic.[53] Mason's so-called savages were left aghast by English barbarity and the colonists' willingness to commit genocide. English colonists were determined to eradicate the entire Pequot nation. They sold some Pequot prisoners of war, including women and children, to slave traders to resell in the Caribbean, and outlawed use of the tribal name, Pequot, after the war.[54]

In 1763, a band of roughly one hundred Scots-Irish men killed twenty Conestogas in Pennsylvania. The Conestogas resided on territory in Lancaster County that their ancestors and the colony's first governor, William Penn, agreed to in 1701. Initially, this land along the Susquehanna River was a remote haven for Conestogas to live peacefully alongside white Mennonite and Quaker inhabitants. They constructed a settlement there with cabins and farms that resembled their white neighbors', and some Conestogas converted to Christianity. But the increasing white population in the eighteenth century resulted in escalating tensions between new white settlers and various Indigenous peoples on what was then considered the Pennsylvania frontier. John Elder, pastor of Paxton Presbyterian Church and one of the leaders of a white militia known as the Paxton Rangers, advocated for the relocation of the Conestogas from their homes in Lancaster County to Philadelphia. Elder contended that the rationale for his proposal was to protect the Conestogas, but he and everyone else understood why the persistent threat of violence existed: white settlers coveted the Conestogas' land and resented how this Indigenous community possessed such valuable territory in a rapidly developing area.

After the rangers first murdered six Conestogas, they encountered one of their Quaker neighbors, Thomas Wright. Wright appealed to Pennsylvania's agreement with the Conestogas, but the rangers retorted with a biblical justification: "Joshua was ordained to drive the heathen out of the land. Do you believe the Scriptures?"[55] Though it is not known whether Elder directly participated in the killing of the Conestogas, the historian Jack Brubaker found one study of the Paxton community that surmises that many of the perpetrators were members of Elder's congregation.[56] Elder himself denied any role in the massacre, but he also stated that nobody could have deterred the rangers. One of Pennsylvania's early historians, Robert Proud, excoriated the rangers in 1798 as "armed demi-savages" who "committed the most horrible massacre . . . under the notion of extirpating the heathen from the earth, as Joshua did of old, that these saints might possess the land alone."[57] Proud also included in his history Benjamin Franklin's account of the massacre (from 1764), in which Franklin lambasted the rangers: "But it seems these people think they have a better justification—nothing less than the word of God." Franklin assailed the rangers as "Christian white savages" due to their "horrid perversion of Scripture and of religion" when defending their remorseless slaughter of defenseless Conestoga women, men, and children.[58]

Both Proud and Franklin acknowledged that land was at the heart of why a band of white Presbyterian settlers brutally annihilated the Conestogas and ultimately drove them from their territory in Lancaster County. Despite Franklin's fury, and the Pennsylvania governor John Penn's public pronouncement that the suspects be arrested and tried in court, none of the Paxton Rangers was ever held accountable for their crimes. The historian Colin G. Calloway underscores how the massacre of the Conestogas, and the subsequent absence of justice, were an indication of an "escalating race hatred" among the broader white population against Indigenous peoples and a diminishing moral fortitude to honor treaties or even treat Indigenous peoples with simple decency. Calloway asks, "If the Conestogas' Christianity could not save them from the wrath of Christians, what basis could there be for coexistence?"[59] White Americans, including Christians, had numerous opportunities to forge pathways for coexistence with Indigenous peoples and enact the principles of justice, mercy, and righteousness.

In 1624, Captain John Smith recalled a conversation he had with Powhatan at a time when the latter's Indigenous confederacy was stronger than the fledgling English colony of Jamestown. Powhatan asked why Smith's people despised the idea of a mutually beneficial coexistence: "What will it avail you to take that by force you may quickly have by love, or to destroy them that provide you food? What can you get by war, when we can hide our provisions and fly to the woods? Whereby you must famish by wronging us your friends."[60] Many other Indigenous individuals and families posed similar queries as the United States emerged as a colonial power, and white Americans continually oppressed them and seized their lands. One of the most important tests of justice and humanity for the United States and its people emerged in the Cherokee Nation. The Cherokees did not want to take anything from white people, but they had already ceded much of their territory by 1830 and had nowhere else to hide their provisions.

"I Wish You to See How Indians Can Live": The Righteous Struggle to Protect Indigenous Land and Preserve the Cherokee Nation

In 1825, Harriett Ruggles Gold, the youngest daughter in a prominent white family of merchants and farmers in Cornwall, Connecticut, decided to marry a Cherokee man, Elias Boudinot. Gold and Boudinot met when he was a student at the Foreign Mission School (FMS), an educational institution in Cornwall founded by the ABCFM in 1817 to prepare young Indigenous, Asian, and Pacific Islander men with a comprehensive education, including reading, writing, math, geography, farming, woodworking, and of course religion, who would then return "to their respective nations with the blessings of civilized and Christianized society."[61] The FMS founders and teachers desired to share the material and spiritual blessings that God had so graciously given them through identifying and equipping the best and brightest young men from other nations within and beyond the United States. They established a boarding school in northwestern Connecticut with the idea of removing young men of color from their "pagan customs" and granting them an immersive pedagogical experience in a "civilized" white society. One FMS supporter explained, "A more thorough education may certainly be given to young heathen in such a school than in one instituted by missionaries in foreign lands; heathen youths may be more completely civilized, more thoroughly Christianized, and their hearts more entirely won over to the missionary cause."[62]

When Boudinot was at the FMS, most students were from Indigenous nations within North America, but the school also enrolled young men from China, Greece, Hawai'i, India, Java, the Marquesas Islands, New Zealand, and Tahiti. In 1821, a visitor marveled at the diversity of students and cultures at the school: "As the eyes and hearts of many of God's dear people are turning towards *Cornwall*, with bright expectation, in consequence of the very interesting assemblage of youth there collected." The visitor then identified Boudinot as among the eight Cherokee students at the FMS.[63] In the same year a different visitor especially praised Boudinot and two other Cherokee students, John Ridge and David Brown, as equal "to the best white young men of their age." This visitor added: "Elias Boudinot, in a declamation, confuted the idea more completely by his appearance than his arguments, that savages are not capable of being civilized and polished."[64]

Boudinot was born in the Cherokee Nation in northwestern Georgia and enrolled at the FMS as a teenager in 1818. He was one of nine children, and his father enrolled him at a Moravian mission school within the Cherokee Nation when he was a young child. In 1817, when Boudinot was roughly thirteen years old, the FMS invited Boudinot and several other Cherokees to study in Connecticut. Already by 1821, only four years into its existence, the FMS was growing in enrollment and gaining favor across churches throughout the United States. They invited benefactors to visit and witness firsthand the marvelous work for foreign missions that was unfolding there.

But something else was happening at FMS that threatened its existence and ultimately led to its demise in 1826. After four years at the school, Boudinot returned home in 1822 to the Cherokee Nation. But his connection to the town of Cornwall endured. Boudinot and Gold corresponded through letters between 1822 and 1825, and a long-distance romantic relationship soon blossomed.

While Boudinot and Gold were writing letters to one another, Boudinot's cousin, John Ridge, remained at the FMS, and Ridge experienced a physical malady with his hip that required him to receive medical attention at the home of one of the school's administrators, John Northrup. As Ridge was recovering there, he befriended Northrup's daughter, Sarah, and the two teenagers fell in love over a span of several months. But once Ridge and Northrup intended to marry, the townspeople in Cornwall, including many of the Christians, opposed it, because they did not support an interracial marriage between a Cherokee man and a white woman. A newspaper editor in nearby Litchfield, Isaiah Bunce, criticized the FMS for fostering an environment that led to what he, and others, viewed as a tragedy. Bunce emphasized what he presumed was the "affliction, mortification, and disgrace" of Northrup's parents at the thought of their white daughter "throwing herself into the arms of an Indian": "To have her thus marry an Indian and taken into the wilderness among savages, must indeed be a heart-rending pang which none can realize except those called to feel it."

Bunce also denounced the horror of a white woman "who has thus made herself a *squaw*, and connected her ancestors to a race of Indians." Squaw is a word traced to the Algonquian language, meaning "woman," that by the 1820s had evolved into a derogatory term that some white Americans used to demean Indigenous women. The newspaper editor did not spare the FMS in his criticism; Bunce directly blamed the school and attributed the interracial marriage as "the fruit of the missionary spirit, and caused by the conduct of the clergymen at that place and its vicinity."[65] Ridge and Northrup wed in Cornwall in 1824 and moved together to the Cherokee Nation, where Ridge belonged to a prominent and powerful family.

One year after this controversial marriage, Gold announced her intentions to marry Boudinot, and many white persons in Cornwall again expressed their displeasure, including FMS administrators and Gold's brother, Stephen Gold.

The school had devoted significant effort to distance themselves from the Ridge-Northrup marriage. In private correspondence and public statements, both FMS and ABCFM leaders expressed that the school did not endorse or teach about interracial marriages. The school was in a difficult position. It did not want to fan the flames of racism and further discourage the men of color studying there.

Daniel S. Butrick, a white missionary among the Cherokees in Georgia, divulged to Evarts that Ridge was angry and dismayed, due to the ferocity of racial hatred against him and Northrup.[66] But the FMS also feared losing the support it had garnered among white Christians, and its administrators also felt the intensity of local white rage. Stephen Gold did not have any qualms about expressing his opposition to his sister's marital plan. He and several others in Cornwall burned likenesses of Gold and Boudinot in effigy in the town square. Harriett Gold's brother-in-law, the Reverend Cornelius Everest of First Congregational Church in Windham, Connecticut, believed the relationship was shameful—"unnatural" and "ungodly business" in his words—and reported that "the best people here, and neighboring clergymen say they would oppose it to the last moments."[67] At the church that the Gold family attended, Harriett was prohibited in Sunday worship from her usual seat in the young women's choir. Nevertheless, she persisted, and Gold and Boudinot wed in 1826. But the FMS closed shortly after their wedding. The school could not continue amid the bad publicity of a second white woman running into the arms of an Indian man.

In addition to the demise of the FMS, relationships between the school and its Cherokee students also suffered. The FMS had delivered a strong denunciation of Boudinot and Gold, identifying them by name in its "unequivocal disapprobation" of their marriage as "an insult to the known feelings of the Christian community" and "the sacred interests of this charitable institution."[68] David Brown therefore wrote a lengthy letter to Evarts reporting how Cherokees in the Southern states were disillusioned upon learning of the fierce opposition to the two interracial marriages. White missionaries from the ABCFM had recruited Cherokee men to study at the FMS and continued to insist that the Christian God created and loved people of all races equally, white and Cherokee alike, but the hostile reception to the Ridge-Northrup and Boudinot-Gold marriages revealed gross contradictions and glaring inconsistencies.

Brown wrote, "We are necessarily led to inquire, whether our friends in New England have always acted from love to us and a desire to do us good. If they loved us, how could they treat us in this manner? They cannot suppose it wicked for white people to marry Cherokees, because members of Baptist, Methodist, and Presbyterian churches have married Cherokee ladies without censure."[69] Brown asked Evarts why white men were permitted to wed Chero-kee women but Cherokee men such as Ridge and Boudinot—Christians who had studied at the premier mission school in the United States—could not marry white women.

Butrick also articulated his own fury at the racism of his fellow white Chris-tians to Evarts, writing in 1826, "We understand that it is now stated in letters from the North, that if our dear brother Boudinot should appear in Corn-wall, half the state would rise against him; and that his life would be in dan-ger. . . . Even the *heathen* world *blushes*, and humanity sickens at the thought."[70] Evarts publicly defended the two interracial marriages and privately chastised the FMS for its overt racism when the school denied any involvement in the Boudinot-Gold relationship.[71]

But Evarts, Brown, Boudinot, and Gold had little time to grapple with the repercussions of the events at Cornwall. With Andrew Jackson's presiden-tial election in 1828, the greater threat of the Indian Removal Act gripped the Cherokee Nation. After their wedding, Boudinot and Gold resided in the Cherokee Nation and had six children together. In letters to her siblings, Gold shared about the joys of marriage and motherhood. But Gold also wrote about the escalating threats of white intrusion into the Cherokee Nation. Dur-ing his presidential campaign, Jackson made clear that he supported legisla-tion to expel Indigenous nations from their lands in the Southern states. After Jackson's election, the state legislature in Georgia moved to take control of Cherokee territory. Even as the Cherokees refused to negotiate with the state's officials, Georgia held land lotteries and began awarding tracts of Cherokee land to its white citizens. Thousands of white settlers, armed with rifles and official titles to land, began pouring into the Cherokee Nation. There were reports of gold in Cherokee territory, and its location in the northwestern corner of the state was along the Tennessee River, which white developers coveted for access to waterway networks northward to the Ohio River and westward to the Mississippi River.[72] A map of Cherokee territory in Georgia from 1831 stated that "this interesting tract of country contains four millions three hundred & sixty six thousand five hundred & fifty four acres, many rich gold mines & many delightful situations & though in some parts mountainous, some of the richest land belonging to the state."[73]

In 1830, the US Congress passed the Indian Removal Act, which autho-rized the president to grant lands west of the Mississippi River in exchange for Indigenous lands within the United States. The historian Claudio Saunt maintains that "removal" is a "soft word" and "artfully vague" because it con-veys no sense of coercion or violence. Saunt therefore uses three other words to describe the Indian Removal Act and other related policies: "deportation,"

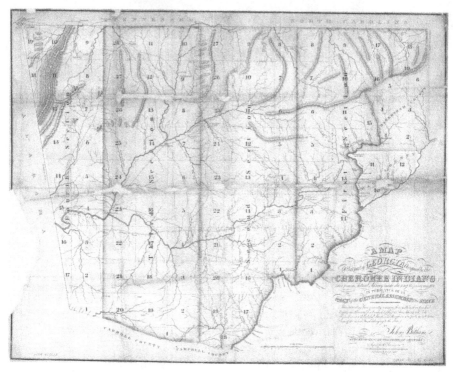

A Map of That Part of Georgia Occupied by the Cherokee Indians, 1831

"expulsion," and "extermination."[74] Gold expressed grave concerns to her sister, Flora Gold Vaill, in 1831: "I am astonished at the apathy which prevails in the States in regard to the Cherokees. The friends of the Indians seem sleeping while their enemies are diligently pursuing their work and the sufferings of the poor Cherokee are daily increased beneath the oppressor's rod." Gold also noted white atrocities against the Mohegans in her native state of Connecticut and asked, "How are the American people ever to atone for the injuries done the original inhabitants of this country?"[75]

Boudinot was a writer and editor of the *Cherokee Phoenix*, the first newspaper published by an Indigenous nation in the United States. He went on a tour throughout the United States in 1826 to raise funds for a printing press and a new secondary school in the Cherokee Nation. Boudinot spoke in many cities, including Charleston (South Carolina), Boston, and Philadelphia. During his stop in Philadelphia, he published the text of the speech he delivered in the city at First Presbyterian Church as a pamphlet entitled "An Address to the Whites." Boudinot began with a lament that "the term *Indian* is pregnant with ideas the most repelling and degrading." He countered, "What is an Indian? Is he not formed of the same materials with yourself? For 'of one blood God created all the nations that dwell on the face of the earth.'" He plaintively observed how many Indigenous communities had suffered greatly after contact with white people: "We have seen, I say, one family after another, one tribe after another, nation after nation, pass away; until only a few solitary creatures are left to tell the sad story of extinction."[76] Yet Boudinot highlighted that the Cherokee Nation was flourishing, with numerous family farms, mission schools, and churches.

In the same year, John Ridge wrote a letter to Albert Gallatin, a Swiss-born politician who served as US secretary of the treasury from 1801 to 1814 and the US minister to France from 1816 to 1823. Ridge reported that there were 13,983 Cherokee persons, 1,277 enslaved Africans, and 220 white persons in the Cherokee Nation. Ridge also described how his Indigenous community was gradually resembling white Southern society with its increasing cotton production, class stratification, and slave ownership: "The African slaves are generally mostly held by [biracial] and full Indians of distinguished talents. In this class the principal value of property is retained and their farms are conducted in the same style with the southern white farmers of equal ability in point of property."[77]

Boudinot did not speak of Black enslavement among the Cherokees, but both he and Ridge shared the same concern about white encroachment. Boudinot acknowledged that the Cherokees had changed their lifeways to follow white Southern patterns, because the only other option was extinction.[78] Therefore white Christians also only had two options: to help the Cherokees survive, or do nothing and allow the Cherokees to perish.

Evarts emerged as the most prominent white activist for Cherokee rights. He leveraged his connections as an alumnus of Yale and son-in-law of a national founder to set up meetings with several members of the US Congress. He found strong allies in the Senate, and two senators, Theodore Frelinghuysen and Peleg Sprague, consulted closely with Evarts before delivering their congressional speeches in opposition to the expulsion bill. Evarts also spoke with Andrew Jackson on several occasions in February 1829, when they were both staying at the same boarding house in Washington, DC, when Jackson was president-elect, and garnered a meeting with John Marshall, chief justice of the US Supreme Court, in 1830.[79] Evarts published in 1829 a series of twenty-four essays defending the Cherokees (and sharply criticizing both the expulsion bill and the white politicians who supported it) under the pseudonym of "William Penn," which were first published in a Washington, DC, newspaper and then all together as a pamphlet. He underscored that the

Cherokees were "neither savages nor criminals," but rather they were simply people who possessed lands that white people in Georgia wanted for themselves. Evarts also noted that some Cherokees were "fellow Christians, regular members of Moravian, Presbyterian, Baptist, and Methodist churches" and appealed to a theology of spiritual unity in asking white Christians to consider those Cherokees who were their "fellow citizens with the saints and of the household of God."[80]

Evarts warned all white Americans about the weighty ramifications of the removal bill. He wrote, "Nothing of this kind has ever yet been done, certainly not on a large scale, by Anglo-Americans. To us, as a nation, it will be a new thing under the sun. We have never yet acted upon the principle of seizing the lands of peaceable Indians, and compelling them to remove."[81] Evarts enraged proponents of the Indian Removal Act in the nation's capital. At least one, the Georgia representative Wilson Lumpkin, publicly condemned him in a congressional address and charged that Evarts's essays "have much more of the character of the politician and lawyer than that of a humble missionary."[82] Boudinot and Gold were appreciative of their friend for his efforts, and they named one of their children, William Penn, after Evarts's pseudonym.

Another of Evarts's friends, Catharine E. Beecher, the sister of Harriet Beecher Stowe and Henry Ward Beecher, joined the cause to protect Cherokee land. Beecher recalled in her memoirs that she met Evarts in Boston in 1828 and that, as they talked, Evarts asked her to get involved in Indigenous advocacy. Upon returning to her home in Connecticut, where Beecher was an educator, she published an open letter, "To Benevolent Women of the United States," calling upon white women to oppose the federal government's machinations to deport the Cherokees.[83] More than fourteen hundred women signed petitions, and Beecher's activism marked the first organized political movement from white women in US history.

Because of the activism of Evarts and Beecher, antiremoval petitions inundated the US Congress. Some were printed and others were written with ink. Some had a few signatures, whereas others had several hundred. Some petitions were over seven feet long. These petitions did in fact sway several Northern congressmen in President Jackson's own party, who either voted against expulsion or did not show up to vote. But ultimately, both the Senate and House of Representatives voted to pass the Indian Removal Act. In the Senate, the act was passed by a count of 28 to 19. In the House, it was passed by the slim margin of 102 to 97. A House member from Georgia was vindicated in his conviction that several thousand petitioners "were nothing in comparison with the millions who were silent and satisfied."[84]

In March 1832, nearly two years after the Indian Removal Act was signed into law, Gold wrote to her sister expressing hope after the US Supreme Court's decision in a case about her friend, Samuel Austin Worcester, a white Presbyterian missionary who was imprisoned in Georgia for refusing to take the oath of allegiance that the state required of white persons residing in Cherokee territory. The Supreme Court ruled that Worcester's arrest was illegal because the state of Georgia was infringing upon the sovereignty of the Cherokee Nation to make and enact its own laws. Gold also shared that she had recently given birth to her fourth child: "I am happy to tell you that my health is good as usual, and that all my family of little ones are also well. Eleanor and Mary go to school and are remarkably fond of their teacher and their books. They can both read. Eleanor learns every morning one verse from scripture according to the verse a day system."

Gold then entreated, "Indeed, I wish you *could* see us in our family, in our neighbourhood, and our Nation. You need not say that I possess that disposition of bragging so peculiar to the Gold family—perhaps I do—but I now only mean—I wish you to see how Indians can *live*—how families, and how a *nation* of Indians can live."[85] This is one of Harriett Gold's last preserved letters. The years following this letter were tumultuous for Gold and the Cherokee Nation. Gold grew ill and died in 1836. Andrew Jackson ignored the Supreme Court's ruling in *Worcester v. Georgia*, and the Cherokees were driven from their land in what is sadly remembered as the "Trail of Tears." The unfolding tragedy evokes what one Cherokee leader, Chief Junaluska, remarked when he received a translated version of the Gospel of Matthew: "It seems to be a good book; strange that the white people are not better after having had it so long."[86]

Gold and Boudinot remained faithful to God and true to one another. Boudinot recorded Gold's words to their children on her death bed: "To William, she said, 'I want you to be a good boy—to be a good man when you are grown, and to do a great deal of good while you live. Be kind to your little brothers.'" Gold then addressed all her children and said, "It has been my sole wish and prayer to God, that you may become Christians, and be useful in the world, and be finally happy in the world to come. Be kind to each other and love one another."[87] After the Indian Removal Act was passed in 1830, Evarts also became seriously ill. He sailed to Havana, Cuba, in February 1831 in the hope that the warmer climate would bring him relief. But his health did not improve, and he died three months later from tuberculosis. Some of his friends thought that Evarts worked himself to death in his relentless pursuit of justice for the Cherokees.

One month before his death, a periodical published Evarts's final essay, entitled "Contingent Prospects of Our Country." Evarts agreed that the United States was growing into a powerful nation due to its economic growth and westward expansion. But he also warned of "awful contingencies" because of how his nation oppressed people of color: "I refer to the present condition and prospects of the *African race*, and of the *aboriginal inhabitants*, who are now lying upon us, dependent, helpless, injured."[88] Evarts detested the pervasiveness of racial injustice across his beloved nation, but he also died believing that true Christians could enact a better and more racially just future.

Chapter Four

"And the Mantle of Prejudice Torn from Every American Heart"

Territorial Expansion and the Erosion of Racial Justice within American Christianity

In 1829, William Apess published his autobiography in New York City. Apess, a Pequot born in the rural Massachusetts town of Colrain in 1798, endured a difficult childhood in Connecticut. He grew up in abject poverty within an Indigenous community that had withstood nearly two centuries of settler colonial aggression and white intrusion. After English combatants defeated the Pequots in a brutal war, the Treaty of Hartford in 1638 stipulated that the surviving Pequots, primarily women and children, must live among either the Mohegans or Narragansetts. Before the treaty, some Pequot prisoners of war had been sold to slave traders who engaged in human trafficking throughout the Caribbean. The precise destinations of these enslaved Pequots are unknown, but we know from one account of colonial Massachusetts that at least eighty Pequots were "sent to Bermuda and sold for slaves."[1] The victorious English colonists decreed that the Pequots would "never again inhabit their native country, nor should any of them be called Pequots anymore."[2]

One military official, Captain John Mason, declared that the total obliteration of the Pequots was an appropriate measure and divine vindication for an Indigenous nation that "resolved to destroy all the English and to root their very name out of this country."[3] A Puritan pastor in 1643 attributed the English victory over the Pequots as a sign of "God's hand from heaven," with the result "that the name of the Pequots (as of Amalek) is blotted out from under heaven, there being not one that is, or (at least) dare call himself a Pequot."[4]

But the Pequots in New England reconstituted and maintained two tracts of land in southeastern Connecticut at the time of Apess's birth. And when Apess published his autobiography, *A Son of the Forest*, he clearly stated in the subtitle and on the very first page that he was a Pequot.[5] Apess had spent the previous four years as a Methodist preacher assigned a circuit across Long

Island, the Hudson River Valley, New Bedford, Providence, and Boston, ministering primarily among Indigenous, Black, and multiracial congregations of color.[6] He had received discriminatory treatment from some white Methodists, encountered racial oppression throughout his life, and carried in his body the traumatic history of genocidal violence against his people. Apess therefore wanted the world to know that he was a Pequot and that his people had not been blotted out from their ancestral homeland.

As a child, Apess became a ward of the State of Connecticut and was placed as an indentured servant in a white home. Various Indigenous nations in New England suffered impoverishment due to economic exploitation and racial injustice. The tracts of land they negotiated in treaties progressively dwindled as white populations in their respective areas grew. Government officials assigned to oversee Indigenous communities often abused their authority to advance their own interests. With few local employment opportunities, many Indigenous men left their families for long durations of time to work on white farms or on fishing and whaling ships. This absence of able-bodied men left Indigenous communities vulnerable to white encroachment.

Apess himself explained in 1833, when advocating for Wampanoags in Mashpee, Massachusetts, that white officials misused their power as "guardians of the Indians" to rent parcels of Indigenous land to white settlers, sell natural resources (such as timber) for their own gain, and commit other acts of financial malfeasance that harmed Indigenous families. Apess offered this specific example of what happened to the hard-earned wages of Indigenous whalers: "Sometimes an Indian bound on a whaling voyage would earn four or five hundred dollars, and the shipmaster would account to the overseers for the whole sum. The Indian would get some small part of his due, in order to encourage him to go again and gain more for his white masters, to support themselves and their children with."[7]

As the fortunes of white officials prospered, Apess and other Indigenous children were forced into indentured servitude, because their unstable families and besieged communities could not afford to raise them. Apess did not shy away from divulging the devastating conditions of his childhood, but he also explained that the example of wage theft was "but a specimen of the systematic course taken to degrade the tribe from generation to generation."[8] Apess wanted his hearers and readers to know the systemic causes of indigence, intemperance, and indentured servitude within his and other Indigenous communities.

When Apess was four years of age, he was severely beaten by his intoxicated grandmother and recuperated first with an uncle and then with a white couple, the Furmans, in Salem, Connecticut (then within the bounds of Colchester).

Apess continued to live with the Furmans as the state granted him to them as an indentured servant until the age of twenty-one. Apess expressed ambivalence toward both his grandparents and the Furmans. Prior to living with the Furmans, Apess remembered being frequently "naked, cold, and hungry" and begging neighbors for food. So he thanked the Furmans for providing him a more stable upbringing. Apess acknowledges in his autobiography a likely impression from white readers: "What savage creatures my grandparents were to treat unoffending or helpless children in this manner." Apess did not excuse his grandparents for their failings, but he attributed their mistakes "in part to the whites, because they introduced among my countrymen ardent spirits; seduced them into a love for it, and when under its baleful influence, wronged them out of their lawful possessions—that land where reposed the ashes of their sires."[9]

The Furmans sent Apess to school "for six successive winters," and he thanked them for this educational access by which he learned to read and write, but he also underscored that schooling was a condition of his indenture, and the Furmans permitted him only the contractually mandated rudimentary instruction and no more.[10] The Furmans did not adopt Apess as their child; it was clear that he was their servant. When he misbehaved, the Furman patriarch physically punished Apess and once shouted, "I will learn you, you Indian dog," when whipping him.[11] Some of the floggings that Apess received were because he attended Methodist worship services without permission. The Furmans were Baptists, but their objection to Apess's interest in Methodism was not doctrinal or theological. The reason that "Mr. Furman forbid" Apess from participating was because he thought the young boy only went to make playful mischief with other children.[12]

By his own admission Apess was a rambunctious child, always in search of the next adventure, but his interest in the gospel that the local Methodists were proclaiming was genuine. He continued to attend worship services and as a teenager went to Methodist camp meetings. Apess was enthralled as he listened to lively sermons from itinerant preachers, known as circuit riders, who preached without the manuscripts that local Congregational and Presbyterian pastors in Connecticut brought with them to their pulpits. He recalled participating in an indelible worship experience of fervent praying and exuberant singing as "the power of the Holy Ghost moved forth among the people." Apess expressed, "I felt convinced that Christ died for all mankind—that age, sect, colour, country, or situation, made no difference."[13]

Yet Apess also recognized that too many white Christians did not believe in the same liberating gospel. In 1830, Apess wrote, "I have been asked time and again, whether I did not sincerely believe that God had more respect to the white man, than to the untutored son of the forest? I answer, and always answer such, in the language of Scripture, 'No: God is no respecter of persons.'"[14] Apess rebuked white Christians for misconstruing the gospel with their racism and found it appalling that some thought (and many more acted as if) God created the white race as naturally and providentially superior to Indigenous and Black races. The principles of Christian discipleship were evident to Apess and encapsulated in Matthew 22:37–40, a scriptural passage that recounts Jesus' answer that love for God and love for neighbor are the two greatest commandments.

Apess was troubled because white Christians did little to protest and less to change racially discriminatory laws and practices. All persons of every race in the United States inhabited a "confused world" that because of settler colonialism and slavery was far from God's design. White Christians lived as though they were the "only beloved images of God" and therefore would not be held accountable for stealing Indigenous lands, enslaving Africans and Indigenous peoples, and depriving people of color of their civil rights.[15] Apess demanded a racial reckoning within white Christianity and a reformation in which "noble-hearted" Christians "stop not till this tree of distinction shall be leveled to the earth, and the mantle of prejudice torn from every American heart."[16]

This chapter examines US territorial expansion and the erosion of racial justice within American Christianity. Apess's ministry integrating political engagement and racial justice with evangelical Protestant understandings of conversion and eternal salvation was unsurprising, because this confluence emerged directly and organically from his life circumstances as a Pequot in the United States. The attention to racial justice did not disappear within every American church, but the fierce opposition to Apess's interpretation of the gospel from many white Christians illustrates the ways in which the history and legacy of settler colonialism shaped and remade Christianity in the United States. Scriptural teachings about equality and justice became obscured and even reviled as white Christians prioritized their desires for more land and economic opportunity over their responsibilities to honor their Indigenous neighbors and dismantle racially oppressive structures in their society.

"Grace, not Race, in Christian Missions": The Limitations of Indigenous Evangelization in the Confused World of Settler Colonialism

In 1882, John Cameron Lowrie explained his philosophy of race and evangelization. Lowrie was an experienced Presbyterian missionary who lived in India for two years and served as a leading administrator with the Presbyterian

Church in the U.S.A. Board of Foreign Missions (BFM) from 1850 to 1891. The BFM supported roughly 450 Presbyterian missionaries working among Indigenous nations in North America from 1837 to 1893.[17] In a chapter entitled "Grace, not Race, in Christian Missions," Lowrie debunked the notion of the Anglo-Saxon race as the most productive in promulgating the gospel. He defined the "Anglo-Saxon race" as "English-speaking people, chiefly found in Great Britain and the United States" and countered claims that this race was superior in Christian missions: "If we look only at the Anglo-Saxon race, then we must remember that it has two phases. Its energy and enterprise have been signally displayed in doing evil, perhaps even more than in doing good."

One phase of Anglo-Saxon engagement with Indigenous peoples involved Protestant evangelism and education, but the other phase entailed "numberless aggressions and injuries inflicted on these Indians," such as "the many broken treaties" and "demoralization of native tribes caused by English and American commerce."[18] Lowrie advocated for BFM missionaries to turn away from the racial theories of their day and instead focus on what he considered the deeper spiritual needs of people of color across Africa, Asia, and the Americas. He was wary of racist ideologies that simultaneously regarded white Americans as superior and Indigenous peoples as inferior, but Lowrie failed to adequately grasp the limitations of his "grace, not race" approach in the racialized context of the United States. The task of Christian ministry among Indigenous peoples was primarily a confrontation with the messy sins of settler colonialism, and it was therefore not possible to neatly separate "grace" and "race" as Lowrie proposed.

Two encounters between white missionaries and Seneca leaders in New York demonstrate the manifold and multilayered challenges of ministry among Indigenous peoples. In 1765, Samuel Kirkland, a white Presbyterian missionary, encountered resistance from the Seneca warrior Onoonghwandekha. Shortly after Kirkland had arrived in Kanadasaga, one of the Seneca leaders had suddenly and mysteriously died. When the Senecas gathered to bury and honor their fallen leader (Kirkland was also present), Onoonghwandekha delivered an address warning that Kirkland's presence among them was dangerous. Onoonghwandekha observed that whenever white missionaries entered Indigenous communities, the result was land dispossession and destruction. He implored, "Brethren hear me! I am in earnest because I love my nation and revere the customs and practices of our ancestors and they enjoyed pleasant days." The Bible that Kirkland carried was "the white people's Book" and "never made for Indians." Onoonghwandekha added that the Senecas would "become a miserable abject people" if they listened to Kirkland and converted to Christianity.[19]

In 1805, the Seneca chief Red Jacket (also known as Sagoyewatha) responded to the arrival of the white missionary Jacob Cram in Buffalo. Cram had spoken before a council of Seneca leaders to declare his intentions. Cram believed that the Senecas were living in a state of spiritual darkness. He shared how he was sent by a "missionary society of Boston" to offer religious instruction, not to take their land or money. Red Jacket responded, "Brother, our seats were once large, and yours were very small; you have now become a great people, and we have scarcely a place left to spread our blankets; you have got our country, but are not satisfied; you want to force your religion upon us." The Seneca chief further stated that the Senecas already had "a religion, which was given to our forefathers, and has been handed down to us their children." The Senecas were taught "to be thankful for all the favors we receive; to love each other, and to be united; we never quarrel about religion." But unlike Onoonghwandekha, Red Jacket did not want the white missionary to leave their area entirely. Red Jacket noted that Cram had also been preaching to the nearby white community and advised him to direct his attention there. The Senecas felt the pressures of increasing white encroachment, and Red Jacket believed Cram had ample opportunity to instruct their white neighbors about sin, salvation, and upright living: "Brother, we are told that you have been preaching to white people in this place; these people are our neighbors, we are acquainted with them; we will wait a little while and see what effect your preaching has upon them. If we find it does them good, makes them honest, and less disposed to cheat Indians, we will then consider again what you have said."[20]

Both Red Jacket and Onoonghwandekha revealed how the white message of Christian grace to Indigenous peoples was always accompanied by the racial dynamics and racist consequences of settler colonialism. Red Jacket also identified the problem that white missionaries could not solve. Missionaries were right in their observation that Indigenous communities were imperiled, but they misdiagnosed the situation and offered the wrong remedy. They insisted that conversion was the answer, but it was white Americans, rather than Indigenous peoples, who needed to repent of their sins of greed and racism and enact the Christian principle of neighbor-love.

Another illustration of the limitations of white missionary attempts directed toward Indigenous evangelization is found in Natick, Massachusetts. In 1646, the white Puritan pastor John Eliot began preaching regularly to Indigenous peoples. Eliot arrived in the Massachusetts Bay colony in 1631 and increasingly felt the conviction to minister among Indigenous communities. Though Indigenous evangelization was the stated purpose of the colony, Eliot and other pastors admitted that they gave minimal attention to this task in the early years of establishing their settlement. In 1647, a colleague of Eliot, the Puritan pastor Thomas Shepard, acknowledged growing criticism from England about the failure to convert Indigenous peoples in Massachusetts: "We are oft upbraided by some of our countrymen that so little good is done by our professing planters upon the hearts of Natives."[21] Shepard explained that he, Eliot, and several other pastors had begun taking more deliberate steps to preach to Indigenous peoples, which included attempts to inculcate English cultural norms for appearance, dress, and sexual activity. Shepard asserted that Indigenous peoples must be "brought to some civility before religion can prosper."[22]

These white ministers started working with colonial officials to set up what they called "praying towns" among Massachusett, Mohegan, Narragansett, Nipmuck, Pawtucket, Wampanoag, and other Indigenous peoples across southeastern New England.[23] Colonial authorities granted small tracts of land to Eliot and other white pastors to construct and control an enclosed community of Indigenous Christians. The white pastors used monetary fines to enforce their rules. In one praying town, Indigenous men were penalized twenty shillings for having sexual relations with unmarried women. Indigenous women and men were charged five shillings for improper hairstyles (women had to tie their hair up and men were forbidden from wearing long locks). Indigenous women were also levied two shillings and six pence for appearing in public with "naked breasts."[24]

The praying towns did not resonate with most Indigenous peoples and at their peak comprised roughly 1,100 Indigenous residents, called "praying Indians," across fourteen separate sites in 1674.[25] And the praying Indians did not practice Christianity in the ways that their white missionary teachers desired. In Jean M. O'Brien's analysis of the praying town of Natick, the historian explains the multifarious motivations of its Indigenous residents. They determined that "the crucial nexus of personal relationships, kinship, community, and land could be preserved through English Calvinism." O'Brien contends that the Indigenous residents accepted the "cultural compromises" enforced at Natick because they desired security and stability amid escalating colonial encroachment with increasing English migration.[26]

In one of Eliot's several accounts of Indigenous conversions, an Indigenous man named John Speen recounted that he prayed "because I saw the English took much ground, and I thought if I prayed, the English would not take away my ground."[27] Another Indigenous man, Nishohkou, turned to God when wrestling with what Apess identified as the "confused world" of settler colonialism. Nishohkou remembered the freedom of his life before English colonization and prayed for solace when considering the devastating losses for his people: "When my heart is troubled about our Land and about riches, I quiet my heart with these meditations."[28]

Of all the praying towns, Natick was the most contentious, because the tract of land where Eliot constructed it was within the English legal boundaries of the town of Dedham. The dispute between Eliot and the English residents of Dedham exposed several tensions among the colonists. The contest for Natick also demonstrated how its Indigenous residents leveraged the praying town as a colonial means to achieve their communal ends. O'Brien explains that the word "Natick" means "my land" in the Algonquian language of the Narragansetts.[29] Between 1650 and 1662, Eliot and the town of Dedham negotiated before the General Court of colonial Massachusetts on the specific acreage and precise location of Natick. But even when Eliot made an agreement with Dedham to move locations, he failed to convince the Indigenous residents to abide by the decision, because some of them wanted to stay on the territory that belonged to their ancestors.

Though Eliot returned to the General Court with an appeal to divine providence—testifying that the praying Indians did not want to move because they believed "it was [God's] pleasure we should begin this work" in the site where they had already settled—he understood that he would likely lose many Indigenous residents if Natick had to relocate.[30] The General Court finally ruled in Natick's favor in 1662, but enraged white residents from Dedham continued to antagonize their Indigenous neighbors and eventually displaced all of Natick's Indigenous residents by the end of the eighteenth century.

In addition to the praying towns, English colonists and Indigenous peoples engaged in negotiations to create several other Indigenous mission stations in Massachusetts. In 1730, Jonathan Belcher, the governor of Massachusetts, approached the London-based Company for Propagation of the Gospel in New England and the Parts Adjacent in America (called the New England Company in 1770) for funds to support a new mission station. Belcher lamented that the colonial government had "done so little from the first settlement of the country to this day for the conversion of the Indian Natives to the true Christian faith."[31] Belcher therefore sought roughly 2,000 pounds to build a church and a school as well as to compensate a pastor and a school principal.

Belcher envisioned a multiracial community and included in his budget two separate line items, "Encouragement to the first tradesmen to settle" and "Presents to the Indians" (apportioning 350 pounds to each), because financial incentives for English and Indigenous alike were required in the initial stage.[32] Four years later, John Stoddard, a government official who purchased Indigenous lands for the colony, met with the Housatonic Mohicans in an effort to enact Belcher's proposal in Stockbridge. After several months of negotiations, the two parties came to an agreement in 1736.

The Mohicans were wary of Stoddard's intentions and feared that white settlers would grow to outnumber and overpower them in Stockbridge. They also considered how their alliance with the English could impair their relations with surrounding Indigenous peoples. In 1735, one of the Mohican leaders, Umpachenee, divulged to Stoddard that a few things "appeared dark in his eyes." Umpachenee questioned why the colony had now expressed interest in offering his people religious instruction and not anytime previously over the long duration that they lived among one another. The Mohican leader also asked Stoddard why the ostensibly Christian colony had many white settlers who acted immorally. Umpachenee wondered how there "should be so many professors" of Christianity who nonetheless "lived such vicious lives, and so contrary to what he was told were the rules of it." Yet Umpachenee and other Mohican leaders ultimately agreed to exchange their fifty-two-square-mile tract of land for thirty-six square miles.[33] They accepted both the reduction in land and the presence of a white pastor because they believed that the town of Stockbridge was the best option to preserve their ancestral homeland within the constrained pathways before them.

In 1751, Jonathan Edwards became the pastor in Stockbridge. It was a surprising turn of events, because up to this point in his life Edwards had not expressed any serious interest in ministry among Indigenous peoples. Unlike other missionaries, such as John Eliot, Edwards did not make any effort to learn the Mohican language and relied upon a Mohican translator, John Wauwaumppequunnaunt, when preaching. During his first months at Stockbridge, Edwards surmised that his priority was to teach the Mohicans to read and write in English as "their own barbarous languages" were, in his estimation, "barren and very unfit to express moral and divine things."[34]

Edwards was a gifted preacher and prolific writer, but he sometimes failed to exhibit the interpersonal skills required of an effective pastoral leader. In 1750, the congregation in Northampton, Massachusetts, voted to dismiss Edwards as its pastor.[35] Edwards was not unfeeling toward the Mohicans at Stockbridge, but he was mainly drawn to the pastorate there because he wanted to devote more time to writing and liked that his salary would come from the colonial government rather than the tithes and offerings of unreliable church members.

Edwards did adjust his preaching to the Mohicans in several ways. One immediate change was necessitated by his unwillingness to learn the Mohican language. Several scholars of Edwards observe that his sermons to Indigenous hearers had shorter sentences and more concise statements because he was preaching alongside a translator.[36] The content of Edwards's sermons also differed. In Rachel Wheeler's study of Stockbridge, the historian maintains that Edwards drew more heavily on the New Testament, especially the Gospels of Matthew and Luke, than his more balanced homiletical approach of expounding texts from both Old and New Testaments to English congregations. Edwards found the metaphors to nature within the parables of Jesus, such as teachings about seeds and trees as well as briars and fish, helped him convey Calvinist doctrines to the Mohicans and other Indigenous peoples.[37] He continued to preach about the consequences of sin and the terrors of eternal damnation, but he emphasized divine love and compassion more than he did in his previous pastorates.

He altered a sermon, "Sinners in the Hands of an Angry God," which he had first delivered in 1741 to a congregation in Enfield, Connecticut, when he preached it a decade later at Stockbridge. Wheeler explains: "But whereas in the Enfield sermon, the sinner dangles as a spider held over the pit of hell with the flames of God's wrath lapping at the fragile thread, suspended only by God's mercy . . . in his Stockbridge sermon, a bleeding Christ stands at the door of the sinner and knocks."[38] In both versions of Edwards's sermon he beckoned his listeners to behold simultaneously God's wrathful justice and bountiful grace, but in Stockbridge there was a greater concentration on the invitation of Christ to sinners. Edwards did not provide an explicit rationale for his shift that emphasized divine grace more than retributive justice in the revised sermon. Yet Wheeler suggests that Edwards's change indicated his growing awareness of the devastating consequences of settler colonialism.[39] Edwards may have chosen to accentuate the image of the bleeding Christ in his sermon to the Mohicans because he desired to express compassion to them as they endured disease, warfare, and ongoing colonial aggression.

But Edwards struggled to adequately address one issue that puzzled the Mohicans, because it did not exist in their Indigenous community: the phenomenon of nominal faith among English Christians. Umpachenee had interrogated Stoddard about why so many self-professing English Christians did not live in accordance with scriptural teachings. Red Jacket resisted white missionaries because his people, the Senecas, already had a religion with a code of morals and rituals that guided their entire community. For some Indigenous peoples, the concept of religion as primarily individualistic, rather than communal, engagement with the sacred was foreign. But even when they comprehended the Protestant theology of individual conversion, Indigenous peoples still thought it was strange how English Christians gave only lip service to their faith commitments. Indigenous peoples understood that some humans obeyed their religious teachings, and others disobeyed them, but the notion of (in this historian's framing) "sometimes obey when it is convenient but always assert that English Protestantism is superior to all other religions" was a bizarre aberration.

Edwards endeavored to elucidate nominal Christianity to the Mohicans, when he preached, "There are a great many that own the Christian religion, and say they believe there is but one God, and that Christ is the Son of God and Savior of sinners, that don't truly believe in Christ."[40] Edwards added that these persons were not in fact Christians, because the indicators of genuine faith were believers who were "willing to leave all for Christ . . . to forsake father and mother, wife and children, brothers and sisters, houses and lands, yea, and their own lives."[41] Edwards's inclusion of forsaking land as a measure of faith was, whether intentional or not, telling. One implication is that the Mohicans and other Indigenous peoples were among the Christian faithful because they had forsaken land (though by coercion and not by choice). Because very few among the English colonists in North America were willing to give up land, another implication is that "a great many" of them were not truly Christian.

"And This Is What Makes the Indians So Uneasy in Their Minds": The Rise of the English, the Fall of the French, and the Disappearing Middle Ground

Jonathan Edwards was the pastor at Stockbridge for roughly seven years, and his ministry among the Mohicans illumines the ways in which both he and the Mohicans navigated the conditions of settler colonialism. Indigenous peoples across North America agreed to mission stations such as Stockbridge, sometimes willingly and more often reluctantly, for a combination of spiritual, material, and political reasons. In 1702, a community of Mohawks in New York asked colonial officials for English pastors "to teach them religion and establish traffic amongst them [so] that they might be able to purchase a coat and not go to church in bear skins."[42]

When Edwards arrived at Stockbridge, there were approximately 250 Mohican and several other Mohawk residents. Some went to the church to hear Edwards preach, but many more chose to live in Stockbridge because it was a haven where they could support their families through employment opportunities in transatlantic trade. Edwards himself acknowledged the importance of trade in his sermons. In 1751, he preached a sermon that directly addressed the colonial interests and sins of the Dutch, English, and French. Edwards chose 2 Peter 1:19 as his text, a verse that describes the gospel as a trustworthy prophetic message and compares Christianity to a light shining in a dark place. He confessed that "the white people have not behaved like Christians," because they did not teach Indigenous peoples how to read the Bible. Edwards conceded, "So that although 'tis about 140 years since the white people came over here, there are but few of the poor Indians have been thoroughly instructed to this very day." He criticized French Catholic missionaries as devious teachers who "pretend to teach the Indians religion," because he thought that they withheld the Scriptures in their ministries. Dutch and English colonists possessed the true gospel, in Edwards's Protestant opinion, but they did not share it with Indigenous peoples because of their economic interests. Edwards stated, "And many of the English and Dutch are against your being instructed. They choose to keep you in the dark for the sake of making a gain of you. For as long as they keep you in ignorance, 'tis more easy to cheat you in trading with you."[43] Edwards utilized the imagery of Indigenous peoples languishing in the dark to describe both their spiritual and material conditions.

In private letters, Edwards also grappled with the political ramifications of Stockbridge and other English missionary endeavors. In 1752, he contrasted the vigorous presence of French Catholic missionaries among Indigenous peoples to the near complete absence of Indigenous evangelization in the English colonies. English failures "in so neglecting the instruction of the Indians" were also "extremely impolitic," because Edwards worried that alliances between the French and several Indigenous nations could defeat the English in military warfare. Edwards also complained that too many English traders dealt unfairly with their Indigenous partners and these exploitative practices were enflaming "distrust" and "aversion" among Indigenous peoples toward the English.[44]

Four years later, Edwards assessed the ongoing war between England and France in North America (that began in 1754 and ended in 1763) with concerns that the vastly outnumbered French colonists—he estimated "the French are twenty times less than we [English] are in number"—could nonetheless emerge victorious because they forged stronger alliances with Indigenous nations due to their greater familiarity with Indigenous cultures and deeper relationships with Indigenous peoples.[45] Edwards insisted in these letters that his pastorate among the Mohicans and Mohawks in Stockbridge gave him distinctive insight on diplomacy in addition to theology.

Edwards was not the only English pastor with antipathy toward the French Catholic missionaries in North America. In 1774, when Kirkland was among the Oneidas in New York, he found that some Oneidas opposed his presence because they identified as Catholic from previous contact with French missionaries in their territory. Kirkland complained in his journal that the Oneidas were "more or less infected with the Roman Catholic religion" and "easily captivated with those things that are showy," by which he meant bells, relics, rosaries, and other holy objects common to Catholicism. He reluctantly conceded that it was "prudent and necessary in many instances to condescend to the imperfect prejudices" of the Oneidas because of "their early acquaintance with the French," and to conduct his Protestant mission with more sensitivity to Catholicism than was expected among his ministerial colleagues.[46]

Roughly twenty-five years before Kirkland, the Swedish botanist Pehr Kalm visited New York and reported that the Oneidas (along with the Cayugas, Mohawks, Onondagas, and Senecas) told the colony's governor that the French missionaries were better than the English ones. Kalm stated how one Indigenous leader remarked "that the English do not pay so much attention to a work of so much consequence as the French" and "do not send such able men to instruct the Indians."[47] Kirkland hinted at the reasons why many Indigenous peoples preferred the missionary teachings of French Catholics over English Protestants, but he focused too simplistically on religious doctrines without a fuller excavation of the complex matrices of Indigenous spiritual, material, and political motivations.

Two significant differences between English and French colonization in North America were the size and scope of their aims. The French developed trade networks, whereas the English established settlements with exceedingly larger numbers of colonists. Edwards's estimation of a 20 to 1 ratio between the two European populations in North America was accurate. In 1750, there were 1,500,000 English colonists compared to 70,000 French colonists. The historian Richard White therefore contends that French colonists and Indigenous peoples together created a "middle ground" in the Great Lakes region. The French called this area the *Pays d'en Haut* (an expression in French meaning "upper country") to demarcate their trade network in North America. The middle ground was born because the smaller number of French colonists could not simply overpower various Indigenous nations. And some Indigenous peoples welcomed the opportunity to exchange their natural resources for European goods with foreigners who did not seek to expel them from their lands. White argues that the middle ground "involved a process of mutual invention" among the French and Indigenous parties because neither side could "gain their ends through force"; therefore both groups had "to understand the world and the reasoning of others and to assimilate enough of that reasoning to put it to their own purposes."[48] Another contrast between English and French colonization was that there were more frequent marriages between French men and Indigenous women, because of the scarcity of French women in North America until the 1730s.[49]

At least some French colonists internally held the same racist attitudes of many English settlers, but they externally acted with more openness toward

Indigenous peoples and their cultures. One example is the participation of French colonial officials and traders in Indigenous practices of gift-giving and condoling. Both practices were important communal acts within many Indigenous nations. When a community gathered for a celebration or a meal, individuals and families brought gifts to honor the tribal leaders. And when a person harmed another living being, such as stealing crops from another human or killing animals in excess, the guilty person publicly confessed and received communal forgiveness in a condoling ceremony. When representatives of different Indigenous nations met, there were similarly lavish presentations of gift-giving and sometimes condoling ceremonies after members of one nation had trespassed persons belonging to another nation.

As the French continued to trade with Indigenous peoples, and as some of them married and raised children together with Indigenous women, they learned both the overt meanings and less obvious subtleties of such practices. They rarely competed with Indigenous peoples for game or fish, because they understood in the middle ground that hunting and fishing were how their Indigenous partners maintained their livelihoods in transatlantic trade. When a rogue French trader infringed upon these Indigenous spaces, a small group of colonial officials brought gifts and public apologies to the respective Indigenous community.

But as English colonists and later American settlers penetrated the *Pays d'en Haut* from 1750 to 1820, they disrupted and ultimately expunged the middle ground. Beginning in 1759, two English military leaders, Thomas Gage and Jeffery Amherst, implemented a different approach to relations with Indigenous peoples after their victory over French and allied Indigenous forces. Gage stated that the English did not need to respect Indigenous cultures and practices, especially gift-giving: "All North America in the hands of a single power robs them [Indigenous peoples] of their consequence, presents, and pay."[50] Amherst instituted a policy that specifically eliminated gift-giving in diplomatic engagements. He did not oppose charitable support to Indigenous communities in cases of dire need or payment for services rendered, but he despised gift-giving as a wasteful practice that he thought encouraged torpor and superficiality.[51]

Relations between the English and Indigenous peoples in the Great Lakes region predictably deteriorated. In 1763, one Shawnee leader shared his frustration with an English colonial official and revealed a longing for the disappearing middle ground: "All the Indian nations are very jealous of the English, they see you have a great many forts in this country, and you are not so kind to them as they expected. The French were very generous to the Indians and always gave them clothing, and powder and lead in plenty, but you don't do that Brothers, and this is what makes the Indians so uneasy in their minds."[52]

Indigenous peoples did not have nostalgia for French colonization, but they found it easier to navigate relations with French foreigners because of their smaller population and their priority of trade rather than settlement. French colonialism wrought devastation across Africa and Asia, and French traders in the *Pays d'en Haut* had exploitative intentions, but the English comprised the more deadly threat to Indigenous North America.

French Catholic missionaries, especially those belonging to the Society of Jesus (more commonly known as the Jesuits), also exhibited a greater willingness than the English to learn about Indigenous cultures. Several historians have described this broad-minded approach as accommodation, as French missionaries made room for Indigenous lifeways and rituals in their thinking and teaching about Christianity. The historian Tracy Neal Leavelle expounds the creativity and flexibility of both French Jesuits and [Indigenous] Illinois women in the eighteenth century. As the two parties interacted with one another, the Jesuits grew in their understanding of how the rosary emerged as a sacred object alongside those that Illinois medicine men employed, such as animal skins and feathers, and many Illinois women forged dynamic spiritual pathways that integrated Christian prayer, worship, and the rosary with existing Indigenous practices to exert their newfound religious authority.[53]

The Jesuits also revised their translation of the Pater Noster (Lord's Prayer) because they grasped how the concept of sinning against God was foreign to the Illinois. The Jesuits found that the Illinois, like some other Indigenous nations, understood sin primarily within the realm of committing harmful actions against other living beings, rather than a confluence of evil thoughts, words, and actions deserving divine wrath. The missionaries therefore translated the sections seeking God's forgiveness while also forgiving others and asking for deliverance from evil in the Pater Noster as "We do not think of the things or people who anger us, and you must not think things of those who make us angry" and "Defend us from all bad things."[54]

English missionaries also endeavored to learn Indigenous lifeways, but it was more difficult for them to make room for Indigenous cultures in their hearts and minds. French missionaries inhabited cross-cultural contexts in which Indigenous peoples outnumbered them. The power dynamics did not always tilt toward Indigenous peoples, but the accompanying realities of living as the minority population generated more immersive experiences for those French ministering among Indigenous communities. The English missionaries, on the other hand, belonged to the majority population in their cross-cultural ministries. Some attempted to learn Indigenous languages, and more endeavored to express scriptural teachings with images and idioms that resonated with Indigenous peoples. John Eliot worked diligently with three Indigenous men, Job Nesutan, John Sassamon, and James Printer, to translate the Bible into the Algonquian language of the Massachusetts in 1663.[55] Jonathan Edwards altered his sermons when preaching to Mohican and Mohawk residents at Stockbridge. But Eliot, Edwards, and other English missionaries were participants in a colonial enterprise that actively displaced Indigenous peoples and violently dispossessed them of their territories.

Eliot had devoted over two decades of his ministry developing praying towns for Indigenous Christians, but the entire project was immediately crushed in 1675 when a war broke out between the English colonists and a coalition of Indigenous forces under the command of the Wampanoag sachem Metacom. Although some Indigenous residents in the praying towns remained neutral or supported the English, English colonists nevertheless regarded them with suspicion—changing their name from "praying Indians" to "preying Indians"—and the colonial government remanded Indigenous residents from every praying town to an unforgiving internment camp on Deer Island with limited food supplies and poor shelter during the frigid winter months of 1675 and 1676.[56]

English missionaries did not blithely despise Indigenous peoples, but they also considered their white race as superior and insisted that Christian conversion be coupled with cultural assimilation. The historian Heather Miyano Kopelson contends that nearly all English colonists, including missionaries, failed to adequately grasp Indigenous cultures. Even when the English praised the generosity of Indigenous feasts in which everyone received crops from a communal harvest, they missed the hierarchical patterns of redistribution rituals that reinforced the authority of tribal leaders.[57]

The English military officer Jeffery Amherst derided Indigenous rituals of gift-giving as the decadent nonsense of a primitive society, but the English had their own social hierarchies that cut across every facet of their lives, including Christian worship. Some white churches in the English colonies (and later United States) had either formal or informal seating arrangements by class, race, familial ties, and other social markers. The communion ritual within Puritan congregations involved the deacons giving the elements first to those of highest social rank. During a celebration of the Lord's Supper in 1724, the colonial Massachusetts judge Samuel Sewall was insulted when a deacon first offered the cup of wine to a worshiper whom Sewall considered to be of lower status.[58]

But Sewall was among the few who questioned the merits of Indigenous evangelization amid English settler colonialism. In 1700, he advocated for the colonial government to protect "convenient tracts of land" for Indigenous communities by enforcing stronger penalties for white encroachment. Sewall was concerned that the increasing English settler population would "want more room" and "will never leave till they have crowded them [Indigenous peoples] quite out of all their Lands." He then added, "And it will be a vain attempt for us to offer Heaven to them, if they take up prejudices against us, as if we did grudge them a living upon their own earth."[59] Sewall understood, at least in part, that he and his fellow settlers were insulting both their Indigenous neighbors and their Christian God.

"How Changed Is Every Scene": The Rise of the Americans, the Fall of the British, and the Breaking of Indigenous Worlds

In 1823, the Ojibwe poet Jane Johnston Schoolcraft (also known as Bame-wawagezhikaquay) wrote the following verse in "The Contrast": "But ah! how soon the scene has chang'd, Since I in love's mazes rang'd." Schoolcraft was born in 1800 to an Ojibwe mother and Irish-born father in the upper peninsula of Michigan Territory. Schoolcraft, recognized as the first known Indigenous woman author in the United States, wrote approximately fifty poems in English and Ojibwe, penned several songs and nonfiction essays, and transcribed and translated Ojibwe oral stories. Schoolcraft had seven siblings (three sisters and four brothers), and their family experienced the tumult of a changing world from the middle ground of Ojibwe and French interaction to English colonialism and then US federal rule.[60]

"The Contrast" captured these disruptive shifts as Schoolcraft began the poem, "With pen in hand I shall contrast, What I have felt—what now has past!" In a later version of the same poem Schoolcraft revised the line "But ah! how soon the scene has chang'd" to "But ah! how changed is every scene," and ended the poem differently with a new verse that specifically addressed the United States: "Discover a new dominion nigh, And half in joy, half in fear, Welcome the proud Republic here."[61] Schoolcraft rewrote the poem to illustrate the totality of changes resulting from American annexation (Michigan became a state in 1837) and the influx of white settlers.

Every scene from her childhood was altered, and many were eradicated, as Schoolcraft limned the razing of trees and Indigenous homes. In another poem, written from Castle Island in Lake Superior, Schoolcraft longed for a world in which "nature only reigns" and "no crimes, no misery, no tears" as well as "no laws to treat my people ill."[62] Indigenous peoples and a few white Americans, ranging from government officers to missionaries, endeavored to make a nation that preserved Indigenous lifeways and protected Indigenous territories, but they encountered innumerable obstacles and ultimately failed.

In 1881, the white woman author Helen Hunt Jackson published the groundbreaking book *A Century of Dishonor*. Jackson devoted years to examining firsthand accounts and government records of white-Indigenous interactions and ultimately concluded that the government of the United States had acted wrongly at every turn in their unfair policies and broken promises. She explained that the "Indian problem"—for this was how many white Americans discussed and interpreted the history and ongoing presence of Indigenous peoples in their country—was in fact a *white Christian problem*. Jackson recognized the same challenge that Sewall identified in 1700. Unless white Christians first repented of their racism and then actively worked to change racially unjust policies and confront racist white persons, white ministries among Indigenous peoples could reap only a "small harvest."[63] But the white population in the United States proved to be the most difficult mission field.

One of the most formidable challenges for government officers and missionaries alike involved the "settler" part of settler colonialism. As transatlantic migration soared, so too did white encroachment on Indigenous territories in North America. Before the American Revolutionary War, England tried to maintain good (or at least passable) relations with Indigenous nations in its North American colonies and understood that restraining the growing white population was a main component in diplomacy. In 1763, King George therefore issued a proclamation establishing the Appalachian Mountains as the boundary between English settlements and Indigenous lands. Five years prior, English military officers had assured their Indigenous allies in Ohio Territory at the Treaty of Easton that their lands would be protected after they defeated the French.[64]

But at other times, colonial authorities leveraged recently arriving settlers to strengthen their position by infiltrating and weakening Indigenous communities. For example, Scots-Irish settlers in Pennsylvania and Virginia, many of whom came to North America with nothing but their belongings, due to economic hardship at home, were given free or inexpensive tracts of land in remote areas as the means to expand each colony's geographical reach and protect the wealthier residents of densely populated cities. In 1774, the Virginia governor John Murray, Lord Dunmore sold tracts of land near Pennsylvania for what one historian notes was "the trifling sum" of 2 shillings and 6 pence (roughly $24 US in 2023) and did not strongly enforce payment.[65] Dunmore's true aim was to secure more territory for Virginia in its land dispute with

Pennsylvania. The Philadelphia mayor James Logan acknowledged in 1729 that Scots-Irish settlers in the Pennsylvania frontier were also useful as a shield against Indigenous peoples because they inhabited the frontlines of potential military conflicts.[66] In 1876, William Henry Egle described these Scots-Irish settlers in his *Illustrated History of the Commonwealth of Pennsylvania* as Presbyterians who "came with their Bibles, their [Westminster] Confession of Faith, their catechisms, and their rifles."[67]

White settlers also migrated west of the Appalachian Mountains, and by 1774 there were tens of thousands of them, despite King George's Proclamation of 1763. Shortly before the Revolutionary War, Thomas Gage complained that these westward settlers were "too numerous, too lawless and licentious ever to be restrained."[68] But Gage was not revealing a new problem. Some white settlers had long broken treaties and abused Indigenous peoples east of the Appalachian Mountains. The English missionary David Brainerd thoroughly criticized the white neighbors of Indigenous communities in New York, New Jersey, and Pennsylvania in his diary and journal from 1743 to 1746. Brainerd found that white persons "behaved more indecently than any Indians" whom he encountered. On one occasion, an Indigenous leader asked Brainerd why he "desired the Indians to become Christians" when "the Christians were so much worse than the Indians."[69]

To this Indigenous leader, Brainerd was the exception to the rule, as most white people he knew were liars and robbers. But Indigenous peoples sometimes discovered that missionaries too could behave like thieves. Samuel Kirkland encouraged Oneida and other Haudenosaunee representatives to accept the US government's proposal of enormous land cessions in the 1780s. The tragic result of these unfair dealings was that white settlers had overwhelmed the Oneidas by 1792. Kirkland was one of the settlers, as he received roughly 6,000 acres of land in upstate New York for his crucial role in negotiations. Kirkland founded Hamilton College on his new property.[70]

Some government officers and missionaries shared the conviction that the only solution to white oppression of Indigenous peoples was strong intervention from the federal government. The first US secretary of war, Henry Knox, wrestled with the ethical and political quandaries of white settler colonial aggression. Knox was raised in a Scots-Irish Presbyterian family in Massachusetts and was a descendant of William Knox (the older brother of John Knox, the renowned sixteenth-century Protestant reformer and early leader of Presbyterianism in Scotland). Henry Knox's parents helped to plant a Presbyterian congregation in Boston in the 1730s.[71] In his duties as secretary of war, Knox sought to deescalate the rising tension between white settlers and Indigenous peoples in Ohio and throughout the Great Lakes region. He believed that both parties held "deep rooted prejudices" against the other because of the constant fighting over land.[72] But Knox also felt that the white settlers deserved more severe censure, because they were relentless and merciless in antagonizing, attacking, and cheating Indigenous peoples. He found himself agreeing with Indigenous leaders when they came to him with their grievances. In 1794, he delivered a frank assessment to President George Washington: "The desires of too many frontier white people to seize by force or fraud upon the neighbouring Indian lands has been and still continues to be an unceasing cause of jealousy and hatred on the part of the Indians." Knox lamented in a "melancholy reflection" that "our modes of population have been more destructive to the Indian natives than the conduct of the conquerors of Mexico and Peru."[73]

The inclusion of Mexico and Peru was likely intentional, as Knox was surely familiar with English colonial (and later American) justifications for settler colonialism based on the thought of eighteenth-century Swiss-born legal theorist Emer de Vattel. In 1758, Vattel argued that the Spanish conquests of Mexico and Peru were unjust because the Indigenous peoples there (Aztecs in the former and Incas in the latter) were firmly rooted in civilizations they had long ago established. But Vattel supported European colonization in the United States and Canada because the Indigenous peoples in these regions roamed over, rather than cultivated, the land.[74] Although Knox wanted the federal government to do more to protect Indigenous peoples and prosecute white intruders, he also understood that the government had accrued significant debt during the Revolutionary War and lacked both the armed forces and financial resources to execute such an extensive and expensive plan.[75]

The historian Richard White discloses the consequences of government inaction as white settlers and Indigenous peoples incessantly killed one another: "Given the size and success of the [Indigenous] raids that ravaged the backcountry, the desire for [white] revenge against an often brutal enemy was understandable enough, but Indian hating did not concentrate on enemies. Indian haters killed Indians who warned them of raids. They killed Indians who scouted for their military expeditions. They killed Indian women and children."[76] Knox believed his new nation had squandered an opportunity and failed in its responsibility to treat Indigenous peoples "with kindness and even liberality" and wondered how "a future historian" would write about the unfolding calamity of intensifying racial oppression and lethal violence.[77]

Some white Christians believed the greatest danger to Indigenous peoples was spiritual, and the most grievous errors of white-Indigenous relations came from the inattentiveness of white Christians to evangelism. In 1723, Solomon Stoddard, a Congregational pastor in Massachusetts (and grandfather of Jonathan Edwards), published a pamphlet asking "[w]hether God is not Angry with the Country for doing so little towards the conversion of the Indians?" Stoddard cited Mark 16:15, a verse in which the resurrected Christ beckons the disciples to preach the gospel to all nations, and he confessed that the English colonists were not fulfilling this mission. Although the seal of the Massachusetts Bay colony featured the Macedonian call in Acts 16:9 (in which the apostle Paul receives a vision of a man from Macedonia saying to him, "Come over and help us"), the colonists prioritized their own economic profits and were "more careful to make a booty" from Indigenous peoples than to convert them to Christianity. He reminded the colonists that England was also "formerly under heathen darkness, as these Indians" and their ancestors worshiped Germanic deities such as Freya, Odin, Thor, and Tuisto until foreigners "brought the gospel" to them.

Stoddard gently acknowledged the violence that accompanied foreign intrusions into England, such as the Norman invasion in the eleventh century, and grudgingly conceded that the French, Portuguese, and Spanish had displayed more commitment than the English to Indigenous evangelization in the Americas. The vicious consequences of military conquest attending settler colonialism did not trouble Stoddard. However, the pastor was furious that the English colonists were not concerned about saving Indigenous souls with the "true religion" that they carried with them from England.[78] Missionaries continued to emphasize the hope of eternal salvation and encouraged Indigenous peoples to look heavenward for comfort as white settlers encroached on their lands. As white Americans encountered Indigenous peoples west of the Rocky Mountains in the second half of the nineteenth century, one Shoshone tribal leader told a missionary that he did not want to go to the Christian heaven if white people were also there: "If it is a good world, as you say, the white man would soon come along, and, if he saw I had a good place, he would want it for himself."[79]

"This Wrong Must Be Righted": When Christian Ministry Demands the Integration of Preaching and Political Advocacy

A few missionaries understood that their ministry among Indigenous peoples required addressing and integrating spiritual, material, and political concerns. William G. McLoughlin, in his history of Cherokee Christianity from 1789 to 1839, contends that the white Baptist missionary Evan Jones distinguished his ministry from white Methodist and Presbyterian efforts because of his growing recognition that evangelism and racial justice were not oppositional aims.[80] To preach about God's grace to the Cherokees also demanded political advocacy to combat racist actions and policies against them. Jones did not learn this important truth in a seminary classroom, but realized it as he lived among the Cherokees.

In the nineteenth century, Baptist pastors generally had less access to formal education than Presbyterians, and they also lacked the institutional resources of the more numerous and hierarchically structured Methodists. Another historian, George A. Schultz, explains, "When a Baptist preacher wished to found a church in the wilderness, he simply did so, asking leave of no one. . . . [T]he typical Baptist minister was self-supporting. Usually he was a farmer who wrestled with rocks and roots during the week and then took on Satan on Sunday."[81] Evan Jones did not have the educational credentials of some other missionaries, but he was not less intelligent than they were. He was in fact rare among them for at least two reasons: he learned the Cherokee language well enough to preach in it without a translator; and he empowered Cherokee preachers, including his former interpreters who taught him the language, by treating them as equal partners, rather than forever pupils.

As the US Congress debated the Indian Removal Act between 1828 and 1830, so too did Christian denominations. In 1829 Jones unequivocally denounced the expulsion bill, noting that the Cherokees were "determined not to yield up their lands, and they consider the acts which are employed to persuade them as vexatious and unjust."[82] He also agreed in the same year to help prepare a Cherokee delegation for their trip to Washington, DC, by translating documents for them. Jones was deeply engaged in the tasks of preaching and political advocacy, as each informed the other. His political advocacy shaped his preaching—he once delivered a sermon on the topic "If Providence does not favor a nation, it cannot prosper"—and his love for the Cherokees deepened as he joined them in protesting their expulsion. When the ABCFM missionary Sophia Sawyer visited Jones in 1832, the breadth of his ministry surprised her. It was unlike anything Sawyer had ever witnessed.[83]

Another white Baptist missionary, Isaac McCoy, was also convinced that political advocacy was necessary for ministry among Indigenous peoples. But McCoy disagreed with Jones about US government policies regarding Indigenous removal. McCoy, who lived among the Kickapoo, Potawatomi, Shawnee, Wea, and several other Indigenous nations across several midwestern states, such as Indiana, Michigan, and Missouri, from roughly 1818 to 1842, became convinced that Indigenous colonization was the solution to the incessant tensions and pervasive problems of white encroachment on Indigenous lands.

In every mission station that McCoy established—he named one in Potawatomi territory the "Carey Mission" in honor of William Carey, the well-known English Baptist missionary in India—white settlers always disturbed and sometimes defeated his ministry efforts by driving out entire Indigenous communities.[84] McCoy therefore wanted more, not less, direct involvement from the US federal government. He advocated for the creation of an "Indian Territory" west of the Mississippi River in which the federal government would grant a significant land allotment to various Indigenous nations. The federal government already negotiated with individual Indigenous nations, such as the Muscogees in Georgia, and forcibly relocated them westward in exchange for their eastern lands, but McCoy desired a more universal policy in which all persons from the different Indigenous nations lived together in one common territory. He also called for the federal government to strongly enforce this territory's borders, likely with white military personnel, to repel white settlers.

McCoy's proposal, published in 1827, sharply criticized the United States and its white citizens. Like Henry Knox, McCoy pointed his finger at white settlers, not Indigenous peoples, as the source of every Indigenous oppression. He began with a searing rebuke of the "right of discovery." Because white Americans continued to deploy the same legal and theological justifications from the age of European colonization in the Americas, such as the argument that Indigenous peoples did not have a rightful claim to lands they did not cultivate (McCoy noted the ongoing appeal to Vattel's theory from 1758), the missionary was compelled to make an obvious counterargument that he felt any rational person could not deny: "Speak we of the right of discovery? The Indians are the Aborigines of the country. We have not discovered an uninhabited region, but a peopled country."

He then presented a hypothetical scenario and wondered how white Americans would respond if a fleet of Chinese ships arrived at Jamestown and made a similar claim about discovering and owning "the whole of the United States territories."[85] The main thrust of McCoy's proposal was that Indigenous colonization was necessary to prevent white settlers from intruding upon and ultimately destroying every Indigenous community. He reasoned that white racism toward Indigenous peoples was as undeniable as it was impervious to remedy: "At first sight of Indians by Europeans, there became fixed in the latter a consciousness of superiority, which still exists, and is evinced in all our conduct in relation to them. We never meet an Indian on a level, as we meet a white man; we always look *down* upon him."[86]

McCoy was expressing a sentiment that other missionaries observed as well. White settlers did not treat every white person they met kindly or respectfully, but their disgust and hatred for Indigenous peoples was immediate and inveterate. McCoy therefore contended that Indigenous peoples could flourish only if the federal government placed them in a hermetically sealed territory free of and from white people. He acknowledged that his proposal was radical, but a large-scale problem required a commensurate solution. Previous reforms failed because they applied only "emollients to the surface of the sore," instead of "probing the wound to the bottom." McCoy then conveyed a bitter truth that many of his white readers probably blanched at with either shock or fury: "There is something among us, not among the Indians, radically wrong in this business: this wrong *must* be righted, or the Indians must be ruined, and Christians reproached."[87]

The missionary also admitted the limits of Indigenous evangelization. McCoy anticipated that some of his Christian readers would surmise that the right response was to further support missionary organizations. But he maintained that missionaries alone "cannot be expected to change the wilderness in which they are located," because "this power is vested alone in Government."[88] McCoy prayed and advocated for his federal government to intervene, address, and fix these systemic injustices.

McCoy ran into several obstacles as he pushed for Indigenous colonization. Some white Christians accused him of betraying his spiritual vocation as a missionary by his outspoken political engagement. The Cherokees and Evan Jones vehemently disagreed with his proposal calling for the deportation of all Indigenous peoples east of the Mississippi River. They also feared that supporters of the Indian Removal Act would welcome McCoy's insistence that Indigenous communities could not survive in the same vicinity as white people. When debating the expulsion bill before the Congress, Georgia representative Wilson Lumpkin cited McCoy's work to bolster his argument for the Indian Removal Act.[89] Other politicians opposed McCoy's plan because they believed that the growing white population, with increasing numbers of immigrants from Europe, necessitated westward expansion. Ohio's Senator William Allen declared that he would reject every measure intending to give Indigenous peoples "eternity of residence" in territory east or west of the Mississippi River.[90]

McCoy wavered between hope and despair. In 1840, he surmised in his *History of Baptist Indian Missions* that white Americans would not be so cruel that they would deny Indigenous peoples even a small portion of the vast westward territory.[91] One year later he despondently wrote in his private journal: "Where are the friends of the Indians. . . . [A]re they never to find a permanent home in America?"[92]

In 1830, at a town meeting in Philadelphia four months before the Indian Removal Act was passed, a group of concerned white citizens defending Cherokee rights lambasted the "insatiable covetousness of the people of the United States" and the "feebleness and ill faith of their government." The group also grappled with the westward expansion of white settlements and speculated that the Cherokees would never be safe from expulsion unless the federal government enacted clear and enduring policies: "Is it not first to be chased beyond the Mississippi, next beyond the Rocky Mountains, and finally to be driven into the Pacific? Is there any permanent asylum for them on this side [of] the grave?"[93] Though this group was referring specifically to the Cherokees, its haunting message was a harbinger of all white-Indigenous relations.

The Pequot Methodist preacher William Apess emphasized that the work of antiracism was both spiritual and political. But Apess was also witness to the long erosion of racial justice within white Christianity. To tear the mantle of prejudice from every American heart required faithful preaching and fervent prayer as well as civic participation and legislative action. In 1833 and 1834, when Apess was laboring alongside the Wampanoags in Massachusetts, he believed that they would prevail if the "true spirit" of Christianity began "to reign in the hearts of the people, and those who compose their legislative bodies."[94]

Apess also challenged those white Christians in Massachusetts who criticized Andrew Jackson, Wilson Lumpkin, and the proponents of Cherokee expulsion to examine themselves: "You plead for the Cherokees, will you not raise your voice for the red man of Mashpee [Massachusetts]?"[95] Apess certainly wanted white Christians to disavow any racial prejudices that existed in their individual hearts and minds, but he also desired that they discern the consequences of settler colonialism in their society and act to dismantle racially unjust structures.

Yet Apess found that many white Christians simply did not want to grapple with racial injustice, especially when they were in their churches, and they severed civic participation from their Christian beliefs and practices. These white Christians did not want to consider how they and their ancestors acquired the land where they resided. They recognized the prevalence of white racism toward Indigenous peoples, but they also made great strides to avoid discussion about (let alone action toward) antiracism in their congregations.

In 1835 and 1836, Apess delivered a public address in Portsmouth (New Hampshire) and Boston, his last publication before his death in 1841. Apess's lecture was a eulogy for Metacom, the Wampanoag sachem who was killed in the decisive war from 1675 to 1676 that enabled the English colonists to exert complete dominion over Indigenous peoples in Massachusetts. Apess looked back at history and questioned why so many white Americans celebrated the Pilgrims, the Puritans, the *Mayflower*, and other curated memories of the colonial past. For it was this very history in which "the seed of iniquity and prejudice was sown" and could still be seen in the "deep-rooted popular opinion in the hearts of many" that Indigenous peoples were made "on purpose for destruction, to be driven out by white Christians, and they to take their places; and that God had decreed it from all eternity." At the end of his lecture, Apess thanked those in attendance and wished for them to know that he did not hold them guilty for the sins of their ancestors—"you and I have to rejoice that we have not to answer for our fathers' crimes"—but that they were responsible for the world in which they lived, and it was not too late to undo the inherited mistakes.[96]

Most in the audience probably responded with thunderous applause and felt good that they heard the fiery message of the eloquent Indigenous speaker. And Apess likely experienced a rush of gratitude for the glowing reception to a lecture that was the product of many hours of research and writing. But Apess yearned for more. He wanted white Christians to come over and help him remake the confused world of settler colonialism and racial oppression with the love and justice of God.

Slavery

Chapter Five

"Churches Dreaded Abolitionism"

The Rise of Slavery and Racism in White American Churches

After the American Civil War, Henry Ward Beecher reflected on the relationship between churches and Black liberation. Beecher belonged to a family of abolitionists, including his more famous sister, Harriet Beecher Stowe, author of *Uncle Tom's Cabin*, but he sometimes hesitated to support the cause when he was the pastor of several congregations, most notably Second Presbyterian Church in Indianapolis and Plymouth Church in Brooklyn, New York. Though the movement pursued God's justice in seeking to end slavery, Beecher remembered: "Churches dreaded abolitionism, parties hated abolitionism, commerce abhorred abolitionism. Mobs rioted around the meetings, and threatened the dwellings, the stores, and the very persons of Abolitionists."[1]

Black and white Christians as well as Black churches participated in abolitionism, but very few white churches were active in one of the most significant social justice movements in US history. Though white churches in the Southern states vehemently resisted abolitionism, Beecher was emphasizing the tenacious opposition to Black emancipation in the Northern states. Beecher was neither exaggerating nor misremembering the facts of history. The obvious absence of white churches in the righteous struggle for Black liberation has been diluted over time to the point that this truth has nearly disappeared in the national memory. In a strange and perverse turn, some Americans today hold the inverse to be true and think that white churches occupied a central and crucial role in abolitionism.

This is one of several oddities in how the history of slavery and abolition is transmitted in the United States. Black and white abolitionists are celebrated as courageous heroes who valiantly risked their lives for a noble cause, but there is far less attention to the implications of this truth. We are quick to

109

praise the abolitionists, but we fail to reckon with the opposition they encountered when they advocated ending something as horrible and unjust as slavery. The abolitionists inhabited a world in which it was dangerous to publicly state that it was wrong to enslave Black people. One of the most perilous places for them to speak was in white churches.

As a white pastor, Beecher acknowledged that there were congregational constraints to his preaching. In 1837, after graduating from Lane Theological Seminary in Cincinnati, he accepted his first call, to First Presbyterian Church in the small town of Lawrenceburg, Indiana. His father, Lyman Beecher, was the seminary's president, and Henry's years of study coincided with tumult and controversy because of escalating tensions due to the abolition movement. In 1834, fifty-one students withdrew from the seminary after several months of conflict with the school's board of trustees. Disapproving of how these students integrated their pursuit of Christian ministry with Black liberation, the trustees called upon Lyman Beecher to enforce stricter regulations that removed abolitionism from the seminary's classrooms and campus life.

Lyman Beecher tried and ultimately failed to broker a compromise that satisfied the demands of the trustees and the convictions of his students, but Henry took to heart several lessons from his Lane education. Henry Ward Beecher disavowed his support for the American Colonization Society and realized the sinfulness of its efforts to send free Black Americans to Liberia and its propagation of the idea that racial integration between Black and white Americans was imprudent. He had once preached a sermon explaining that the removal of Black Americans from the country was better for them than the alternative of perpetually living as inferior to the white citizens of the United States. Beecher became convinced of the wrongfulness of slavery and anti-Black prejudice. He wrote in one of his sermon notebooks in 1837 that "the radical sin of American Slavery is that it denies manhood to those on whom Christ bestowed it."[2]

Beecher denounced the popular and pervasive notion of the Black race as inherently and permanently inferior to the white race, as antithetical to Christianity. But in his final weeks at Lane, Beecher also penned in his journal, "Remember! You can gain more easily if you get around . . . [people's] prejudices and put truth in their minds. But never if you attack prejudice."[3] As Beecher prepared for his first call, he resolved to steer clear of direct engagement with abolitionism as a pastor.

After two years in Lawrenceburg, Beecher moved to Indianapolis in 1839 to become the pastor of Second Presbyterian Church. The larger city presented Beecher with more opportunities to minister among parishioners in the middle and upper classes; his annual salary increased from $500 to $800.[4]

But Beecher continued to refrain from preaching on abolitionism. During his first year as the pastor of Second Presbyterian, Beecher endeavored to learn as much as he could about his church members and the larger context of Indianapolis. He pored over the book of Acts in the New Testament and was convinced that the ministerial accomplishments of Christ's apostles and Paul were due to their commitment to understand the feelings and perspectives of the people they sought to convert.

Beecher recalled, "And I studied the sermons until I got this idea: that the apostles were accustomed first to feel for a ground on which the people and they stood together; a common ground where they could meet."[5] In his search for common ground, Beecher discerned an antipathy toward abolitionism. When Indiana was annexed into statehood in 1816, the state constitution banned slavery. But like other midwestern and western states, Indiana desired neither white enslavers nor free Black persons. Most of its white citizens disagreed with those abolitionists who advocated for the civil rights of free Black Americans, which included equal access to education, employment, voting, and residence.

In 1851, Indiana incorporated firm anti-Black migration provisions into its state constitution. Illinois and Oregon also enacted discriminatory policies restricting Black residency. The historian Leon F. Litwack delineates how these states either explicitly barred Black Americans from residency or introduced the stipulation of a bond requirement "ranging from $500 to $1,000" (which was not required for new white residents) that "amounted to practical exclusion."[6] During the state convention to revise Indiana's constitution, James Rariden, a delegate from Wayne County, argued that the overwhelming public sentiment among the state's white population against racially integrated public schools illustrated the need for more restrictive policies deterring Black residents.

When Black parents attempted to send their children to the same schools as white children, Rariden stated that "the whites rose *en masse*, and said, your children shall not go to school with our children, and they [the Black pupils] were consequently expelled." Rariden detested Black enslavement and was glad that it did not exist in Indiana, but he also defended the "feeling of pride that elevates the white man over the black man" as natural, not the sin that some within the abolition movement were calling upon all white Americans to repent of in their hearts and change in their laws. He explained that this push for racial integration was why he opposed abolitionism.[7] Beecher found that many in Indianapolis, including at his church, held similar views to Rariden: "Nobody was allowed to say a word on the subject of slavery. They were all red-hot out there then; and one of my elders said, 'If an Abolitionist comes here I will head a mob to put him down.'"[8] So Beecher waited seven years and preached his first sermon on slavery at Second Presbyterian in 1846.

One year later, Beecher received invitations from two East Coast churches, Park Street Church in Boston and Plymouth Church in Brooklyn, seeking his pastoral leadership. He had honed his preaching skills in Indianapolis, and other churches had begun to take notice. Beecher ultimately chose the pastorate of Plymouth Church and eagerly embraced the urban surroundings and possibilities of his new ministry. In his first sermon there, Beecher declared that his obligation was to preach Christ "in his personal relations to individual men," which included the "right and duty to introduce into the pulpit every subject" that concerned the congregation, such as "the morals of trade, of commerce, or politics."[9] Beecher therefore addressed slavery more directly than he did in his prior pastorates, but he continued to avoid the problems of racial prejudice in cities such as Brooklyn and across the Northern states. In 1851, Beecher protested the Compromise of 1850 and the Fugitive Slave Act, which compelled white residents in Northern states to assist in the recapture and return of enslaved persons to the enslavers they had escaped. He opposed how some politicians appealed to the compromises that preserved slavery at the initial Constitutional Convention in 1787 as precedent for the continuation and extension of Black enslavement in the 1850s. He insisted that the founders agreed to compromise only because they thought slavery was declining "like the late snows in April" and "would soon melt away" with gradual emancipatory measures.

But the increasing profitability of cotton, rice, and sugar production had changed the fortunes of enslavers in the Southern states and manufacturers in the Northern states in ways that the founders did not foresee. And white American Christians also did not meet the challenge of abolishing slavery in the face of a soaring gross domestic product and growing national economy. Beecher explained: "Although Christianity can do much to control commerce and temper commerce, and does do much, yet where the gains are large, there is no power which can restrain it throughout the whole community."[10]

Beecher also highlighted the presence of two competing Christian religions operating in the United States, which he identified as "a Christianity of the Bible" and "a Christianity of the Church," and lamented that "the latter does not always express the fullness or spirit of the former."[11] Yet Beecher himself succumbed to churchly compromises in his own journey to ministerial success. He did not preach as fervently and frequently on the many injustices of racial discrimination in his immediate vicinity, even though he witnessed these anti-Christian realities all the time: "When I came here there was no place for colored men and women in the theatre except the negro pen; no place in the opera; no place in the church except the negro pew; no place in any lecture-hall; no place in the first-class car on the railways. The white omnibus of Fulton Ferry would not allow colored persons to ride in it."[12]

In 1839, Andrew Harris, a Black Presbyterian pastor in Philadelphia and the first Black graduate of the University of Vermont, identified three compounding sins in Black enslavement: monetary greed, slavery itself, and anti-Black racism. Harris asserted, "The Bible says the love of money is the root of all evil. . . . Yet, without disputing the correctness of the declaration, it seems to me that slavery has developed a passion in the human heart that is stronger than the love of money." Harris maintained that the "deeper root" of slavery's evils was the enduring racial prejudice of the white population.[13] White people in the Northern states acted against their own economic interests when they turned away Black persons who were willing to pay for rides on public transportation, meals in restaurants, and seats in the theatre and other entertainment venues.

But the larger point Harris was making entailed how white people were betraying the principles of justice and humanity as they denied Black people equal access to education, employment, and every other pathway to dignity and flourishing. Beecher likely agreed, but he also knew the limits of his vocation. White preachers, especially successful ones, could not fill the pews of their churches if they preached the full gospel of abolitionism.

This chapter covers the rise of slavery and racism in white American churches. As slavery emerged in the North American colonies, there were a few white Christians who deployed scriptural arguments to protest the pernicious sins of the transatlantic slave trade and slave ownership. But many more either publicly defended slavery or privately made moral compromises as the system of slavery became engrafted onto their cultural, economic, social, and religious foundations. Many white churches in the Northern states dreaded abolitionism, because it required them to confront the ongoing consequences of slavery in their contexts. The racially discriminatory attitudes and policies that white Americans, including white Christians, held against Black Americans illustrated their failures to construct a racially just society after abolishing slavery.

"This Silence Soon Becomes Acquiescence": The Beginnings of Black Enslavement in Colonial New England

Alvan Stewart, a white lawyer and abolitionist, admonished a gathering of Presbyterian clergy in 1839 for their "moral cowardice" in failing to preach on slavery. Stewart believed that "the ministers of Christ should stand on the watchtowers of the nation" and point out those laws and practices that were contrary to "the ordinances of Heaven." Stewart's use of the watchtower surely struck a chord with his hearers, as it was a powerful allusion to the prophetic literature in the Hebrew Bible. The pastors likely could recount specific passages, such as Isaiah 21:8 and Habakkuk 2:1, in which the biblical prophets commit themselves to standing on the watchtower to proclaim God's messages of truth and justice.

Stewart warned the ministers that their decision to remain silent on slavery would result in greater evils: "This silence soon becomes acquiescence, which soon is apology, which is soon defense, which is soon vindication, which at last turns into a political truth maintained by the authority of the Holy Scriptures."[14] Stewart traced the history of how slavery informed and deformed American Christianity. The white Christian defense of Black enslavement evolved from quiet acquiescence weighing economics and racism against faith and morality to bold declaration insisting that persons of African descent were racially inferior to white people and divinely ordained for perpetual slavery in the United States.

Black enslavement was introduced in Massachusetts between 1623 and 1638. Some historians point to the arrival of Samuel Maverick, the son of an Anglican minister who built his own private fort on Massachusetts Bay in 1623. Maverick was an enslaver who owned at least three enslaved Africans. Other historians maintain that the first enslaved Africans arrived in Massachusetts in 1638 on a ship that the colony's governor John Winthrop recorded as having cargo that included "salt, cotton, tobacco and Negroes."[15]

Another early account of Black enslavement in Massachusetts comes from the English naturalist John Josselyn. Josselyn visited the northeastern region of North America twice, first in 1638 through 1639 and again from 1663 to 1671. In 1674, he published an account of his two trips that included his encounter with one of Maverick's enslaved persons. An enslaved woman approached Josselyn to ask for his help. Josselyn learned that Maverick was forcing her to have sex with an enslaved man against her will, because the enslaver wanted her to produce children and increase his holdings in human property. Josselyn wrote, "Mr. Maverick was desirous to have a breed of Negroes, and therefore seeing she would not yield by persuasions to company with a Negro young man he had in his house; he commanded him will'd she nill'd she to go to bed to her."[16]

This shameful episode was one of several that caused Josselyn to criticize English colonization. Josselyn recognized that those Puritan settlers who wrote glowing reports of how they were introducing the wonders of the Christian gospel to the Indigenous inhabitants of North America were actually engaging in cunning and deceit. The colonial racial capitalism of the transatlantic trade exploited both Indigenous and Black persons to enrich the English settlers.

Josselyn observed, "Thus instead of bringing of them [Indigenous peoples] to the knowledge of Christianity, we have taught them to commit the beastly and crying sins of our Nation, for a little profit."[17] In seeking more profit, Maverick turned to sexual violence.

The historian David Hackett Fischer finds Josselyn's account of "African slavery in Massachusetts Bay" illustrates how it was "a lawless system of extreme inhumanity" in which "a cruel master bred his slaves as if they were animals, and did so by violence, assault, and rape that violated many canons of Christian ethics."[18] In 1640, roughly two years after Josselyn met the aggrieved enslaved woman belonging to Maverick, Boston gave a land grant of 600 acres to Maverick, which was the highest allotment offered to any individual.[19]

Puritan settlers in New England responded differently to criticisms of Black enslavement and Indigenous land dispossession. They mounted vigorous theological justifications for the latter, such as John Winthrop's division in 1629 of natural and civil rights, to claim that Indigenous peoples did not own their territories, but they did not publish treatises to defend the former until 1701. Puritan clergy such as John Eliot and Cotton Mather gently encouraged enslavers to treat enslaved persons without undue cruelty and advocated for Black evangelization. At least some pastors desired for enslaved Africans to receive Christian instruction and participate in congregational worship.

These ministers wanted to save African souls, but they also recognized that enslaved persons were to be separated from the English settlers because of their race. Churches practiced racial segregation in both their houses of worship and their cemeteries.[20] Enslaved Africans, even in their graves, could not rest among English settlers. But the Puritan clergy refrained from publicly defending slavery, even when one of its leading theologians, Richard Baxter, published a searing indictment against Black enslavement in 1673. Baxter was probably the most read Puritan writer in the seventeenth century. Though he never traveled to North America, Baxter sharply lambasted slavery across the English colonies in the Americas as unjust. He asserted that enslavers who purchased African captives and "use them as beasts for their mere commodity" were "fitter to be called incarnate devils" than Christians.[21] Two years later, the colony of Rhode Island in 1675 reinforced laws from 1652 that prohibited slavery and restricted Black and white servitude to ten years. The colonial government also extended the ten-year limitation to Indigenous servitude, but the laws were inconsistently enforced and devolved into dead letters by 1708.[22]

In 1700 and 1701, the stirrings of antislavery prompted a formal defense expressing the compatibility of Black enslavement with English Protestant Christianity. In Massachusetts, an enslaved man named Adam publicly protested his legal status. His enslaver, John Saffin, was a prominent merchant in

Boston. One component of Saffin's business enterprise was human trafficking in the transatlantic slave trade. In 1680, he and four partners dispatched the ship *Elizabeth* on a voyage to Africa to transport enslaved persons. Saffin and Adam had an agreement by which Saffin would grant Adam his freedom for seven years of faithful service. Adam was therefore aggrieved when Saffin determined to lease Adam to another enslaver as the end of his seventh year of enslavement was approaching. Adam claimed that Saffin had reneged on their contract, but Saffin argued that Adam was the one who had first betrayed their agreement because of his negligent work ethic and disobedient attitude.[23]

After Adam shared his travails with Samuel Sewall, the judge in colonial Massachusetts who raised questions about English settler colonialism, Sewall published in 1700 an antislavery tract entitled "The Selling of Joseph." In addition to his judicial role, Sewall also belonged to one of the wealthiest merchant families in Boston. Thus, he had deep familiarity with both slavery and the transatlantic slave trade. Before learning of Adam's case against Saffin, Sewall confided in his diary that he had been "long and much dissatisfied with the trade of fetching Negroes from Guinea and had a strong inclination to write something about it."[24] Sewall finally published an antislavery pamphlet, which he began by writing, "The numerousness of slaves at this day in the province, and the uneasiness of them under their slavery, hath put many upon thinking whether the foundation of it be firmly and well laid; so as to sustain the vast weight that is built upon it."[25] He appealed to Genesis 37 and found that the blatant immorality of Joseph's brothers when they sold him into slavery illustrated the wrongness of Black enslavement. Sewall argued from Psalm 115:16 and Acts 17:26–29 to underscore how persons of African descent were the children of God with an "equal right unto liberty" no different than English persons.

He then pointed out the sinful horrors of Black enslavement. Enslaved families were forcibly separated from one another—"husbands from their wives, parents from their children"—in the sales and transfers of enslaved persons. Some enslavers gave into the "temptations masters are under" and sexually violated enslaved women. Sewall disputed the interpretation that the transatlantic slave trade had a providentially favorable outcome due to the opportunity for Black evangelization in North America. In Genesis 50:19–21, Joseph reassures his brothers that God had turned their evil intentions into good purposes. Some English Christians asserted that the slave trade was like this scriptural account, because enslaved Africans were "brought out of a pagan country, into places where the gospel is preached." Sewall reasoned that captivity and human trafficking were not godly means for Christian mission and questioned whether "the rigor of perpetual bondage" and the dehumanizing conditions of Black enslavement permitted fruitful pathways for evangelism.[26]

Saffin responded in 1701 with a pamphlet of his own defending slavery. Saffin found ample support for his position in the Bible. Slavery was practiced throughout the Old and New Testaments. The ancient Israelites, including the patriarch Abraham, owned enslaved persons. Saffin emphasized Leviticus 25:44–46, a scriptural passage that forbids ancient Israel from enslaving its own people: "Though the Israelites were forbidden (ordinarily) to make bond men and women of their own nation, but of strangers they might."[27]

Saffin concurred with Sewall about one faulty misinterpretation of the Bible that was sometimes employed to justify Black enslavement: the curse of Ham from Genesis 9:24–27. European and white American interpreters defended both slavery and racism through this biblical text in which Noah, in an inebriated stupor, angrily curses his son Ham, after Ham witnesses his father naked. Noah pronounces favor on his elder sons, Japheth and Shem, and states that Ham's son, Canaan, will be the slave of Japheth and Shem. Interpreters argued that persons of African descent were the descendants of Ham and carried with them the Noahic curse in the forms of slavery and racial inferiority.

This dubious line of thinking required interdisciplinary malpractice across biblical, ethnological, and genealogical studies. For the ongoing application of the curse against Ham to make sense, persons of European descent had to be proven the descendants of Ham's brothers, Japheth and Shem. Sewall refuted the curse of Ham theory as genealogically incorrect and morally depraved. He believed persons of African descent were the descendants of Cush, not Canaan, and moreover wondered how any Christian could worship a God who vindictively punished an entire race of humans with perpetual slavery because of one unfortunate incident between Noah and Ham.[28]

Saffin did not bother to dispute Sewall on this point, but Saffin countered that Sewall missed the larger message from the Old Testament: "Any lawful captives of other heathen nations may be made bond men as hath been proved."[29] European Christians had divine permission to enslave Africans because they were foreigners from nations that were not Christian. Saffin regarded all the theological attention to four verses from Genesis 9 as unnecessary, when it seemed to him that the entirety of Scripture upheld Black enslavement.

Another area of agreement between Sewall and Saffin concerned English prejudice against persons of African descent. Both men acknowledged that the greatest obstacle to abolitionism in Massachusetts was that the English settler population abhorred the presence of free Black persons. English settlers tolerated the existence of enslaved Africans because of their economic contributions in labor and valuations as human capital. They not only performed uncompensated service for their enslavers, but they and their children could be resold in the marketplace or bequeathed to an enslaver's family members. In one section of his pamphlet, Sewall strongly argued that Africans were made in the *imago Dei* and shared the same desires for dignity and liberty as the English. But in a subsequent paragraph Sewall asserted the impossibility of racial integration, writing about persons of African descent in his colonial society: "And there is such a disparity in their conditions, color, and hair, that they can never embody with us, and grow up into orderly families, to the peopling of the land."[30]

Saffin commented on this precise point from Sewall and added a second barrier to Black liberation: financial reparations to enslavers. Saffin believed that abolishing slavery also required compensation to enslavers. If the colonial government expropriated other forms of capital (such as real estate or animals) from the settlers for the sake of the public good, it would do so only with fair remuneration to those individuals. Yet Saffin added that racial prejudice was the more challenging problem. Even if enslavers were "reimbursed out of the public treasury," Saffin questioned the feasibility of removing all persons of African descent from the colony. He inveighed, "And it is to be feared that those Negroes that are free, if there be not some strict course taken with them by authority, they will be a plague to this country."[31]

Saffin's pamphlet illustrated the contradictory impulses of evangelical duty and racial hatred that coursed throughout English colonization in North America. On the one hand, English enslavers were exhorted to convert their enslaved Africans. On the other hand, Saffin railed against "the Negroes' character" as "libidinous, deceitful, false, and rude" and claimed that cowardice and cruelty were among the "innate" attributes of the Black race.[32] Sewall was more measured in his assessment of Black persons. They were angry, surly, and untrustworthy because of their enslaved conditions. It was the racial oppressions from the English, rather than any innate racial characteristics, that caused the tensions between enslavers and the enslaved in the colony.

Saffin addressed the economics of Black enslavement more directly than Sewall, but a closer examination of Sewall's life reveals that he was just as involved in the human trafficking of colonial racial capitalism as Saffin. Sewall's abolitionism in print did not accord with his business practices. The historian Zachary McLeod Hutchins finds that Sewall placed at least fourteen advertisements in local Boston newspapers with intentions to sell over twenty-four enslaved Africans. In 1715, Sewall announced in the *Boston News-Letter* the sale of "a Negro boy and two young Negro women." One year later the same newspaper posted: "Two fine lusty Negro men to be sold by Mr. Samuel

Sewall Merchant, and to be seen at the Swing-Bridge in Merchants-Row Boston." In 1725, the *Boston Gazette* published: "To be sold by Mr. Samuel Sewall Merchant, a young likely Negro man and a young Negro woman, just arrived, to be seen at his house in the Common."[33] Hutchins argues that Sewall's protracted involvement in the buying and selling of enslaved persons necessarily complicates his legacy as an advocate for Black emancipation.[34]

Sewall's pamphlet is recognized as the first printed abolitionist essay in North America, but the author joined other wealthy merchants in accruing income from transatlantic trade, which included enslaved Africans alongside other commodities such as fish, lumber, rum, sugar, and tobacco. Slave markets in Boston and other cities such as Newport in Rhode Island were morally revolting, but they were also socially respectable in the sense that the English colonists who gathered there were from the middle and upper classes.

In addition to purchasing the labor and capital of enslaved Africans, English colonists pursued slave ownership because it was a social marker of success. One historian of slavery in colonial New England observes that nearly every prominent white family across Boston, Hartford, New Haven, Providence, and other towns and cities possessed enslaved persons.[35] Perhaps Sewall expressed aloud qualms about slavery that some of his peers divulged privately, but the slave merchants themselves did not reside in the shadows. Men such as Sewall and Saffin were economic, political, and social leaders in their communities. Sewall's social context does not excuse his gross hypocrisy as an antislavery advocate who sold enslaved persons for financial gain, but it helps to explain how Sewall opposed slavery in print yet participated in the business of the slave trade.

"If the Slavery in Which We Hold the Blacks Is Wrong": Rum Distilleries, White Churches, and the Business of Slavery in Colonial New England

In 1731, Jonathan Edwards traveled from his Massachusetts home in Northampton to a slave market in Newport, Rhode Island. Why did this twenty-seven-year-old pastor of a Congregational church make the long journey, probably by an arduous combination of coach, sloop, and horseback, spanning 130 miles? It was not to join an assembly of fellow ministers for a theological conference or to preach at a revival meeting, which one would think were the most common reasons for Edwards's trip. Rather, Edwards arrived in Newport to purchase an enslaved person. Newport emerged as a leading site for the transatlantic slave trade in the eighteenth century. Between 1750 and 1775, approximately 90 percent of all slave ships dispatched from

Boston, New York City, and Newport. Newport alone accounted for 62 percent of the total, as more than 350 vessels dispatched from this small but significant seaside city in Rhode Island.[36]

Edwards determined to buy an enslaved person in Newport for at least three reasons. Two are certain and the third is likely. Elite white families in Northampton owned a small number of enslaved persons for domestic labor and fieldwork. Edwards had married Sarah Pierpont in 1727, and together they had eleven children. Therefore, Edwards desired to own an enslaved person for assistance with daily chores in his home. But Edwards also acquired a "Negro girl named Venus" for eighty pounds to enhance his social standing.[37] Edwards invested 40 percent of his annual salary in 1731 to join the ranks of the gentry in the town where he worked as a pastor.[38] There is no record to prove the third rationale, but perhaps the reason Edwards traveled all the way to Newport, when there were ample opportunities for him to purchase an enslaved person in Boston, was linked to cost and choice. There were more enslaved persons at lower prices in Newport's slave markets than in those venues closer to Northampton.

Edwards's position on slavery was multilayered but straightforward. Even his hypocrisy is readily discernable. Edwards was a renowned Protestant leader. One historian lavishes Edwards with effusive praise: "Edwards was extraordinary. By many estimates, he was the most acute early American philosopher and the most brilliant of all American theologians." Some Christians today, not only in the United States but around the world, either explain away Edwards's participation in Black enslavement by dismissing his sinfulness as the product of his social (and historical) location as a man of his times, or overemphasize the contradictions he freely admitted as an example of his ingenious mind at work in grappling with complexity.[39]

Another approach has been to simply ignore that Edwards was an enslaver and defender of slavery. In the index of a book comprising fifteen different scholarly essays assessing the legacy of "Jonathan Edwards at home and abroad," there is one subentry for slavery with a single locator, whereas there are multiple locators for "Calvinist theology," "divine providence," and "original sin."[40] The solitary essay that dares to mention slavery quickly excuses Edwards's slave ownership as the result of his existence in a colonial world in which "not many Euro-Americans yet felt their consciences pricked by the fundamental evil of slavery." The essay then moves to focus on three abolitionists—Lemuel Haynes, Samuel Hopkins, and Sarah Osborn—who are identified as belonging to the "Edwardsian tradition."[41] This Edwardsian categorization is specious, because Hopkins was the only one of the three to have had personal contact with Edwards, and there is scant evidence connecting the racial justice work of Haynes and Osborn directly to Edwards's writings.

In 1741, Edwards jotted some notes in response to a controversy over slavery in the town of Northfield in Massachusetts. At a Congregational church there, several parishioners assailed their pastor, Benjamin Doolittle, for owning an enslaved person. Edwards publicly supported Doolittle and privately penned his thoughts on a defense of Black enslavement. His notes never materialized into the form of a published work, but they illumine at least three strands of Edwards's thinking.

One is that Edwards criticized the immorality of the transatlantic slave trade but not slavery in the North American colonies. He found that the parishioners denouncing Doolittle were complicit in "a far more cruel slavery than that which they object against in those that have slaves here" because they were consumers of transatlantic trade products even though they knew that the human trafficking of African captives was an integral component of this economy.[42]

Another is that Edwards was wary of the literalist approach to biblical exegesis that proslavery Christian thinkers such as Saffin employed. He charged that finding instances of slavery in the Old Testament did not necessarily justify Black enslavement. He asked himself whether the Bible permitted Christians to enslave people who were not Christian and determined that passages such as Deuteronomy 15:6, in which God promises that ancient Israel will rule over other nations, did not apply to the early modern context of Africa, Europe, and the Americas. Edwards also conveyed a sense of progressive revelation, with the conviction that the Christian God increasingly revealed more wisdom to humans over time. He interpreted Paul's epistles in the New Testament as textual evidence that God "winked at" some past injustices "in those times of darkness" but no longer did so in Edwards's age.[43] Further revelation from God to humans meant that humans were consequently more accountable to act justly.

A third insight from Edwards's notes on slavery illustrates a willful inconsistency. The transatlantic slave trade was wrong, but it was permissible for Edwards, Doolittle, and other enslavers to retain their enslaved persons. Christians were responsible for doing good and opposing evil because God had stopped winking at the cruel and barbaric practices that prevailed in antiquity. Yet Edwards made no effort, not even with his quill in private commentary, to dismantle Black enslavement as it existed in colonial New England.

The historian Kenneth P. Minkema rightly assesses the life and legacy of Jonathan Edwards: "Edwards's journey to Newport implies that in 1731 he had no qualms about the African slave trade. His notes a decade later, however, show that he had changed his mind about buying newly imported slaves. Nonetheless, he remained an unapologetic defender of slavery as an institution and continued owning slaves himself."[44] In 1748, Benjamin Doolittle emancipated Abijah Prince, the enslaved man in his possession, and gave to Prince a tract of his land in Northfield.[45] Edwards never relinquished his human property.

In 1769, the First Congregational Church in Newport was seeking a new pastor. Its previous minister, William Vinal, was forced to resign due to criticisms about his impiety, namely his apparent insobriety, and the church had grown weary of the rotation of supply preachers occupying its pulpit for roughly two years. One of its members, Sarah Osborn, advocated within the congregation for Samuel Hopkins to be its next pastor. Osborn had lived in Newport since 1729 and was a prominent figure in both the church and city. When she was twenty-three years old, Osborn became a member of the church in 1737, and four years later she organized a women's society at First Congregational. Osborn also led Christian meetings for persons of African descent in the city. Both free and enslaved Black persons gathered weekly at her home—free persons on Tuesday evenings and enslaved persons on Sunday evenings—for Bible study and prayer. Osborn endorsed Hopkins because she felt that his sermons entailed a powerful blending of sound Reformed theology with sharp emotional sensibilities that simultaneously gripped the mind and touched the heart. And Osborn also believed that Hopkins would support her ministry among Black persons, which some white Christians in Newport opposed.

Both Hopkins and First Congregational initially wavered when the church first extended an invitation to Hopkins to serve as its pastor. Hopkins had preached for five consecutive Sundays before receiving the offer, but he also knew that the congregation's voting members (they were all men, as women were not granted this authority) had doubts about him. Of the twelve voting members, only seven approved of him. Three voted against Hopkins and the other two abstained from voting. Hopkins declined the congregation's invitation and preached a farewell sermon there in 1770.

But Osborn and other women from the church lobbied furiously for Hopkins. Hopkins had visited Osborn's home on a Sunday evening for her Bible study and prayer meeting with enslaved persons, and she was further convinced that he was the right minister for her church. Eight days after Hopkins's farewell sermon, the congregation held a second vote on reissuing a call to Hopkins, and there were no votes in opposition. The historian Sheryl A. Kujawa-Holbrook wryly comments, "Members who had previously voted against Hopkins had now either changed their minds about him or else did not wish to interfere with the plans of Sarah Osborn and her female society."[46] Osborn's faith was rewarded. Her new pastor stayed at First Congregational until his death in 1803 and Hopkins emerged as one of the fiercest abolitionists, not only in Newport but also the United States.

Before ministering in Newport, Hopkins was a pastor in the Massachusetts town of Great Barrington for over twenty years and never expressed disapproval of slavery. Like other white pastors, he owned an enslaved person and accepted Black enslavement as a socially acceptable component of his society. He admired Jonathan Edwards and arrived at his doorstep in 1741. After graduating from Yale College, Hopkins desired to study under Edwards and did so in Northampton for several months before moving to Great Barrington in 1743. But Hopkins's awakening to the sinfulness of Black enslavement did not arise from deep biblical study with Edwards or an epiphany after reading tomes of theological scholarship. As Hopkins resided in Newport, he witnessed the horrors of the transatlantic slave trade and then decided that slavery must be abolished.

In Joseph Conforti's analysis of Hopkins's life, the historian maintains that Hopkins's evolution to abolitionism began in Newport: "For the first time in his life the backcountry minister confronted the slave trade's grim reality. Chained Africans were sometimes unloaded in Newport and sold before his eyes."[47] Hopkins began preaching against slavery in 1771 and five years later published a pamphlet entitled "A Dialogue Concerning the Slavery of the Africans." Hopkins dedicated the pamphlet to the Continental Congress and beseeched its delegates to consider the emancipation of more than 500,000 enslaved Black persons in the thirteen North American colonies as they pursued liberty from British rule. Hopkins affirmed the congressional resolution from 1774 denouncing the transatlantic slave trade and hoped it was not issued "merely from political reasons" but also "from a conviction of the unrighteousness and cruelty of that trade." He highlighted the moral inconsistency of "promoting the slavery of the Africans, at the same time we are asserting our own civil liberty at the risk of our fortunes and lives."[48]

In his criticism of Black enslavement as "a very great and public sin," Hopkins incorporated a metaphor that illustrates how his own experiences in Newport reshaped his Christian faith and theology. He refuted popular white notions that slavery was either a permissible institution that required minor reforms to curb abusive enslavers or an unjust system of lesser priority amid the colonists' many grievances against British tyranny. Hopkins compared the abolition of slavery to a dire situation on a ship: "If the slavery in which we hold the blacks is wrong . . . this is acting like the mariner, who when his ship is filling with water, neglects to stop the leak, or ply the pump, that he may mend his sails."[49] Hopkins saw ships and mariners all the time, and he had grown intimately familiar with the centrality of human trafficking within the business of slavery in Newport.

In his abolitionist tract Hopkins acknowledged that the transatlantic slave trade predated Rhode Island and the North American colonies. The English had long competed with Dutch, French, Portuguese, and Spanish slave traders, but Hopkins highlighted how the colonists in New England committed a distinctive plethora of evils in their participation in this unjust trade. The commodity they principally exchanged for African captives was rum. In addition to "the inhuman practice" of human trafficking, the colonists compounded this sin with their bartering of alcohol. Hopkins referenced a scriptural verse, Habakkuk 2:15, that condemns the ancient Babylonians for exporting alcohol to other nations.[50] The production of cane spirits in the Americas began in the seventeenth century, and colonial New England became the center of rum distilling.

In Christy Clark-Pujara's treatment of slavery in Rhode Island, the historian explains how merchants in the colony's two biggest cities, Newport and Providence, transported local agricultural products, such as cheese and livestock, to sugar plantations in the Caribbean in exchange for molasses. The same merchants then sold the molasses to local distillers to make rum that was sent to the West African coast to exchange for African captives. In 1740, one report stated that over 120 vessels dispatched from Rhode Island, and all but ten of them carried enslaved persons. In 1773, the *Adventure* ship dispatched from Newport with 24,380 gallons of rum, which enabled the ship's traders to obtain sixty-two African captives. The average cost for enslaved men and women was 220 and 190 gallons, respectively.[51] Hopkins interpreted the divine condemnation on profiting from liquor vending as applicable to the slave merchants in Rhode Island. He did not believe any Christian could justify the exploitation of "incredible quantities of rum, and molasses which has been distilled into rum among ourselves" to acquire and transport enslaved Africans to the Americas.[52]

Abolitionists in England also identified how the consumption of coffee, rum, sugar, tobacco, and other imported products in their nation contributed to the transatlantic slave trade. In 1791 and 1792, there were several pamphlets published in London and Manchester calling for a boycott of rum and sugar specifically. One pamphlet, entitled "An Address to the People of Great Britain, Proving the Necessity of Refraining from Sugar and Rum, in order to Abolish the African Slave Trade," provided an outline of the boycott strategy. Abstaining from a product such as rum or sugar would "have a powerful effect by sinking the price of the commodity; and thereby take away the temptation to import additional slaves."[53]

Another pamphlet addressed to Christians "of every denomination" emphasized the "impropriety of consuming" rum and sugar because it was "produced by the oppressive labour of slaves." It appealed to James 1:27, a verse in the New Testament revealing that pure religion entailed care for afflicted orphans and widows, and explained how a boycott of rum and sugar fulfilled this Christian duty. The cost of these imported products was more than English money because the transatlantic economy necessitated African captivity, family separation, corporal punishment, and other exploitative labor injustices.[54]

A third pamphlet encouraged Londoners to drink brandy, wine, or a "good strong beer" instead of rum and to drink their tea without sugar as was customary in China.[55] In Rhode Island, consumption of the products in question was not a pressing issue, because rum was the central driver of its economy. By 1730, most professions in Rhode Island were connected to the slave trade. Clark-Pujara sketches a helpful delineation of everyday life in Rhode Island: "Slave traders employed shipbuilders, sailors, caulkers, sailmakers, carpenters, rope makers, painters, and stevedores (those who loaded and unloaded ships). Coopers made the barrels that stored the rum. . . . [C]lerks, scribes, and warehouse overseers conducted the business of the trade."[56] In cities such as Newport, all the persons in these occupations paid taxes, which along with the duties collected on transactions in the slave markets provided the funds for public works and utilities. And the salaries of local pastors also came from the tithes and offerings of church members who were employed in professions tied to the business of slavery.

"Lord God Almighty, I Pray Thee, Teach Me Duty": Sarah Osborn, Samuel Hopkins, and a Constantly Moving Circular Faith

Hopkins, like other clergy in his context, was certainly cognizant of the intersection between the business of slavery and church financial budgets that included pastoral compensation. He once frankly observed, "The inhabitants of Rhode Island, especially those of Newport, have had by far the greater share in this traffic of all these United States. This trade in the human species has been the first wheel of commerce in Newport, on which every other movement in business has chiefly depended."[57] Yet Hopkins also understood that the wickedness of slavery demanded that Christians act to abolish it. And God provided pastors with pulpits to speak out against injustice and educate parishioners. He therefore surmised, "And why should the ministers of the gospel hold their peace and not testify against this great and public iniquity, which we have reason to think is one great cause of the public calamities we are now under?" He dared his ministerial colleagues to examine their souls and pray on whether it was right for them to "refuse to plead the cause of these oppressed poor against the cruel oppressor." Hopkins admitted that some pastors feared the consequences of disrupting the economic foundations of their society. He also conceded that other pastors were enslavers who did not want to lose their human property.[58]

In 1751, James MacSparran, the Episcopal rector of St. Paul's Church in the Rhode Island town of Narragansett, wrote in his diary of how both he and his wife, Hannah Gardiner MacSparran, physically punished one of their enslaved persons, a man named Hannibal, for leaving their residence after nightfall without permission. He wrote, "I got up this morning early, and finding Hannibal had been out. . . . I stript and gave him a few lashes till he begged. As Harry [another enslaved man] was untying him, my poor passionate dear, saying I had not given him enough, gave him a lash or two, upon which he ran." Upon Hannibal's recapture, James MacSparran marked Hannibal with "pothooks put about his neck" and complained that "it has been a very uneasy day with us."[59] Hannibal was further whipped several days later, and he again fled MacSparran's residence. A member of MacSparran's church, Christopher Phillips, found and returned Hannibal to MacSparran with a note asking the pastor to exhibit more compassion toward Hannibal. Phillips was also an enslaver, but he gently admonished his pastor for what he considered as abusive mistreatment of enslaved persons. MacSparran agreed to "spare" Hannibal "upon his promise of better behaviour."[60]

MacSparran's diary also reveals that St. Paul's Church was a multiracial congregation in which he baptized persons of African descent. In 1899, Daniel Goodwin, the rector of the same church, published MacSparran's diary with additional commentary integrating other congregational records. Goodwin found in the parish register this sentence on April 26, 1748: "Phillis, daughter of Negro Moll, was baptized by ye Doctor, *before he sold her* to Daniel Dennison."[61] In Goodwin's explanation of the fact that MacSparran baptized and sold an enslaved child, the editor of MacSparran's diary asks the reader to remember that slavery was "a marked institution of Narragansett and no doubt contributed largely to the wealth of the planters as well as to the aristocratic atmosphere of the region."[62] In 1998, when the Rhode Island Heritage Hall of Fame inducted MacSparran, it acknowledged his slave ownership as a "major blemish on MacSparran's record," but noted that he was not the only slaveholding inductee and cited one historian's favorable assessment of MacSparran's ministry among enslaved persons.[63]

The evidence for this positive rendering of MacSparran's ministry is a simplistic nod to the presence of enslaved persons among the membership of St. Paul's Church. But the justification to excuse MacSparran's enslaving sins and honor his legacy quickly unravels with even just a little bit of deeper inquiry. In addition to the account in MacSparran's diary of his cruelty as an enslaver, other Christian leaders in the eighteenth century refuted the argument that the ministry of Black evangelization lessened the evils of slavery.

In 1769, Osborn first introduced Hopkins to enslaved and free persons of African descent in Newport. In one of her first letters to Hopkins, Osborn noted the pastor's passion for Bible study and invited him to her home to witness something he had never encountered: "God has also providentially gathered a number of black people, servants and free, that have usually attended on reading, catechizing, &c., on Sabbath evenings at our house who will also be glad of your instructions."[64] In short time, Hopkins shared Osborn's conviction that slavery was a "horrid sin."[65] And Hopkins soon despised the intractably ubiquitous argument among English Christians in North America that defended slavery by counting Black converts. He summarized the false justification with precision, probably because he heard it so often: "Sir, there is one important circumstance in favor of the slave trade, or which will at least serve to counterbalance many of the evils you mention, and that is, we bring these slaves from a heathen land to places of gospel light, and so put them under special advantages to be saved."[66]

Hopkins dismantled this fallacy with two counterarguments in 1776. Hopkins first asserted that enslaved and free persons of African descent had more reason to denounce English Christianity than to convert to a gospel that slavery corrupted. Hopkins averred that enslaved Black persons beheld a nominal Christianity that betrayed Christ's teachings and "only serves to prejudice them in the highest degree against the Christian religion": "For they not only see the abominably wicked lives of most of those who are called Christians, but are constantly oppressed by them, and receive as cruel treatment from them as they could from the worst of beings."[67] He then imagined a hypothetical scenario in which "all the slaves brought from Africa" converted to Christianity and reasoned that even this occurrence would not justify Black enslavement, because the transatlantic slave trade, as "a direct and gross violation of the laws of Christ," was not an ethical method to fulfill the Great Commission.[68]

In 1793, Hopkins published a speech he had delivered to an abolitionist society in Providence that revealed an evolution in his thinking on Black Christianity in North America. He continued to rail against the fallacy of Black evangelization as a defense of slavery, but Hopkins grappled more directly with the reality of an emerging Black Christian presence than he had in his previous writings. In a reflection that likely revealed the white pastor's increasing contact with Black Christians, Hopkins wrote that their genuine faith, "in circumstances tending so strongly to prejudice against it," was an indication of "the extraordinary, wonderful, and no less than miraculous interposition of divine power and grace."[69] Hopkins recognized that the gospel of Black Christianity had overcome the moral contradictions and theological perversions of white Christian America, but he continued to worry that white Christians would interpret the increasing number of Black believers as a means to one of two ends: either to fortify their proslavery convictions, or to soothe their consciences about the injustices of slavery.

Osborn and Hopkins developed a strong working relationship and friendship in Newport. The two met for tea every Saturday after spending their mornings in private devotionals of prayer and Bible reading. In the later years of Osborn's life, when she could not attend worship at First Congregational Church due to her declining health, Hopkins led services at her home. Both were serious about personal piety and social reform. Their worship of God inspired their civic engagement. They were agitators who were willing to disrupt the social order of their world because of the revelations and stirrings they experienced in private meditation, public worship, interaction with persons of African descent, and conversation with one another. Theirs was a constantly moving circular faith as their unfolding experiences informed how they read the Bible and their scriptural interpretations in turn influenced their daily decision-making.

In 1767, Osborn wrote in her diary, "Lord God Almighty, I pray thee, teach me duty. . . . O, thou guide of my youth, thou staff of my age, thou determiner of my doubtful ways, thou that hast upheld me upon a precipice all my days—keep me from falling on the right hand or left."[70] Hopkins relied upon Osborn for support and edification, which encompassed seeking her guidance on ministerial matters such as sermon preparation and church leadership. In 1784, First Congregational publicly denounced slavery, including the transatlantic slave trade that Hopkins identified as the first wheel of commerce in Newport, as "a gross violation of the righteousness and benevolence which are so much inculcated in the gospel" and resolved: "Therefore we will not tolerate it [slavery] in this church."[71] Several Quaker meetings made similar antislavery resolutions, some preceding First Congregational, but few mainstream Protestant churches did so.

One historian surmises that Hopkins's abolitionism was encouraged, or at least permitted, at First Congregational because the church comprised more members of lower income in comparison to the larger and wealthier Second Congregational Church and several other Protestant churches in Newport.[72]

The women's society that Osborn led raised funds to help cover Hopkins's annual income in some years when the church's budget fell short, but Hopkins also relied on donations from supporters outside of Newport.[73]

Osborn and Hopkins are certainly worthy of the praise they receive today as exceptional Americans and Christians. But there are at least two problematic interpretations of their abolitionist legacies. One misapplication is to draw inaccurate or overstated conclusions about the past. Neither Osborn nor Hopkins represents the prevailing currents of white American Christianity in the late eighteenth century. Few white Christians, and fewer churches, exhibited abolitionist convictions as they did. A church history lesson on slavery and Christianity in Rhode Island that featured Osborn and Hopkins at the center would be inspiring, but it would also be misleading.

To return to an earlier observation about one historian utilizing Osborn and Hopkins to burnish the legacy of Jonathan Edwards, it is simply not the case that Edwards's theological insights propelled the racial justice endeavors of Osborn and Hopkins. Another historian raises the possibility that Edwards was a "proto-abolitionist" even though "he owned slaves and explicitly defended slaveholding," because of the work of Hopkins and other Calvinist abolitionists who labored long after Edwards's life.[74] Rather than admit the truth about Edwards and reckon with the implications of his enslaving legacy, these historians obfuscate and misdirect with their provocative theories.

The second error concerns asking the wrong questions. We focus our attention on abolitionists such as Osborn and Hopkins and ponder their motivations and life circumstances as if their religious journeys are shrouded in mystery. Yet the answer is plainly evident. Osborn and Hopkins were faithful Christians who worked to abolish slavery because they believed it was wrong to kidnap, transport, sell, oppress, and enslave Africans. The more obvious query is also more challenging. What does it mean that so many white Christians either defended or remained complicit in maintaining something so cruel and immoral as Black enslavement? The answers force us to confront the vulnerabilities of Christianity when it is practiced by people inhabiting and benefiting from unjust economic, racial, social, and national contexts.

One other interpretive deflection when studying the history of slavery in the United States is an insistence on blaming the biblical literalism of past Christian expositors. Because there is discomfort in addressing the immorality of white Christian America in upholding Black enslavement, it is easier for some to attribute the sins of slavery to deficient theological education and insinuate that these white Christian ancestors would have read the Bible differently if they had access to the growing corpus of hermeneutical methodologies, such as historical criticism, that emerged beginning in the late nineteenth century. Ignorance, rather than immorality, becomes the primary cause of white Christian participation in slavery.

Yet Hopkins, in 1776, dismissed the regnant biblical justifications for slavery as both ethically and intellectually faulty. He sharply criticized the appeals to isolated scriptural verses containing regulations for Hebrew servitude and Greco-Roman slavery as well as the deployment of the Noahic curse against Ham as self-interested interpretations that were "glaringly contrary to the whole tenor of divine revelation."[75] Hopkins countered that any Christian who studied the Bible, with a full view of the entirety of the Scriptures, would arrive at the conclusion that Black enslavement was sinful. He charged, "I hope you will not appeal to the Holy Scripture in support of a practice which you and everyone else must allow to be so inexpressibly unjust, inhuman, and cruel, as is the slave trade."[76]

Hopkins then analyzed several common scriptural passages that proslavery Christians deployed, such as Colossians 4:1, which gave the following instruction in the English translation of the Bible that Hopkins cited: "Masters, give unto your servants that which is just and equal."[77] He applied the verse to the system of indenture, which was one of two primary forms of compensated labor in the late eighteenth century. In addition to wage labor, in which employers provided employees with financial pay for specific tasks or hours of work, indentured servitude was a contractual system in which a person agreed to labor for another person for a mutually agreed upon amount of time to repay a loan. In the North American colonies, some migrants from Europe worked for several years in exchange for the provisions of their transatlantic voyage, lodging, and food.[78] Hopkins found that Colossians 4:1 offered mandates to regulate indentured servitude but not Black enslavement. Hopkins surmised, "The master who conformed to this rule must not only treat his servants with equity in all instances, but must set at liberty all who were evidently unjustly enslaved, and therefore had a right to their freedom."[79] Enslavers could not give their enslaved persons what was just and equal because the latter party comprised African captives and their descendants who did not consent to a labor contract.

"Was Not Our Blessed Lord a Political Preacher?": Lemuel Haynes and White Christian Resistance to a More Perfect Union

Another Congregational pastor in New England arrived at the same interpretive conclusions as Hopkins. In 1776, Lemuel Haynes, born to a white mother and Black father, wrote an essay entitled "Liberty Further Extended: Or Free

Thoughts on the Illegality of Slave-keeping." Haynes was the pastor of small and predominantly white congregations in Connecticut, Vermont, and New York for more than forty years from roughly 1785 to 1833. Haynes was born in Hartford, Connecticut, in 1753, but little is known of his parents. The historian Helen MacLam observes that "the identity of Haynes's parents remains a matter of conjecture."[80] Historians believe his father was either enslaved or a free Black man working as a waiter in a hotel. One possibility for Haynes's mother is Alice Fitch, an indentured servant of Scottish descent who worked for a man named John Haynes. Another early biographer of Haynes, Timothy Mather Cooley, identifies Haynes's mother as an unnamed "white woman of respectable ancestry in New England."[81]

Haynes was given over as a ward of the state of Connecticut as an infant and lived under the indenture system within a white family. The patriarch of this family, David Rose, was a farmer from the Connecticut town of Durham, who relocated with his wife, Eliazbeth Fowler Rose, their children, and Haynes to Granville, Massachusetts. Formal schooling opportunities in the rural milieu of Granville were scarce, but Haynes expressed deep appreciation to the Rose family for teaching him "the principles of religion" at their home and credited Fowler Rose for caring for him "as though I was her own child."[82] Haynes assiduously studied the Bible and could recite from memory a good number of the scriptural texts explaining the doctrine of grace. He also memorized the hymns of Isaac Watts and pored over published sermons from popular preachers such as Philip Doddridge and George Whitefield. Haynes completed his indenture at the age of twenty-one in 1774 and enlisted in the military to fight for the continental army in the American Revolutionary War.[83]

In "Liberty Further Extended" Haynes referenced both the Declaration of Independence and several scriptural passages. Haynes vigorously supported the patriot cause, but he also desired a morally consistent revolution that simultaneously sought American independence from England and Black emancipation. Haynes argued that it was important for the patriots to work toward abolishing slavery as they protested and battled against British and loyalist forces for the unalienable rights of life, liberty, and the pursuit of happiness. Haynes concurred that liberty was a right "granted to us by the Divine Being" and "a jewel which was handed down to man from the cabinet of heaven." He cited Acts 17:26 and wrote, "It hath pleased God to make of one blood all nations of men . . . to dwell upon the face of the Earth."

Haynes therefore maintained that persons of African descent had no less a right to liberty than the white colonists. He acknowledged the prevalence of Christian justifications of slavery, but Haynes dismissed "even those of the most cogent kind" as "essentially deficient" and a "lamentable consequence" of the imputation of sin after the fall of humankind, a Calvinist doctrine tracing human depravity to the trespasses of Adam and Eve in the book of Genesis. English Christians deceived themselves and betrayed the gospel in using the glorious truths of the Bible to defend the "vile and atrocious" injustices of the transatlantic slave trade and "slave-keeping" in the North American colonies. Haynes excoriated the harsh realities of family separation in Black enslavement, in which spouses were separated from one another as well as parents from children. He charged that enslaved parents were unable to love their children according to scriptural instruction, and enslaved spouses could not fulfill the duties that were assigned to couples "whom God hath joined together."

Slavery was a monstrous sin that not only destroyed Black lives and families, but also stained Christian witness: "And thus it [slavery] brings ignominy upon our holy religion, and makes the name of Christians sound odious in the ears of the heathen. O Christianity, how art thou disgraced, how art thou reproached, by the vicious practices of those upon whom thou dost smile!"[84] Haynes worshiped a merciful God, but he also believed this same God judged individuals and nations with divine blessing and retribution according to their actions. The historians James P. Byrd and James Hudnut-Beumler observe that Haynes urged the patriots "to oppose both the British tyranny and also tyrannical slavery," as he saw both causes as worthy of even a violent rebellion.[85]

Haynes and Hopkins shared the conviction that pastors had the responsibility to preach about social justice. The doctrine of divine sovereignty informed how both men understood pulpit ministry. Because God ruled over all things, the preacher sought to illumine how current events revealed both the wondrous love and holy rebuke of Jesus Christ. In an ordination sermon in 1791 for Reuben Parmelee, the new minister of First Congregational Church in Hinesburg, Vermont, Haynes described the pastorate as a watchtower. Every minister was a "spiritual watchman" who declared the whole counsel of God.[86] Haynes ardently believed that pastors could not fulfill their duty on the watchtower without engaging politics from the pulpit. In 1813 Haynes preached that it was inappropriate for "ministers of the gospel" to be "noisy and clamorous" in "party disputes." But Haynes found it was also impossible for clergy to educate congregations on the civic responsibilities of Christians without directly addressing political matters. Haynes cited Christ's warnings against the oppressive actions of governing rulers in Matthew 23 and exhorted, "Was not our blessed Lord a political preacher, when he reproved those in authority?"[87]

Hopkins attributed the victory of American independence from England to divine favor and greatly admired the US Constitution in its proclamation of striving "to form a more perfect Union." At the same time, Hopkins also criticized the Constitutional Convention for its decision to postpone for twenty years a ban on the transatlantic slave trade. In 1787, he wrote to Moses Brown, a former slave merchant turned abolitionist, whose family helped to found Brown University, to complain about the convention's acquiescence to the demands of "some of the southern delegates." Hopkins compared the delay in ending the slave trade to the biblical figure Achan, an ancient Israelite solider who disobeyed Joshua's command and plundered gold and silver from a fallen Jericho: "I fear this is an Achan, which will bring a curse, so that we cannot prosper." Yet Hopkins also understood the realpolitik of forming a new nation and prayed that God would move the United States toward Black emancipation and "vindicate the oppressed, and break the arm of the oppressor, in his own way and time."[88]

Hopkins also publicly taught about the integration of Christian discipleship with American patriotism. He endeavored to instruct others about the necessity of holding fidelity to God and nation in productive tension. Hopkins interpreted the "whole contest" of the American Revolution as vindication of the patriots' "deep and lasting sense of the worth of liberty," but he also did not hesitate to condemn "our unrighteousness and cruelty towards the Africans."[89] White American Christians did not reject the whole tenor of Hopkins's preaching. Many accepted the assurance of divine favor and rejected the admonition about slavery.

Haynes and Hopkins did not minister in large and affluent Protestant churches. Neither pastor had the reach or renown of prominent clergy in their day, such as Ezra Stiles, the minister of Second Congregational Church in Newport from 1755 until he departed to assume the presidency of Yale College in 1778, or Henry Ward Beecher a generation later. Beecher regularly preached in majestic sanctuaries overflowing with scores of white worshipers, whereas Haynes and Hopkins delivered sermons before smaller groups of people in modest churches that sometimes struggled to collect sufficient tithes and offerings to pay their salaries. Perhaps Beecher's greater ministerial success can be attributed to his rhetorical gifts and interpersonal capacities in understanding people, but Haynes and Hopkins were also powerful speakers who displayed interpretive brilliance in reading the Scriptures and assessing their contexts. Haynes and Hopkins comprehended Beecher's insight that white churches dreaded abolitionism, but they pushed the limits of the pastoral vocation in white Christian America and never gave up in their efforts to mobilize churches for racial justice.

Haynes and Hopkins continually encountered fierce resistance. Hopkins lamented that white racism against Black people was one of the most pernicious and potentially enduring consequences of slavery. Many white American

Christians did not want to end slavery, because the enslaved were Black, not white. The reason for white Christian apathy and antipathy to abolitionism was "obvious" to him: "It is because they are negroes, and fit for nothing but slaves, and we have been used to look on them in a mean, contemptible light, and our education has filled us with strong prejudices against them." He added that too many white Americans regarded persons of African descent as subhuman and "another species of animals, made only to serve us and our children, and as happy in bondage as in any other state."[90]

Haynes experienced firsthand the tenacity and ferocity of anti-Black racism. The words, "African," "black," "mulatto," and "nigger" were wielded and slung at him as racial epithets. One church in Connecticut was impressed with Haynes's preaching but did not select him to be its pastor, because it feared inflaming racial tensions in the town. A church in Vermont removed Haynes after roughly thirty years of service, and at least one of Haynes's contemporaries believed the reason was because influential church members felt that a white pastor would attract more worshipers amid the increasing white migration into the town.[91] Haynes referred to himself in the third person and remarked with biting sarcasm that the church dismissed him after thirty years because "they found out he was *a nigger*, and so turned him away."[92] One lasting mark of American slavery, even in the states that had either abolished it or never permitted it, was the unrelenting racial oppression of Black people.

Chapter Six

"These Things Have Fired My Soul
with a Holy Indignation"

Black Christianity Confronts American Racism
and the Long Shadow of Slavery

In the fall of 1831, a free Black woman entered the office of *The Liberator* newspaper in Boston. Maria W. Stewart did not have an appointment, and the newspaper's two white editors, William Lloyd Garrison and Isaac Knapp, were surprised to see her. But the editors welcomed Stewart into their modest headquarters befitting a start-up that launched its first issue on January 1, 1831. One colleague remembered the office where Garrison and Knapp began their abolitionist newspaper: "The dingy walls; the small windows, bespattered with printer's ink; the press standing in one corner; the composing stands opposite; the long editorial and mailing table, covered with newspapers; the bed of the editor and publisher on the floor."[1]

Garrison introduced *The Liberator* in the first issue as a periodical devoted to the cause of Black liberation and the immediate abolition of slavery. He described the resistance that he encountered from white Americans in the Northern states during a recent lecture tour as "contempt more bitter, opposition more active, detraction more relentless, prejudice more stubborn, and apathy more frozen, than among slave owners themselves." But Garrison informed readers of *The Liberator* that its pages would report the whole truth about the oppression of slavery and how these injustices betrayed American democracy and Christianity. As its editor, Garrison promised to be "as harsh as truth, and as uncompromising as justice," and he warned, "Let southern oppressors tremble—let their secret abettors tremble—let their northern apologists tremble—let all the enemies of the persecuted blacks tremble."[2]

Stewart was one of the fledgling newspaper's readers, but she was also a writer and held in her hands a manuscript to submit to Garrison and Knapp. The three individuals shared the same convictions and were close in age, as each was in their mid-twenties—Stewart was born in 1803, Knapp in 1804, and Garrison in 1805—but Stewart stood apart because of her race and gender. Black women like Stewart had important and powerful messages to convey, but they inhabited a world dominated by white men. Many people did not believe that either Black men or white women belonged in the domains of public speaking and writing. The notion of publishing an essay from a Black woman therefore probably seemed outrageous. But as Garrison and Knapp read Stewart's work, they determined it was worthy of a wider audience. Stewart's writings were first included in issues of *The Liberator* and then published as separate pamphlets.[3]

The two years preceding Stewart's visit to Garrison and Knapp were difficult and traumatic for her. Stewart was born in Greenwich, Connecticut, to Black parents named Caesar and Lib on September 4, 1803. Nothing more is known of her parents than their names and race, "Caesar & Lib (negro)," as indicated from birth records that the scholar Kristin Waters recently unearthed.[4] An orphan at five years of age, Stewart was indentured to a white pastor in Hartford from roughly 1808 to 1818. Stewart did not disclose more about the pastor's identity beyond writing that she "was bound out in a clergyman's family."[5]

Due to Waters's painstaking research, we now know more about the possibilities of Stewart's childhood years as an indentured servant. Waters convincingly suggests that Stewart lived with the white Congregational minister Abel Flint and his wife, Amelia Bissell Flint. Flint, a graduate of Yale College, was the pastor of Second (South) Congregational Church in Hartford from 1791 to 1824. He was widely admired in Hartford and remembered as "every inch a gentleman" and a formidable preacher. Waters surmises that while Stewart likely received "some familial love and care" from the family holding her indenture, her domestic labor was "severe and demanding."[6] The little that Stewart herself wrote about her childhood indicates how much she despised her indentured conditions. She found it awful that people were forced to "spend their lives and bury their talents in performing mean, servile labor" with "no possibility" of "rising above the condition of servant."[7]

After her indenture, Stewart labored in domestic work for several more years in Connecticut until she had saved enough money to relocate to Boston. In 1826, she married James W. Stewart, a Black naval veteran who performed military service in the War of 1812 and then worked as a shipping agent at the port of Boston. James died suddenly of heart failure in 1829, and several of his white business associates exploited his unexpected death to subsequently cheat Maria from receiving her rightful claim to his estate.

As Maria W. Stewart grieved the loss of her husband, she began to write. She also practiced a vigorous devotional life, with many hours spent in prayer and Bible reading. Among Stewart's first writings is a series of fourteen spiritual meditations grappling with the wonders and mysteries of divinity, humanity, grace, sin, redemption, and providence. In a brief introduction to the published pamphlet, Stewart explained in 1832 that the meditations were the result of a recommitment to Christianity after her husband's death, as she felt Jesus speaking "peace to my troubled soul": "Soon after I presented myself before the Lord in the holy ordinance of baptism, my soul became filled with holy meditations and sublime ideas; and my ardent wish and desire have ever been, that I might become a humble instrument in the hands of God."[8]

In one of her meditations, Stewart denounced the presence of many Christians "who profess the name of Jesus" but did not exhibit the evidences of goodness and righteousness in their conduct. She alluded to Matthew 23:27 and compared these false Christians to "whited sepulchers" with beautiful external appearances but filth, decay, and "all manner of uncleanliness" internally.[9] Stewart was convinced that "the chains of slavery and ignorance" would not be broken until both Black and white American Christians truly repented of their sins and practiced pure and holy lives that demonstrated the moral virtues of the gospel.[10] Stewart was also convinced that she was divinely called to be a herald of this prophetic message. Was it possible for a recently widowed Black woman with the bare credentials of indentured servitude and domestic labor on her resume to become a published author, public speaker, and civil rights leader? Stewart dared to believe that all things were possible for one who had faith.

Shortly after Stewart approached Garrison and Knapp, the editors published her essay entitled "Religion and the Pure Principles of Morality, the Sure Foundation on Which We Must Build." On October 8, 1831, Garrison and Knapp included a notice in *The Liberator* indicating that Stewart's tract was on sale at the newspaper's office for six cents.[11] In the essay Stewart advanced a multifaceted argument that addressed racism, nationalism, Christianity, individual responsibility, and communal possibility. Stewart expressed complex but discernable convictions that defy easy categorization. She celebrated the principles of American democracy and admired the United States as a nation that provided economic opportunities for people from the lower classes of society to improve their stations in life and attain higher levels of flourishing.

But she also criticized white Americans for their woeful neglect of their Black neighbors. She noted, "But how very few are there among them that bestow one thought upon the benighted sons and daughters of Africa, who have enriched the soils of America with their tears and blood: few to promote their cause, none to encourage their talents."[12] Enslaved Africans were unjustly transported to North America, and they and their descendants had certainly contributed to the making of the United States. Some fought for the patriots in the American Revolutionary War, and others to protect the new republic in the War of 1812. Yet white Americans continued to enslave Black persons in the Southern states. And free Black Americans everywhere were denied the same rights and opportunities as the white population. There were few jobs for Black Americans. The historians Stephen Kendrick and Paul Kendrick maintain that Black Bostonians in the 1830s were "almost completely blocked from professional roles in law and medicine" and also faced structural obstacles to vocations as cabinetmakers, carvers, caulkers, chandlers, mechanics, plumbers, polishers, roofers, upholsterers, and in other industrial labor. Black persons in Boston therefore worked as barbers, hairdressers, clothing retailers, tailors, sailors, shipping agents, and in domestic labor.[13]

Stewart surveyed the failures of Black emancipation in the Northern states, including the racial oppressions she encountered throughout her life, and charged, "Oh, America, America, foul and indelible is thy stain! Dark and dismal is the cloud that hangs over thee, for thy cruel wrongs and injuries to the fallen sons of Africa."[14] One year later, Stewart wrote an article for *The Liberator* demonstrating her affection for the United States, because it was founded on the "pure principles" of justice and liberty for all: "O, America, America! Thou land of my birth! I love and admire thy virtues as much as I abhor and detest thy vices; and I am in hopes that thy stains will soon be wiped away, and thy cruelties forgotten."[15] Stewart weighed her abiding patriotism alongside her resolute Christian faith. In doing so, she identified the racial sins of her nation and demanded that its white citizenry actively work to remove the many stains of slavery.

Stewart also challenged her fellow Black Americans with nuanced counsel that simultaneously assailed profligate vices and encouraged racial solidarity. She confronted how centuries of racial oppression had resulted in a milieu in which most white persons and even some Black persons believed in the spurious notion of an innate Black racial inferiority. Stewart observed, "Many think, because your skins are tinged with a sable hue, that you are an inferior race of beings; but God does not consider you as such."[16]

In 1832, Stewart delivered a lecture in Boston's Franklin Hall before a racially diverse audience of Black and white persons. Biographers of Stewart highlight this lecture as one of the earliest political addresses in US history from a woman before an inclusive public gathering across race and gender. Stewart spoke on the topics of abolition, the colonization movement to send free Black

Americans to Liberia, and Black civil rights.[17] She refuted racist ideologies that demeaned persons of African descent as inherently less capable than white people. Slavery and ongoing racial oppression were the causes of poverty and despair within the Black community in cities such as Boston. Stewart asserted, "I have learnt, by bitter experience, that continual hard labor deadens the energies of the soul, and benumbs the faculties of the mind; the ideas become confined, the mind barren, and, like the scorching sands of Arabia, produces nothing." She assessed her own racial community as "neither lazy nor idle" and found that the economic and intellectual achievements of some Black persons were in fact remarkable when considering the innumerable barriers to success they overcame and "how little we have to excite or stimulate us." Stewart also acknowledged that some free Black persons were engaged in what she regarded as shameful habits, such as drinking and gambling, and "never were and never will be serviceable to society." Yet in the very next breath, Stewart asked the white listeners in the public hall, "And have you not a similar class among yourselves?"[18]

The prevailing message from Stewart was a resilient hope fueled by a righteous anger. In 1833, she stated that the fullness of the abolitionist movement—the pursuit not only to end slavery in the Southern states but also to enact racial equality throughout the nation—was pulsating in the hearts of every Black American. Stewart declared, "These things have fired my soul with a holy indignation, and compelled me thus to come forward, and endeavor to turn their attention to knowledge and improvement; for knowledge is power."[19]

This chapter surveys how Black Christianity confronted American racism and the long shadow of slavery in the Northern states. There were Black, Indigenous, and white Christians in the United States who shared Maria W. Stewart's holy indignation, but they comprised a small minority within American Christianity, and they encountered hostility from other white Christians as they sought racial justice in the states that had abolished slavery. The free Black population in the United States rose from roughly 60,000 persons in 1790 to 488,000 in 1860, but even this larger number of free Black Americans in 1860 comprised less than 2 percent of the overall US population. Black Christians appealed to the Bible in their pursuit of dignity, equality, and flourishing. A few white Christians actively supported these Black Christians, and one shining example of multiracial mutuality is evident in the building of the first Black church in Philadelphia. But the rarity of such partnerships also illustrates the tenacity and ferocity of racial discrimination across towns, cities, neighborhoods, and churches within the antebellum United States.

"Tell Us No More of Southern Slavery": Racial Prejudice and the Long Shadow of Slavery in the Northern United States

The center of Black abolitionism was in the Northern states and comprised a diversity of individuals. Some were born into slavery and either escaped their enslavers or purchased their freedom in agreements with their enslavers. Frederick Douglass was one of many "fugitive slaves." He fled from enslavement in 1838 and traveled northward to pursue a life of freedom and dignity. A fugitive slave had committed an illegal act, according to the US legal system, because the enslaved person was human property that belonged to an enslaver. Enslavers had documentation to prove that a fugitive slave was rightfully theirs via purchase, inheritance, or other legal means. In 1845, Douglass went to Europe after the publication of his autobiography. He had become one of the most powerful speakers and popular writers in the United States (he sold 5,000 copies of his autobiography within the first four months of its publication and roughly 30,000 copies in five years) and therefore sought to expand his lecture circuit abroad in a transnational strategy to mobilize further support for American abolitionism in England, Ireland, and Scotland.

But Douglass was also concerned about his own illegal status as a fugitive slave. In 1846, he explained to an audience in London what American slavery entailed: "Slavery in the United States is the granting of that power by which one man exercises and enforces a right of property in the body and soul of another. The condition of a slave is simply that of the brute beast. He is a piece of property—a marketable commodity in the language of the law." Douglass also emphasized how the US Constitution "makes it the duty of the northern states to return the slave if he attempts to escape," which meant that he remained in danger of recapture and return to his enslaver, Hugh Auld. Friends of Douglass in England collected money to purchase his freedom. In the United States, Auld agreed to emancipate Douglass after receiving 150 British pounds in payment.[20]

Other Black abolitionists were born as free persons in a Northern state. Lemuel Haynes and Maria W. Stewart were orphans who grew up as indentured servants in white families. Others, such as James Forten in Philadelphia and Theodore S. Wright in New York City, were nurtured and raised by Black parents. Black abolitionism was not a monolith, as different individuals pursued various strategies for emancipation. Some worked more closely with white allies than others. After the Compromise of 1850 and the passage of the Fugitive Slave Act, a few Black leaders, such as Mary Ann Shadd Cary and Samuel Ringgold Ward, advocated for emigration to Canada and Jamaica, because they felt the rising scourge of racial discrimination thwarted opportunities for Black flourishing in the United States.

One common thread within the variegated tapestry of Black abolitionism was the recognition that it was a nationwide struggle that encompassed both ending slavery in the Southern states and enacting racial justice to fulfill the promises of abolition in the Northern states. Stewart captured both the agonies and aspirations of the free Black population in 1832, when she proclaimed, "Tell us no more of southern slavery; for with few exceptions . . . I consider our condition but little better than that." She derided her own limited access to education and employment during her hard years in domestic labor as one example of the plight of so many Black women who were restricted to "lives of continual drudgery and toil." She and other Black women like her possessed "noble souls" with dreams to exert their creativity and genius, but "the powerful force of prejudice" crushed their spirits as they spent their days "as house-domestics, washing windows, shaking carpets, brushing boots, or tending upon gentlemen's tables." Stewart was careful to note that she did not wish to demean domestic work per se, because it required the acquisition of sundry skills and provided "an honest livelihood" for some persons.[21] The problem lay not in the occupation of domestic labor but rather in the absence of other vocational opportunities for Black women.

Stewart and Douglass also identified white Christianity as a source of Black oppression after emancipation in the Northern states. Stewart's call to hear less from white abolitionists about "southern slavery" was not because she felt that they overstated its cruelties and immoralities. Instead, Stewart grew weary of the insufficient attention that white abolitionists devoted to reforming their own Northern racist society. Stewart observed the same weakness in white abolitionism that the Pequot pastor William Apess found in white reform movements toward Indigenous rights.

White reformers in New England railed against the sins that white Georgians had perpetrated in the forced deportation of the Cherokee Nation and brutal enslavement of Black persons, but they inconsistently elided their own histories of settler colonialism and slavery. What was worse was their hypocrisy in failing to address the ongoing discrimination against Indigenous and Black persons in their own communities. In 1833, Stewart compared the United States with scriptural depictions of ancient Babylon. So many white American Christians, including abolitionists, drew inspiration from connecting their new nation with ancient Israel. Yet Stewart countered, "It appears to me that America has become like the great city of Babylon. . . . She is, indeed, a seller of slaves and the souls of men." Stewart recounted a national history that ran contrary to the principles of justice and humanity: "The unfriendly whites first drove the native American from his much loved home. Then they stole our fathers from their peaceful and quiet dwellings, and brought them hither, and made bond-men and bond-women of them and their little ones."[22] She now desired for white Christians to continue the work of constructing a more racially just society in states such as Connecticut and Massachusetts.

Stewart was frustrated that white women storeowners in Boston generally did not employ Black women. Some of these white women attended abolitionist meetings, raised funds for abolitionist causes, and declared that they would do whatever they could to help the poor and oppressed slave. But when Stewart asked them to hire Black women, they politely refused her request. Stewart summarized their responses: "Their reply has been—for their own part, they had no objection; but as it was not the custom, were they to take them into their employ, they would be in danger of losing the public patronage."[23] The white women insisted that they were not racist and pleaded for Stewart to understand their quandary. They worshiped a God who was no respecter of persons and believed that both slavery and racial prejudice were wrong, but they also felt that their personal reputations and professional businesses would sink if they hired a Black employee.

Douglass explained how the dehumanizing conditions of slavery continued to traumatize even the formerly enslaved now residing as free persons in the Northern states. He wrote in his autobiography of the starvation that he experienced in his childhood, the corporal punishment that he endured as a young man, and the mentally deadening effects of slavery on the human mind. He recalled an occasion in Maryland when he and other enslaved persons suffered the humiliations of a valuation after their enslaver's death: "Men and women, old and young, married and single, were ranked with horses, sheep, and swine. There were horses and men, cattle and women, pigs and children, all holding the same rank in the scale of being, and were all subjected to the same narrow examination." Douglass emphasized how every enslaved woman was subject to "the same indelicate inspection," an invasive process in which enslavers, slave traders, and prospective buyers assessed the sometimes fully nude bodies of women.[24] Like Stewart, he also recounted how the drudgery and hopelessness of hard labor with no prospect of advancement obliterated the Black mind, body, and soul: "My natural elasticity was crushed, my intellect languished, the disposition to read departed, the cheerful spark that lingered about my eye died; the dark night of slavery closed in upon me; and behold a man transformed into a brute!"[25]

Even after Douglass escaped the dark night of slavery, he encountered its long shadow in the Northern states. He was denied access to public transportation or forced to sit in the "Jim Crow" car on trains, which was also referred to as "the dirt car." He worshiped in churches that designated a section in their sanctuaries for Black persons, known as "the negro pew," and was invited to the communion table only after all the white worshipers had partaken of the elements. He witnessed in Boston how Black persons were blocked from professions in caulking, a skill that he cultivated as an enslaved man in Baltimore. In 1841, Douglass protested racial segregation on the New England railways and refused to leave his seat beside a white colleague, John A. Collins, when the conductor ordered him to the Jim Crow car.[26]

Twelve years later Douglass delivered a speech before an abolitionist society in New York City in which he surmised that the aims of Black liberation would not be met until white reformers devoted further attention to racial justice throughout the Northern states. He noted that Black Americans were "becoming a nation, in the midst of a nation which disowns them," and believed that the abolitionist movement had the duty and capacity to pursue a multiplicity of injustices all at once. Douglass's own life journey was an embodiment of Black America "both slave and free." He pointed to Luke 4:18 and invoked Jesus Christ, "who came to preach deliverance to the captives, and to set at liberty them who are bound," as a wellspring of hope and strength in a "corrupt and selfish world." Yet Douglass also differentiated between the liberating Jesus and the "hollow and hypocritical church" of white American Christianity.[27]

In 1813, James Forten was prompted to publish a pamphlet in response to deliberations on a bill in the state legislature of his native Pennsylvania. Forten was not a writer, but he was a respected leader in the Black community of Philadelphia. Born in a free Black family in 1766, Forten learned how to make sails from his father and enlisted in the naval forces for the patriots during the American Revolutionary War. British naval officers tried in vain to recruit Forten; he declined their offer of a scholarship to study in England. Forten was resolute in his devotion to the revolutionary cause and the nation that was forged in resistance to achieve democratic liberty. He was known for saying, "America, with thy faults, I love thee still."[28]

Forten later owned a lucrative sail-making business and became one of the wealthiest people in Philadelphia. He nonetheless encountered racism at every turn and witnessed how discriminatory forces and policies restricted Black access to education and employment. Forten's own children received private education from tutors because there was no adequate school for Black pupils. Pennsylvania passed a gradual abolition law in 1780 that guaranteed emancipation to enslaved persons born after the act's passing when they turned twenty-eight years of age. But emancipatory laws in the Northern states did not produce racial equality. The results in cities such as Philadelphia was heightened animosity against Black Americans from the broader white population.

The proposed bill in the Pennsylvania legislature that drew Forten's ire sought to severely restrict Black movement within the state. The historian Julie Winch contends that the measure threatened to "reduce free black citizens to little more than slaves."[29] An enraged Forten sharply criticized the bill and highlighted the inhumanity of granting police officers the authority "to apprehend any black, whether a vagrant or a man of reputable character" and demand to see a certificate confirming their legal status. Forten protested two aspects of this predatory and prejudiced measure. On a legal basis he questioned the fairness of imprisoning a free Black resident sans certificate for terms ranging from six months to seven years and even potentially for sale to an enslaver. Moreover, Forten also challenged the bill on moral grounds, because it illustrated a deep resentment of the Black race and would inflame further racial insult as he envisioned white police officers, and even white bystanders, taunting Black people in public with shouts of "Halloa! Stop the Negro?" and "Hoa, Negro, where is your Certificate!"[30] He lamented that legislators were debating a law that stood in such clear contradistinction to the principles of civil liberty and simple human decency.

Forten appealed to sacred documents to undergird his protest. He connected the Declaration of Independence, Pennsylvania's state constitution, and the Bible in his penetrating call for racial equality. All persons—"the Indian and the European" as well as "the white man and the African"—were divinely created by the Christian God and equally endowed with the same capacities. Forten and all other Black residents had "certain inherent and indefeasible rights," which included unconstrained access to travel throughout the state. Forten asked, "Has the God who made the white man and the black, left any record declaring us a different species? Are we not sustained by the same power, supported by the same food, hurt by the same wounds, pleased with the same delights, and propagated by the same means?"[31] He also offered an expansive interpretation of the founders and averred that their compromises on slavery at the Constitutional Convention presented Black and white Pennsylvanians with an opportunity to demonstrate how a nation enacting Christian virtues and democratic principles could construct a racially just society after abolition.

Forten argued that the founders did not abolish slavery and establish racial equality in the United States, but they knowingly set a pathway for Black liberation in their deflections and omissions. The delegates at the Constitutional Convention agreed that "all men" were created equal but "did not particularize white and black." Whereas many Americans interpreted the Declaration of Independence as confined to white citizens, Forten maintained the absence of explicit classification was an indication of a just future for Black

Americans after slavery. He surmised, "They [the founders] knew we [Black Americans] were deeper skinned than they were, but they acknowledged us as men, and found that many an honest heart beat beneath a dusky bosom. They felt that they had no more authority to enslave us, than England had to tyrannize over them."[32]

Forten was a fiercely patriotic military veteran and ardent Christian believer. He understood the difficulties of Black flourishing after generations of enslavement and conceded that some free Black persons had failed to rise above the arduous conditions. He, like other Black abolitionists, did not stipulate that the Black race was inherently exceptional, or that every Black person would thrive if given the opportunity. The Black race was equal to the white race and other races. Forten did not suggest that the outcome of racial equality in the United States would be Black perfection, but rather he anticipated that many Black persons would become "useful members of society" and there would be "a number of worthless men belonging to our colour," as there were in white communities.[33] Forten held together in his heart and mind a confluence of despair and optimism, with the hopeful conviction that his city, his state, and ultimately his nation would embody the promises that he had fought for as a young man and continued to believe in with abiding faith.

Forten's dream was radical and conservative all at once. His call for racial justice was countercultural in his immediate context of Philadelphia at the turn of the nineteenth century. When the state legislature of Pennsylvania passed its gradual abolition act, the final bill was the product of compromise, and a good number of white Christian representatives nevertheless voted against it. George Bryan, a Scots-Irish Presbyterian merchant in Philadelphia, emerged to political prominence in 1778 and drafted the initial abolition bill. Bryan proposed that all enslaved persons born after the passage of the act receive emancipation at the ages of eighteen (for women) and twenty-one (for men). But Bryan ran into significant resistance from enslavers who wanted a longer duration before liberation, to ensure they received what they felt was adequate labor for their acquisitions of human property. The state legislature passed the bill two years later, after the emancipation age for both enslaved women and men was raised to twenty-eight.

One commentator derided the age increase as mean and unjust because it deprived enslaved persons of the opportunity to earn incomes and establish livelihoods for themselves in what were crucial years of young adulthood between eighteen to twenty-eight. Perhaps Bryan agreed, but he conceded that this revision was made to meet the demands of enslavers. The historians Gary B. Nash and Jean R. Soderlund find that twenty of the forty-four Episcopalian, Lutheran, Presbyterian, and Reformed representatives opposed the bill in 1780. The bill was voted on three times before its passage by a final count of thirty-four to twenty-one.[34] Black and white abolitionists such as Forten and the white Quaker tailor Isaac T. Hopper continued to advocate for the lower ages of eighteen and twenty-one for Black emancipation. They stated how they were simply asking for the same age restrictions that were placed on indentures for white children in Pennsylvania.

A draft of a bill proposing these lower ages with financial reparations to enslavers (taken from local county treasuries) appeared in the state legislature in 1797 but did not gain momentum. Nash and Soderlund maintain that "this was the first time that compensated emancipation was mentioned in the mid-Atlantic states."[35] But the two historians add that the greater failing of the state legislature was in its woefully inadequate governance toward racial equality after abolition. They assert that many white abolitionists were also "more interested in purging the evil of slavery from their midst than in relieving the oppression of black Pennsylvanians."[36] These reformers devoted little attention to the rise of anti-Black racism. They did not feel the fury and vitriol of this escalating prejudice in the ways that Forten and other free Black persons did, but they also could not claim ignorance, because their lives were also marked by the ubiquitous patterns and rhythms of racial discrimination.

As much as Forten and other Black abolitionists challenged the conventions of a white-dominant society in the Northern states, their scriptural appeals evinced plain and traditional interpretations of Christian teachings on justice, love, and goodness. Forten's exposition of the Constitutional Convention as preparing the way for Black emancipation was disputable and likely an idealistic and romanticized revisionist history of the founders' deliberations. But his arguments that God created all races of humankind as equal in dignity and Jesus instructed his followers to treat one another with fairness and mercy did not comprise a brilliantly provocative new framework for Christian theology. Forten simply listed fundamental truths about Christianity. This insight is not meant to belittle Forten's genius. Instead, it illustrates how deeply Black enslavement corrupted white American Christianity.

Before gradual abolition in states such as Pennsylvania, some white Christians had criticized the transatlantic slave trade and slave ownership as racially unjust. In 1688, a small group of Dutch and German Quakers in Germantown, Pennsylvania, penned a letter protesting slavery to the Quaker meeting in Abington. The four men, Garret Hendericks, Derick op den Graeff, Francis Daniel Pastorius, and Abraham op den Graeff, were writing in a foreign language, English, and sometimes composed awkward phrases. But the message of their missive was clear: It was wrong to buy, sell, and own persons of African descent. They rejected the racially infused doctrine that permitted white enslavement of the Black race, writing, "There is a saying, that we shall do to all men like as we will be done ourselves; making no difference of what generation, descent or colour they are." They suggested that the Quaker meeting should institute a ban against slave ownership among its members and shuddered at the blasphemous testimony if it became known "that ye Quakers do here handle men as they handle there ye cattle."[37]

The historian Kathleen M. Brown points to this Quaker petition from Germantown as an early North American example of how "antislavery advocates took pains to depict the humanity of slaves in a variety of ways, broadcasting their bodily suffering and pain, their full emotional range, their innate 'natural law' morality, and their intellectual capabilities."[38] Christian justifications of slavery in turn rejected the full humanity of enslaved Black persons. Proslavery Christians twisted the Bible to do so, and the result was the warping of many white consciences. If God permitted the enslavement of people with darker skins, then it was also permissible to regard persons of African descent with apathy or even contempt. Forten poignantly captured how racial prejudice was the manifestation of proslavery Christianity: "O miserable [Black] race, born to the same hopes, created with the same feeling, and destined for the same goal, you are reduced by your fellow creatures below the brute. The dog is protected and pampered at the board of his master, while the poor African and his descendant, whether a saint or a felon, is branded with infamy."[39] Some white Christians publicly asserted that their religion had nothing to say about racial equality, and many more quietly assented to this doctrine in their everyday lives.

"And We All Went out of the Church": The Northern Origins of "Jim Crow" and the Emergence of an Independent Black Church in Philadelphia

In the contemporary United States the words "Jim Crow" are commonly affiliated with racial segregation in the Southern region of the country. The foremost images that arise in most minds are of separate water fountains for white and colored people (with the former being of superior quality to the latter) and angry white mobs shouting at young Black children trying to enter all-white Southern schools. We also remember the civil rights movement and think of moments from Alabama in the 1950s and 1960s, such as a forty-two-year-old Black woman named Rosa Parks refusing to give up her seat on a Montgomery city bus in 1955 and the thousands of nonviolent demonstrators marching across the Edmund Pettus Bridge in Selma ten years later. We are slower to recall that racial segregation and Jim Crow laws originated in the Northern states. The historian Steve Luxenberg observes how Jim Crow laws certainly "gained velocity in the South at the end of the nineteenth century" but began in "the free and conflicted North" shortly after the nation's founding.[40] Meticulous and thorough regulations to mark and separate Black people were unnecessary in the states that practiced slavery, as it was a coercive system with its own rules and restrictions. But white Americans in the Northern states instituted racial segregation in schools, restaurants, hotels, churches, neighborhoods, buses, and trains to control the presence of free Black persons.

The phrase "Jim Crow" also first gained currency in the Northern states. Thomas Dartmouth Rice, a playwright and actor born in New York City, emerged as a popular performer in the late 1820s due to his minstrel act in blackface. Rice was not the first white actor to perform in blackface, but he became the most famous one for his fictitious character "Jim Crow." White crowds packed storied venues in New York City, Philadelphia, and across the United States (as well as in Liverpool and London in England) to behold Rice singing, dancing, and talking as a Black man in an exaggerated and racist caricature. One example of Rice's success is found in the ticket sales from the Bowery Theatre in New York City. In addition to Rice's shows, the famous pantomime actor George L. Fox (his most acclaimed role was playing "Humpty Dumpty") and the renowned Shakespearean actor Edwin Forrest were also box-office draws. But Rice "brought more money into the Bowery treasury than any other American performer during the same period."[41] By the 1830s Rice's character also became synonymous with racial segregation. In 1841, Frederick Douglass refused to sit in the Jim Crow car on a train belonging to the Eastern Rail Road company in New England.

The city of Philadelphia was one of the most contested sites of racial segregation in the nation. The Black population in Pennsylvania grew more than in any other Northern state. In 1790, there were 10,274 Black persons in the state, which was the third most populous behind New York (25,978) and New Jersey (14,185). By 1820, Pennsylvania's Black population nearly tripled to 30,413, which trailed only New York (39,367) and surpassed New Jersey (20,017). In 1840, Pennsylvania's Black population of 47,918 was only slightly less than New York's (50,031) and more than double New Jersey's (21,718).[42] Because the center of Black life in the state was found in Philadelphia—the city's Black population rose from roughly 10,000 in 1810 to 15,000 in 1830—it was also where the specter of Jim Crow and racial prejudice loomed largest.

Racial tensions between Black and white Philadelphians began during the American Revolutionary War. Some white residents echoed Black abolitionist calls for a morally consistent movement that fought for both American freedom

Thomas D. Rice Wearing the Costume of His Character "Jim Crow"

from British rule and Black emancipation from slavery. In 1775, the philosopher Thomas Paine supported the revolutionary cause, but also implored his fellow patriots to confront their hypocrisy when "they complain so loudly of attempts to enslave them, while they hold so many hundred thousands in slavery."[43] But other white Philadelphians who favored England wielded this inconsistency to disparage the patriots. The merchant Richard Wells taunted white Philadelphians in 1774 and asked how they could "reconcile the exercise of slavery with our professions of freedom."[44]

When British military forces occupied the city in 1777, some enslaved persons fled their enslavers and joined the British for myriad reasons. Some learned of the proclamation of Virginia governor Lord Dunmore, promising freedom to enslaved men who enlisted in a British regiment. Others wished to exact revenge on their enslavers. One newspaper included a white woman's account of her verbal jostling with an enslaved man. In their exchange of harsh words, the man threatened her with a warning about what would happen if "Lord Dunmore and his black regiment" made it to Philadelphia.[45]

More than Dunmore's proclamation, Pennsylvania's gradual abolition act was the greater source of white animosity against the Black community in Philadelphia. White residents generally struggled to accept the cultural, economic, and social changes that accompanied emancipation. They bristled at and sometimes ridiculed how newly liberated Black persons decided on new names for themselves. The historian Ira Berlin explains that the process of renaming was an important part of how formerly enslaved people engaged a "reconstruction of black life" that entailed self-definition, liberative celebration, and political defiance.[46]

Prior to 1780, two common types of names for enslaved people were African and Greco-Roman. Many enslaved persons therefore had names such as Cuffee, Phibbi, and Quame or Caesar, Diana, and Venus. Upon their emancipation, newly liberated Black persons often gave themselves English names such as Benjamin, James, and Rebecca. In an assertion of their own dignity and respectability after enduring the degrading nicknames that their enslavers sometimes conferred upon them, they also resisted diminutive forms of these names. It was Benjamin, not Ben or Benny, and Rebecca, not Becca or Becky. Enslaved persons rarely had surnames, so a newly liberated Black person often selected one. The popularity of Freeman and Newman as surnames among free Black persons in Philadelphia and throughout the Northern states illustrates how some chose surnames to indicate their liberty and independence.[47] A few picked the same surnames as white enslavers in Philadelphia, but hardly any opted for the surnames of Cadwalader, Wharton, Wistar, and other prominent slave-owning families in the city.[48]

The Black population in Philadelphia, both those born free and those newly liberated, also resolved to achieve economic success and social recognition. These desires were not unusual in the antebellum Northern states. Black women and men simply had the same strivings as white people. They too chased after the American dream and wanted to become, in the words of one historian, respected citizens with "property and standing."[49] But their efforts to attain well-paying jobs and purchase real estate were met with white resistance. At a psychic level some white Philadelphians resented the changing attitudes and countenances of Black people in their city. White people had grown accustomed to enslaved persons who rarely looked them in the eye and were startled at the sight of newly liberated persons walking with more confidence in their steps and fortitude in their faces.

The element that caused more contention than any other was in employment. White migration to Philadelphia also surged in the first half of the nineteenth century as the city's overall population jumped from 100,000 in 1816 to 164,000 in 1830.[50] The growing number of English, German, Irish, and other European immigrants arriving to the city collided with the existing labor force of Black and white workers, to create a fragile and volatile economic context with increasing job competition and decreasing wages. As in Boston and other Northern cities, the burgeoning industrial businesses in Philadelphia, ranging from textile mills to shoe manufactories, restricted employment to white persons. In 1802, one abolitionist society seeking to address Black unemployment reported that it could find work for only 20 of the 102 persons who had turned to it for assistance.[51]

Black Christians in Philadelphia therefore persisted with a holy indignance. They pursued the fullness of life and liberty with gratitude to God, appreciation for white allies, resilient determination, and righteous anger. The church was also a contested site of racial discrimination. In roughly 1792, Richard Allen, Absalom Jones, and several other Black worshipers were accosted at St. George's Methodist Episcopal Church because they refused to sit in a segregated section of a newly built gallery. These Black worshipers had financially contributed during the church's stewardship campaign to renovate the sanctuary and were surprised to learn that one outcome of their giving was an architectural redesign that further separated them from white worshipers. Allen explained that the racist incident occurred on the first Sunday worship service after the renovation was complete. He remembered, "We expected to take the seats over the ones we formerly occupied below, not knowing any better. We took those seats. . . . We had not been long upon our knees before I heard considerable scuffling and low talking." While the Black worshipers were knelt in prayer, a white church member seized Jones and admonished him, "You must get up—you must not kneel here." Jones replied that he and the other Black worshipers would get up and move after the prayer, but another white church member came over to assist the first white man in attempting to physically relocate the Black worshipers to their designated pews in the gallery. Allen described the events that followed: "By this time prayer was over, and we all went out of the church as a body, and they were no more plagued with us in the church. This raised a great excitement and inquiry among the citizens, in so much that I believe they were ashamed of their conduct."[52]

Allen and Jones were two of the eight founding members of the Free African Society (FAS) in 1787, and it was one of the first Black-led organizations in the United States to provide social services, such as job training and medical care, to African Americans. The FAS also successfully advocated for a plot of land in the city's public cemetery, and ministers such as Allen and

Jones officiated at weddings for Black couples. Allen and Jones soon desired an autonomous Black church distinct from white churches in Philadelphia. The two disagreed on the church's denomination—Allen wanted it to be Methodist from the onset, whereas Jones preferred that the FAS remain ecumenical in the fundraising stage and decide on a denomination closer to the church's opening—but both men believed in the importance of an independent Black church in which Black pastors and laity discerned for themselves God's direction in congregational ministry.[53]

The racist confrontation at St. George's Church was therefore not the catalyst that inspired a new Black church in Philadelphia, but the unfortunate episode fortified the conviction that Black Christians would find genuine spiritual flourishing only in their own worship spaces. It is crucial to emphasize the differences between racial separation and racial segregation. This vision for an autonomous church illustrates a self-motivated desire for racial separation in one aspect of Black life. These Black worshipers detested the imposition of racial segregation in formal laws and informal practices that denied them access to equal opportunities in education, employment, and human flourishing. But they also yearned to form their own racially distinct religious community: a Black-led church that fostered authentic and creative expressions of African worship and spirituality in a refuge that stood apart from the pervasive and soul-crushing racial prejudice they encountered in their everyday lives. Allen and Jones relied on white allies for support, and Allen publicly thanked the physician Benjamin Rush and the merchant Robert Ralston for their partnership.[54]

But the FAS received scant support from white churches. Clergy and laity from these churches opposed the creation of a Black church. William White, rector of Christ Church in Philadelphia and bishop of the Protestant Episcopal Church of Pennsylvania, angrily told Rush that "the proposed African church" was ill-conceived because it was an exertion of Black racial "pride."[55] Prior to their departure from St. George's Church, Allen and Jones received harsh opprobrium from white church members upon sharing their desires for a separate Black church. Allen recalled how these white church members "used very degrading and insulting language to us."[56] Rush was dismayed at the apathy and hostility from white churches toward Black Christians. He attended two different Presbyterian churches in the city during the 1770s and 1780s and then worshiped at St. Peter's Episcopal Church, which was likely where he was a member when assisting the FAS. In 1792, he wrote to a friend in Boston, the white Congregational pastor Jeremy Belknap, and expressed his hopes and grievances in the efforts to plant a new Black church. Rush was encouraged that Allen, Jones, and other Black leaders had "adopted articles and a form of church government (purely republican) peculiar to themselves," but he complained that the white churches were not helping and surmised that one reason was because these congregations did not want to lose their Black worshipers.[57]

White Christians in the mainstream Protestant denominations sorely disappointed Rush. They did not help their fellow Black Christians, so Rush turned for financial aid to other white persons, such as John Nicholson, a brash business entrepreneur who did not rub shoulders among the city's coterie of elite white Christian patrons. One historian highlights how "Nicholson provided what none of the established Philadelphia elite would offer—a large loan to begin construction" of the church.[58] Rush shared with Belknap his growing suspicion that the only way to "exercise the true spirit of the gospel nowadays" was to flee from the mainstream Protestant denominations, because they seemed "more devoted to their forms or opinions than to the doctrines and precepts of Jesus Christ."[59]

In Newport, Samuel Hopkins wondered the same thing sixteen years before Rush. Hopkins questioned the hypocrisy of the mainstream denominations in contrast to the Quakers. He noted that mainstream Protestants looked down upon the Quakers because they did not practice communion and further condemned the Religious Society of Friends on several doctrinal matters. Hopkins felt that the omission of communion in Christian worship was wrong, but he nonetheless admired the Quakers for their antislavery strivings, which were far greater than any mainstream denomination, and judged Christian complicity and participation in slavery as "inexpressibly more dishonorable and offensive to Christ" than disputations on the Lord's Supper.[60]

But Hopkins, Rush, and other abolitionists continued to encounter this improper weighing of Christian standards within white churches. Too many white Protestants in the mainstream denominations considered their theological disagreements on issues such as the proper mode of baptism as more determinative of Christian faithfulness than combating the sins of slavery and racial oppression. They chose to contend against one another on infant baptism and debate what biblical evidence supported sprinkling or immersing an adult believer, rather than grappling with abolitionism. Hopkins and Rush knew that these white Protestants were betraying the true spirit of the gospel. Black and white abolitionists also understood that white Christians preferred discussing the intricacies of certain theological doctrines within the comfortable confines of ecclesial gatherings to reckoning with their most pressing societal injustices.

To "Greatly Promote the Cause of the Oppressed": Black Christian Piety and Protest in Productive Tension

Black and white clergy such as Allen, Jones, and Hopkins also took doctrinal matters seriously and exhibited no less a commitment than other pastors to the theological beliefs they held dear, but they did not ignore the demands of abolitionism. Unlike their white counterparts, Black ministers did not have a choice. Pastoral leadership among Black persons in the Northern states required direct engagement with slavery and racial discrimination. Raphael G. Warnock in his dissertation, published as an academic monograph in 2013, traces the history of Black Christianity in the United States and maintains that from its origins two streams of religious interpretation have flowed in its veins. Warnock writes, "The freedom for which the black church has fought has always been both internal and external, expressing itself politically and spiritually, embracing black bodies and souls. This is so because historically the faith of the black church has been shaped and characterized by two complementary yet competing sensibilities: revivalistic piety and radical protest."[61] Warnock delineates how Black churches, pastors, and theologians have variously enacted these two impulses in efforts to fulfill different and sometimes differing conceptions of Christianity. In some times and contexts, Black Christians emphasized one component over the other. At the turn of the nineteenth century in Philadelphia, the streams of individual piety and political advocacy ran together in productive tension within the churches that Allen and Jones pastored.

In 1793, Allen and Jones were both present on the inaugural day of construction for the first Black church in Philadelphia, on Fifth Street between Walnut and Locust Streets. Jones invited Allen to commence the project as a recognition of Allen's relentless work to mobilize people and raise funds. Allen accepted the honor and later reflected, "As I was the first proposer of the African church, I put the first spade in the ground to dig a cellar for the same. This was the first African church or meeting-house that was erected in the United States of America."[62]

But Allen soon left the church after the organizing group selected its denominational affiliation. Allen and Jones both voted for Methodism, but the majority opted for the Episcopal Church. Jones consented and in 1794 became the pastor of the church, named St. Thomas's African Episcopal Church (later named the African Episcopal Church of St. Thomas). Allen departed to form his own church, Bethel African Methodist Episcopal Church (later named Mother Bethel African Methodist Episcopal Church), in the same year. Allen acknowledged that several of his FAS colleagues despised the Methodists after the cruel racism they endured at St. George's Church,

but he resolutely believed that the "Methodist connection," with its rich combination of "plain doctrine" and "good discipline," was the most effective
and faithful pathway for Black Christian flourishing. Even the atrocious witness of some white Methodists did not shake Allen's unwavering commitment
to the Wesleyan tradition.

Allen also navigated the inherent tension between personal piety and political protest. He believed and taught that the ultimate destination of Christians was heaven. Black Christians could thus find hope and comfort in the
assurance that the pains of their earthly sufferings paled in comparison to the
ecstasies of eternity with the angels, saints, and the triune God. Allen wrote,
"What, though I mourn and am afflicted here, and sigh under the miseries of
this world for a time, I am sure that my tears shall one day be turned into joy,
and that joy none shall take from me."[63] But Allen was also convinced that
God empowered every Christian to participate in reforming the earthly societies that they inhabited. Thus, God held white Christians in the United States
accountable for the sins of slavery and racial prejudice. And God also called
Black Christians to work toward racial justice through righteous daily living,
practicing diligence and sobriety, and contributing their time, talent, and treasure to the FAS and other civic organizations.

In 1799, Allen delivered a eulogy for George Washington at his church and
interpreted the legacy of the nation's first president as a principled leader who
had ushered in the full promise of liberty through his life and death. Though
Washington was an enslaver, Allen pointed to Washington's determination in
his will to emancipate his enslaved persons upon the passing of his wife, Mar-
tha Washington, as an indication of the way forward for the nation. Black and
white Christians therefore fulfilled both their civic and religious duties when
they labored to "greatly promote the cause of the oppressed."[64] Allen's preaching knit together a Christian theology with both the sure promise of everlast-
ing life in heaven and the fierce urgency of social justice in his city and nation.

As St. Thomas's African Episcopal Church was being built, its Black and
white organizers decided to host a dinner to celebrate the raising of the
church's roof beams. Over one hundred people gathered under the shade of
large trees on the outskirts of the city. The group comprised bricklayers, carpenters, donors, and merchants. The white participants were served a bountiful meal by fifty or so future Black congregants. After Rush reluctantly agreed
to take his reserved seat at the head of the table, he offered two toasts to rous-
ing cheers, first saying, "Peace on earth and good will to men," and then,
"May African churches everywhere soon succeed to African bondage."[65]

When the white guests finished eating, they arose, and the Black hosts
took their seats. Six of the white persons then served dinner to the Black

Philadelphians. Rush desired to be among the servers, but the Black participants insisted that he and John Nicholson, the white financier whose loan permitted the church building project to move forward, remain in their seats. Rush was moved when William Gray, a prominent Black fruit vendor and FAS leader, "was checked by a flood of tears" as he attempted to deliver a toast. Several Black church members approached Nicholson at the end of the evening to express their heartfelt gratitude. Rush's wife, Julia Stockton Rush, was visiting her mother in New Jersey and not at the event. Rush therefore wrote about it to her from their Philadelphia home: "Never did I witness such a scene of innocent—nay more—such virtuous and philanthropic joy. . . . To me it will be a day to be remembered with pleasure as long as I live." In the letter's postscript, Rush added, "Love as usual. Read this letter to your Mama. She belongs to our African Church."[66]

The dinner was indeed a rare occasion as Black and white Philadelphians celebrated together with attentive kindness and mutual respect. But it was not an event in which racial realities were ignored or forgotten. The purpose of the multiracial gathering was to praise the progress in building the city's first Black church. The white guests who served their Black hosts directly addressed the racial prejudice that marked all their lives and determined to act according to Christian principles. Rush's memory of the event is bittersweet. At one level it is a powerful testimony of what is possible when American Christians across different races resolve to work together and fellowship at the same table. At another level it is a sad indictment of how seldom this happened in Philadelphia and other antebellum Northern cities. Racial animosity, rather than racial reciprocity, was the overwhelming current that charged the early American republic in the states that had gradually abolished slavery.

Philadelphia is the cradle of several Black churches and denominations. In addition to St. Thomas's African Episcopal Church and Bethel African Methodist Episcopal Church, the nation's first Black Presbyterian church and the first Black Baptist church in the Northern states were founded in the city. In 1830, one year before his death, Richard Allen attended the first national Black convention, as approximately forty delegates from nine states assembled at his church.

But the emergence of Black vibrancy in the city was met with ferocious opposition from the broader white population. White mob violence erupted against Black residents on several occasions, especially at public festivals and Black celebrations. In 1805, a violent group of white people attacked the many Black persons who were also present to celebrate the Fourth of July in city streets adjacent to Independence Hall. The white assailants resented how the growing free Black population had (in their racist minds) the audacity to partake in civic festivities. The Fourth of July celebration in the shadow of Independence Hall became an exclusively white gathering over subsequent years.[67]

Some white residents even railed against Black Philadelphians when they created their own galas. In 1828, a band of white hecklers taunted and assaulted Black persons in front of an assembly hall where a Black subscription ball was being held. They tore the gowns of some Black women and struck other guests immediately after they arrived in their coaches. These white persons belonged to the working class and resented the display of Black wealth in the forms of Black couples publicly appearing in elegant dress and elaborate hairstyles with white coach drivers and attendants assisting them.

Middle- and upper-class white Philadelphians also mocked their Black counterparts. Some interpreted the economic struggles of the Black persons in the working class as evidence of Black racial inferiority, but they also assessed Black expressions of rising social stature as garish and unseemly. Just as Thomas Dartmouth Rice enthralled white audiences with his caricature of Jim Crow, several white artists in Philadelphia created satirical cartoons to poke fun at Black residents. Edward Williams Clay published a series of fourteen colored prints in the late 1820s entitled "Life in Philadelphia" that depicted dark-skinned Black Philadelphians in ostentatious, fancy garb trying to mimic white gentility.

Life in Philadelphia, Plate 13, by Edward Williams Clay

The Results of
Abolitionism!

In 1835, a political cartoon entitled "The Results of Abolitionism!" portrayed Black persons commanding white construction workers with phrases such as "Bring up the mortar you white rascals." These responses altogether illustrate the rage and range of white resistance to Black flourishing.

Gary B. Nash rightly identifies the history of Philadelphia in the decades after the gradual abolition act as a "tragedy and triumph." The development of Black churches such as Bethel, which grew from a little over 200 members in 1799 to nearly 1,300 in 1813, is an example of the triumph. But Nash also finds: "The tragedy lay in the unfulfilled promise of a racially equal and harmonious society. . . . As devoted as some white Philadelphians were to the cause of antislavery and racial justice, they proved impotent to control their society at large."[68] White Christians such as Benjamin Rush worked alongside Black religious leaders to reform their city, but this multiracial coalition was outnumbered. And one of their problems was not due to the quantity of white mainstream Protestant churches. There were probably enough white churches to at least make some tangible changes. Rather, the dilemma rested in the poor moral quality of these apathetic congregations.

"That Is the Test": Different Christian Responses to the Challenge of American Racism

Black clergy across the Northern cities encountered racial discrimination from white Christians. After graduating from Princeton Theological Seminary in 1828, Theodore S. Wright pastored First Colored Presbyterian Church (later named Shiloh Presbyterian Church) in New York City. Wright, with his degree from Princeton, likely possessed the most formal theological training of any African American person in his day. He was born in 1797 to free Black parents in New Jersey and lived in Providence (Rhode Island), Schenectady (New York), and New York City as a youth and young adult before enrolling at Princeton Seminary. His years of study there coincided with the rise of the American Colonization Society (ACS), and the seminary's faculty ardently supported this movement to send free Black Americans to Liberia. Several leaders within the ACS were graduates of Princeton University (known as the College of New Jersey until 1896), and the seminary was also a stronghold of the colonization movement. From New York City, the nation's first Black newspaper editors Samuel Eli Cornish and John Brown Russwurm castigated the ACS in *Freedom's Journal.* In 1827, Cornish and Russwurm derided white Christian involvement in African colonization as immoral and antithetical to the gospel.

ACS advocates openly admitted that white prejudice against the Black race was prevalent throughout the Northern states. Princeton Seminary professor Archibald Alexander defended the colonization movement on the grounds that "prejudice of colour" in the United States was unreasonable but also unvanquishable. He therefore encouraged free Black Americans to emigrate to Liberia for opportunities there to pursue the blessings of freedom and dignity. "If I were a coloured man," Alexander surmised, "I would not hesitate a moment to relinquish a country where a black skin and the lowest degree of degradation are so identified, that scarcely any manifestation of talent, or course of good conduct, can entirely overcome the prejudice which exists." Alexander further noted that anti-Black racism was "as strong, if not stronger, in the free, than in the slaveholding states."[69]

Cornish and Russwurm furiously responded to this justification for African colonization as insulting to both Black people and the Christian God. They countered that "to concede so much to prejudice is to deify it" and diminish the omnipotence of the God who reigns over the earth with justice and goodness. The Black editors of the *Freedom's Journal* asserted, "However inveterate prejudice may be, it is still an evil, and we should be as justifiable in saying that drunkenness, Sabbath-breaking and profane swearing exist, and we will compromise with them in our religious efforts, as to say it in the case of prejudice."[70] Cornish and Russwurm questioned why white Christian clergy invested so much of their energy to preach against sins such as cursing and skipping worship on Sundays and so little on racial injustice. Wright worked as an agent for *Freedom's Journal* when he was at Princeton. Another of its professors, Samuel Miller, had warned Cornish and Russwurm to moderate their criticism of the ACS or else they would lose many white subscribers. The Black editors refused Miller's counsel and publicly rebuked him. Miller, in turn, wrote to another New York City newspaper to announce that he was canceling his *Freedom's Journal* subscription because he was "entirely dissatisfied with the spirit and apparent tendency of that paper."[71] Wright was the one who received the notifications from the seminary's students and faculty when they followed Miller's lead and ended their subscriptions.

Wright emerged as a formidable civil rights leader during his years as a pastor in New York City. He was active in several abolitionist societies and was one of the twelve members of the American Anti-Slavery Society's executive committee in its founding year from 1833 to 1834. Wright was instrumental in pushing the abolitionist movement to focus more deeply on racial justice in the Northern states. Like Maria W. Stewart, Wright did not deny the horrors of slavery in the Southern states, but he also recognized that Black liberation required acute and sustained attention to the menace of racial discrimination. In 1836, he expressed his bitter opposition to a white approach to abolitionism that stated, "We must first kill slavery, and leave prejudice to take care of itself."

He argued that no Black person could be truly free until American racism, in addition to American slavery, was eradicated: "No man can really understand this prejudice, unless he feels it crushing him to the dust. . . . [I]t has bolts, scourges, and bars, wherever the colored man goes. It has bolts in all the schools and colleges."[72] Wright lambasted white Americans for the educational and employment barriers they had erected against free Black people. He was careful to point out that his request was not for charity, but rather opportunity. Wright explained, "We do not ask you to break down any of the rules of society. . . . We want you to treat us as honest people. Give us a motive for emulation, industry, and improvement. Leave us the same chance to find our level in society that other men have."[73]

Antebellum Black abolitionists criticized slavery and racial oppression, but they did not seek to dismantle the structures of American capitalism and democracy. Patrick Rael, in his history of Black abolitionism, astutely observes that Black reformers in the antebellum Northern states championed the prevailing middle-class values of "uplift, respectability, civilization, natural rights philosophy, republicanism, [and] liberalism" as their own political convictions, religious prescriptions, and social aspirations.[74] Wright, Stewart, Forten, and other Black abolitionists decried how systemic racism prevented Black people from achieving the American dream, but they believed in this dream as much as, if not more than, white reformers. Wright, like Stewart and Forten, did not promise that every Black American would rise from poverty with racial equality. If treated fairly, the "bright children" among them would "improve and elevate themselves," and others would fail, no different than any other race of people.[75]

Rael accentuates that these Black leaders "did no violence to their own cultural heritage" in their yearnings for inclusion in the American middle class, because they had "helped build those values, just as their labor had helped to build the North's cities."[76] Later generations of Black and Indigenous activists—as well as white, Asian American, and Hispanic American persons and individuals from other racial and ethnic communities—would challenge the capitalist structure undergirding the United States and call for large-scale government action and intervention in addressing inequities of race and class, but it is imprecise to count antebellum Black Christian reformers as among the ranks of this progressive undertaking. Perhaps some of their incisive observations and principled arguments about racism and racial equality lay the groundwork for future progressive movements, but these Black abolitionists endorsed existing American structures and mainly wanted access to them.

Another shared sentiment among these Black Christians was holy indignation. They loved God and felt loved by God. They received spiritual comfort when worshiping in churches alongside fellow believers and when praying in quiet solitude. Yet they were also angry all the time. Stewart was cheated out of her late husband's estate and frustrated that Black women had few labor opportunities beyond domestic work. She despised both the racism she endured from white people and the sexism she encountered from Christian men and women of all races when she endeavored to fulfill a divine call to be a public speaker. Her career as a social reformer in Boston was cut short after only two years because of opposition to her efforts to break gender barriers both in the church and wider society.[77]

Wright's unyielding insistence that white Christians reckon with racism in the Northern states made him unpopular in mainstream Protestant circles. Wright cast vituperative judgments upon even the abolition movement. He charged, "It is an easy thing to task about the vileness of the slavery at the South, but to . . . treat the man of color in all circumstances as a man and a brother—that is the test." He further elaborated with "something for abolitionists to do": "Let every man take his stand, burn out this prejudice, live it down, talk it down, everywhere consider the colored man as a man, in the church, the stage, the steamboat, the public house, in all places, and the death blow to slavery will be struck."[78] Wright's test for his fellow abolitionists and white Christian America illumines a paradox. The answer to the test was simultaneously easy and hard. To treat people of different races as equal was an obvious and indisputably Christian thing to do. Yet the sin of slavery made so many white Christians respond with an unholy indignation.

"It Is a Gospel Paradox"

The Contest between Abolitionism
and Proslavery Christianity

William Lloyd Garrison was a seasoned activist when he published his
tract on the "infidelity" of abolitionism in 1860. He was approaching his
fourth decade of work as a professional abolitionist. His vocation was unusual.
Other abolitionists were lawyers, merchants, pastors, or politicians. Garrison,
however, had no other occupation but, in his words, "to plead the cause of my
colored countrymen" and free them from slavery.[1] In 1831 he launched from
Boston his newspaper, *The Liberator*, and two years later helped to establish the
American Anti-Slavery Society, the most significant abolitionist organization
in the United States. He amassed a modest income from these various endeavors—as an editor, publisher, lecturer, and organizer—to support his family. He
and his wife, Helen Eliza Benson Garrison, had seven children together. Their
daughter, Fanny Garrison Villard, recalled that her father even delivered abolitionist speeches to her and her siblings at home: "I was hardly more than an
infant when my father came to my crib to give me a good-night kiss. He said:
'What a nice warm bed my darling has! The poor little slave child is not so
fortunate and is torn from its mother's arms.'"[2]

Garrison's relentless drive for Black liberation was met by an equally fierce
opposition. Hence, in 1860 Garrison responded to the longstanding accu-
sation that abolitionism was atheistic and anti-Christian. White Christians
branded Garrison as a dangerous heretic who misused the Bible in appeal-
ing for abolition. Garrison explained that he was not surprised that his most
ardent detractors were white Christians. Every nation had distinct societal
injustices that were difficult to reform, precisely because they had grown so
large as to become engrafted to its foundations. Garrison then observed of his
nation: "The one great, distinctive, all-conquering sin in America is its system
of chattel slavery." One demonstration of slavery's force was its reach in white

Christian America, in which "the spirit of slavery was omnipresent, invading every sanctuary, infecting every pulpit, controlling every press, corrupting every household, and blinding every vision." Garrison also noted that proslavery Christianity spawned an ecumenical movement that brought together people of faith from a wide array of denominations and traditions like no other issue.[3] These Christians argued over innumerable doctrines and scriptural interpretations, such as predestination and free will, but they all agreed that American slavery was divinely ordained with undisputable biblical evidence on their side. They rallied against abolitionism as a grave threat to their Christian faith, their American nation, and their white race.

Garrison understood that his task was so difficult to accomplish because abolitionism called upon white American Christians to reckon with three interlocking strands that shaped their lives: religion, patriotism, and racism. Each of the three components separately made for a formidable opponent, but Garrison and other abolitionists were in a struggle against the combination of the three together. Chattel slavery in the United States had grown from approximately 700,000 enslaved persons in 1790 to 4,000,000 in 1860. The overall US population had also increased from roughly 4,000,000 to 31,000,000 in the same time span. There were about 394,000 enslavers in 1860, which amounted to less than 1.5 percent of the total population. Yet American slavery proved to be an intractable enemy that was overcome only by violence, not by persuasion. The number of US military fatalities in the American Civil War—620,000 across Union and Confederate forces—surpassed both the number of enslavers and the combined number of casualties in the First and Second World Wars, Korean War, and Vietnam War. One distinction between the Civil War and the latter military engagements was that in the Civil War every fatality was an American one.

Garrison was an avowed pacifist who promoted nonviolent resistance, but he also recognized that his righteous cause was at odds with powerful forces. He did not hesitate to declare that he and his abolitionist colleagues were engaged in a moral and religious battle. Throughout his life, Garrison answered his many Christian critics by pointing them to the confrontational ministry of Jesus. In 1838, he wrote, "If you would make progress, you must create opposition; if you promote peace on earth, array the father against the son, and the mother against the daughter; if you would save your reputation, lose it. It is a gospel paradox, but nevertheless true—the more peaceable a man becomes, after the pattern of Christ, the more he is inclined to make a disturbance, to be aggressive, to 'turn the world upside down.'"[4]

Garrison reinforced his position in 1860 with the argument that his tactics were the same as the early modern Protestant Reformers, such as Martin

Luther and John Calvin, and that every great reform movement must display "antagonism to public quietude and good order, and make the whole social, political, and religious structure tremble to its foundations."[5] He found inspiration from Isaiah 58:6–12 and desired to be a "repairer of the breach" and "restorer of paths to dwell in," which was not possible unless he also dared to tear down the pillars of proslavery Christianity, provincial patriotism, and anti-Black racism.[6]

In the same year that Garrison published his tract debunking the "infidelity" of abolitionism, Abraham Lincoln was traveling across the country in his presidential campaign as the candidate of the recently formed Republican Party. In speeches throughout New England, Lincoln told a story to illustrate how the love of money corrupted moral sensibilities. Lincoln presented an American parable of two pastors. One pastor pointed to a word in the Bible and asked the other pastor: "Do you see that word?" The other pastor indignantly replied, "Yes, of course." Then the first pastor placed a gold coin over the word and asked, "Do you see it now?" As his audience laughed, Lincoln moved quickly to his antislavery position and explained how enslavers considered the contentious debate over the westward extension of slavery through a financial lens: "Whether the owners of this species of property [enslaved persons] do really see it as it is, it is not for me to say, but if they do, they see it as it is through 2,000,000,000 of dollars, and that is a pretty thick coating."[7]

One of the thorniest obstacles to abolition was the matter of reparations for enslavers. Proponents of slavery argued that Black liberation was impossible, because the federal government did not have sufficient funds to remunerate enslavers for relinquishing their human property. In 1836, South Carolinian politician James Henry Hammond stated in a speech before the US House of Representatives that a plan for Black emancipation comparable to England's reparations to enslavers when they abolished slavery across their Caribbean colonies in 1833 would bankrupt the federal government many times over. The annual budget of the federal government in 1830 was roughly $25,000,000, which equaled the value of only 60,000 enslaved persons.[8]

Abolitionists such as Garrison countered that reparation to enslavers was unnecessary and immoral, because enslavers had already extracted ample profits from slave ownership through the exploitation of enslaved persons as uncompensated laborers. But they were realistic about other accompanying challenges to emancipation. Black abolitionists did not deny that some free persons of African descent were struggling to pursue honest livelihoods and languishing due to their own unproductive habits. But they also insisted that the primary reason for the stumbles within the free Black population was the hard transition from generations of enslavement to liberty amid rampant racial discrimination.

Garrison supported this position and amplified it in his own writing and speaking. He admired Black Americans for their resilience and courage, and he befriended and supported many Black abolitionists, such as William Wells Brown, Frederick Douglass, and Maria W. Stewart, by publishing their work and connecting them to larger transatlantic networks. But Garrison did not idealize the Black race and guarantee that every Black person with the same educational and employment opportunities as white people would flourish. In 1832, Garrison wrote of Black Americans, "It would be absurd to pretend, that, as a class, they maintain a high character: it would be equally foolish to deny, that intemperance, indolence and crime prevail among them to a mournful extent."[9] Black Americans were like any other race of people and would have similar outcomes of success and failure. What enraged Garrison was that slavery and racial prejudice denied Black Americans access to the founding principle of the United States, the democratic promise of life, liberty, and the pursuit of happiness. The ferocity of white racism toward the free Black population in Northern states was further demonstration of slavery's pernicious effects.

Garrison surmised, "As a nation sows, so shall it also reap. The retributive justice of God was never more strikingly manifested than in this all-pervading negrophobia, the dreadful consequence of chattel slavery."[10] He, like other Black and white abolitionists, integrated his Christian faith and his patriotism in productive tension. Garrison loved his country no less than his proslavery Christian opponents, but he refused to compromise his morality to excuse the sins of his nation. In 1854, Garrison protested the recent passage of the Kansas-Nebraska Act in a public Fourth of July celebration by burning a copy of the US Constitution, declaring that it was not a sacred compact that preserved the American union but rather "a covenant with death" and "an agreement with hell" for permitting the expansion of slavery.[11]

In seeking to turn the world upside down, American abolitionists were trying to restore their corrupted churches and sinful society with the principles of goodness and reasonableness. In 1792, the white Presbyterian pastor David Rice delivered a speech before the Kentucky state legislature denouncing slavery on the grounds that it was "inconsistent with justice and good policy."[12] Rice laid out the simple argument that his state should abolish slavery because it was morally wrong. Yet in the following years and decades it became harder, not easier, for many white American Christians to profess this fundamental truth. The white Presbyterian pastor Frederick A. Ross accused the abolitionists in 1857 of what he regarded as a severe crime: They were "torturing the

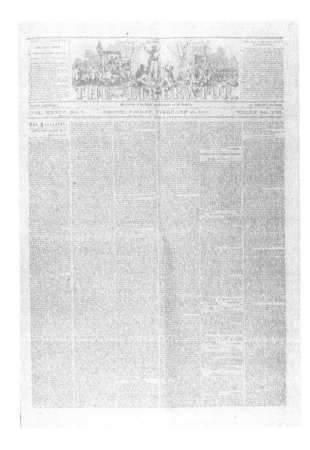

Abraham Lincoln Papers:
Series 1. General Cor-
respondence, 1833–1916:
The Liberator (Boston Newspaper), February 12, 1864

Bible" and twisting it into "an abolition Bible," and even worse, turning the Christian God into "an abolition God."[13] The white Episcopal bishop Stephen Elliott similarly charged four years later that Christian abolitionists were in fact "infidels—men who are clamoring for a new God, and a new Christ, and a new Bible."[14] The sad and perverse irony is that proslavery Christians were the ones who had turned American Christianity upside down.

This chapter analyzes the contest between abolitionism and proslavery Christianity. Abolitionists such as William Lloyd Garrison were seeking to disentangle American Christianity from its wicked and irrational ties to slavery and racial prejudice. They paradoxically stood on the right side of history and the wrong side of many white American churches. As abolitionists constructed a strong movement and crafted compelling scriptural arguments for Black liberation, proslavery Christians rose to the challenge set before them and defended Black enslavement with robust appeals to biblical texts, racist theologies, and patriotic considerations. To return to Lincoln's parable, the abolitionists represented the first pastor, who asked whether the second pastor could see the word in the Bible. But what covered the word was more than a gold coin. It was also an American flag, the ideology of white supremacy, and the mainstream Protestant churches, all of which made for a pretty thick coating indeed.

"Cleaving to the Bible and Taking All Our Decisions about This Matter from Its Inspired Pages": The Rise of Proslavery Biblical Interpretation

One of the clearest indicators of how slavery shaped white American Christianity is found in the rise of proslavery biblical interpretation. Proslavery Christians accused the abolitionists of employing manipulative tactics in their scriptural appeals. In 1837, the white Methodist minister Samuel Dunwody argued that the abolitionists substituted "the plain letter of the word of the Lord" with "a train of metaphysical reasonings."[15] Dunwody and other proslavery clergy charged Garrison and other abolitionists with the interpretive error of misusing several scriptural verses, such as the prophetic call in Isaiah 58:6–12 to repair the breach and the messianic proclamation in Luke 4:18 to set at liberty those who are oppressed, to wield them as weapons attacking the faith and moral standing of enslavers and supporters of slavery. Proslavery pastors criticized the abolitionists for what they saw as a biased methodology that entailed the selection of verses that would serve one's ends without sufficient attention to the original contexts in which these verses were written.

In 1822, the white Baptist pastor Richard Furman refuted the abolitionist appeal to the "Christian golden rule" in Matthew 7:12, which records Christ's teaching to treat others as one desired to be treated, as a naive and incomplete interpretation. Furman countered that the abolitionists were wrong to insist that this verse was "an unanswerable argument against holding slaves," because the Golden Rule needed to be measured alongside other scriptural instruction about God's intended "order of things" within the hierarchical structures of society. Parents and children did not treat each other as equals, because the former exercised authority over the latter. Another example Furman provided was the existence of class differences throughout biblical history, such that not every wealthy individual was commanded to distribute one's material riches among those who were impoverished.

Furman did not mention the scriptural recounting of Jesus directing a rich young man to sell all his possessions (in Matt. 19:16–30, Mark 10:17–31, and Luke 18:18–30), but it is likely that Furman would have weighed this episode within the spectrum of his larger conviction that the racial and social inequalities in the United States were providential. Persons with authority and power were instructed to be just and responsible, not to overturn the systems and structures that they inhabited. Because slavery was mandated in the Scriptures, the application of the Golden Rule in the American context was not the abolition of slavery.

Instead, Christian enslavers were taught to do unto their enslaved persons as they would desire to be treated if they were enslaved: "A bond-servant may be treated with justice and humanity as a servant; and a master may, in an important sense, be the guardian and even father of his slaves."[16] Furman's use of the word "may" to describe how enslaved persons were to be treated illustrates that he and other proslavery Christians knew that some enslavers abused their authority. Furman conceded that American slavery was a cruel and oppressive system that bred a vicious catalogue of physical, psychological, and spiritual sins. But even "the fullest proof of these facts" did not mean that slavery was incompatible with Christianity. Furman noted that the existence of wicked husbands and fathers who abused their spouses and children did not prompt a widespread call for the dismantling of marital and familial structures.[17]

Furman was the pastor of the First Baptist Church in Charleston, South Carolina, and a significant early leader in the wider Baptist tradition. In 1814 he was elected president at the first meeting of the Baptist Triennial Convention in Philadelphia. Three years later he was reelected as president when American Baptists from across the nation gathered again in the same city for the Triennial Convention's second meeting. After completing his two presidential terms, Furman was elected the first president of the South Carolina Baptist Convention in 1821. As a young man, Furman detested slavery and called it "undoubtedly an evil."[18] Another prominent white Baptist pastor in Charleston, Basil Manly Sr., when he was a student at the University of South Carolina, also maintained that slavery was "evil" and "utterly repugnant to the spirit of our republican institutions."[19]

But both men became defenders of slavery after they became pastors. As much as Furman and Manly insisted that their scriptural justifications for slavery were the results of a direct exegetical approach that aimed for a plain reading of the Bible, their own life journeys contradict this assertion. Their moral sensibilities first intuited that slavery was wrong and later evolved into reasoning it as divinely sanctioned in the Scriptures. Manly, like Furman, was also keenly aware of slavery's many oppressions. During his first three years as the pastor of First Baptist Church, from 1826 to 1828, Manly kept a private journal in which he divulged his joys and hardships in ministry. One especially perplexing dilemma arose in his ministerial work among enslaved persons who worshiped at the church. An enslaved woman confided to Manly that she did not participate in communion because she feared God's punishment for her sin. But Manly then learned of the specific sin: the enslaver who owned this enslaved woman was raping her, or as Manly described the sexual violence, "her master *compels* her to live in constant adultery with him."[20]

Yet Manly continued to publicly assert that Christianity authorized slavery and that abolitionism was heretical. He and Furman ministered in one of the wealthiest cities in the antebellum United States, due to Charleston's seaport location and the transatlantic slave trade. Even after the international slave trade was abolished in 1808, Charleston remained a central hub for human trafficking with its many slave markets. Manly and Furman therefore witnessed the worst of American slavery. Early in their lives, they believed that Black enslavement was an evil system and repugnant to the spirit of both Christianity and American democracy. But as the two men became more successful in ministry, they discovered that the Bible was a proslavery document. Furman died in Charleston in 1825, and the South Carolina Baptist Convention named its first college after him one year later. Manly left his church in Charleston in 1837, after eleven years, to become the president of the University of Alabama in Tuscaloosa.

Protestant clergy, especially in the Southern states, emerged as the most vociferous speakers and prolific writers in support of American slavery. The historian Larry E. Tise finds that "ministers wrote almost half of all defenses of slavery published in America."[21] This fact is horrifying, but not beyond belief. There are readily discernable answers to explain why pastors led the way in promoting slavery, and in turn, denigrating Black people, in the contest between abolitionists and enslavers. One reason for the centrality of pastors among the proslavery ranks is because the abolitionist movement drew so heavily on the Bible and other sources within the Christian tradition.

Garrison had helped to inspire a generation of activists for Black emancipation when he wrote in the inaugural issue of *The Liberator* that he did not wish "to think, or speak, or write, with moderation." He compared the moral crisis of slavery to three perilous metaphors: "Tell a man whose house is on fire, to give a moderate alarm; tell him to moderately rescue his wife from the hands of the ravisher; tell the mother to gradually extricate her babe from the fire into which it has fallen." Garrison also promised that he would neither equivocate nor "retreat a single inch."[22] The religious arguments of American abolitionism therefore required a religious response that would be just as persuasive, passionate, and forceful. The proponents best equipped to defend slavery at the necessary levels of moral certitude and rhetorical ferocity were pastors.

Another reason is found in the religious and social dynamics of the Southern states. Clergy throughout the nation aspired to attain social respectability.

Jonathan Edwards and other pastors in colonial New England purchased enslaved persons partly for assistance with domestic labor, but also as evidence of their elite standing within the regnant social milieu. E. Brooks Holifield, in his study of American theology and culture in the antebellum Southern states, observes: "The social ladder therefore leaned heavily against the church house door, and a consciousness of social position affected the tone of church life as well as its external trappings."[23] The moral cost of social favor was incredibly high for clergy. The price was more than slave ownership, because it also entailed delivering the finest and fiercest public defenses of slavery in print and from the pulpit. One of the surest pathways for pastors seeking a larger congregation, greater income, and higher social standing was through acquiring a reputation as a skilled defender of slavery.

Many pastors therefore invested a significant amount of their time and energy to craft their proslavery treatises. These clergy pored over not just the Bible but also a plethora of other works across many disciplines, ranging from philosophy to theology, to publish books and proclaim sermons that would abate the rising tide of abolitionism, keep enslaved persons in bondage, and lead them to attain further social prestige. The greatest tragedies of American slavery are without question the oppression of millions of Black women, men, and children and the persistence of anti-Black racism. But a lesser tragedy can be found in the moral capitulation of white proslavery clergy to the cultural, economic, and social forces of slavery. Generations of pastors and theologians devoted their hearts and minds to figuring out how to present the evil atrocities of slavery as good, holy, and pleasing to God. Their legacies are deservedly in ruins today, but it is also important to note that at least some of their contemporaries, such as abolitionists and enslaved persons, judged them as harshly as we do in the present.

After Harriet Tubman escaped from her enslaver in Maryland, she asserted that American slavery was "the next thing to hell." Tubman courageously assisted at least seventy other formerly enslaved persons by means of the Underground Railroad and maintained that she "never saw one who was willing to go back and be a slave." She ultimately reasoned, "If a person would send another into bondage, he would, it appears to me, be bad enough to send him into hell, if he could."[24] Many white pastors and theologians were bad enough to declare that slavery was a gift from heaven and abolitionism was a curse from hell.

The proslavery writings of Thornton Stringfellow, a white Baptist pastor in Virginia, illustrate how the merging of cultural, political, racial, and social forces determined the direction of his ministry. In 1841 Stringfellow published an extensive article in the Richmond *Religious Herald* offering a systematic defense of slavery from the Bible. The article was reprinted in a pamphlet several years later; in 1856 Stringfellow published a revised and enhanced version of it in a book entitled *Scriptural and Statistical Views of Slavery*. Stringfellow published in 1861 a second book further examining the origin, nature, and history of slavery.[25] Throughout his work, Stringfellow acknowledged that the abolitionist movement had made slavery a contentious issue that imperiled the union between the Northern and Southern states.

Because the abolitionists identified slavery as "the greatest of sins that exist in the nation," Stringfellow professed in 1841 to be an impartial interpreter of the Bible who sought to arrive at a faithful conclusion that was not swayed by selfish motives or political interests. Stringfellow and his proslavery ministerial colleagues had no other agenda but to "be seen cleaving to the Bible and taking all our decisions about this matter from its inspired pages."[26] Many proslavery apologists utilized this notion of impartiality. Stringfellow and other pastors drew a contrast between their self-described evenhandedness and the hot-tempered abolitionists, who presupposed the moral rectitude of Black liberation when opening their Bibles.

James Henley Thornwell, a white Presbyterian theologian from South Carolina, argued in 1851 that the biblical authors themselves wrote about slavery in "cool, dispassioned, [and] didactic" language without a hint of the vitriol that the abolitionists employed: "The master is nowhere rebuked as a monster of cruelty and tyranny, the slave nowhere exhibited as the object of peculiar compassion and sympathy."[27] But Stringfellow and Thornwell had their own perspectives and prejudices. Both men were enslavers who ministered in a slaveholding society. That their scriptural exposition was impartial was simply a myth. Every interpreter examines the Bible through the lens of one's cultural context and with one's moral (and immoral) sensibilities. Proslavery Christians accused their opponents of reading with the spectacles of abolition, but they were wearing the same exact spectacles. Abolitionist and proslavery Christians alike were analyzing the Bible through the lens of American slavery. The two sides turned the same pages but arrived at different conclusions.

Stringfellow offered a robust fourfold defense of slavery. The first prong detailed how slavery was sanctioned in the Hebrew Bible. The second prong illustrated the existence of slavery in ancient Israel. Stringfellow argued that the laws in the Old Testament comprised "the only national constitution emanating from the Almighty" and evinced ample support for involuntary slavery. The third prong demonstrated how the New Testament regulated slavery as a permanent relationship no different than marriage and family. The fourth prong maintained that "the institution of slavery is full of mercy."

Stringfellow defined slavery as the "state, condition, or relation" in which "one human being is held without his consent by another, as property, to be bought, sold, and transferred, together with the increase, as property, forever."[28] This definition itself was a refutation of the abolitionist argument that American slavery was dissimilar to the system authorized in the Hebrew Bible. In 1836 the white Quaker abolitionist Angelina Emily Grimké contended that "the laws of Moses" prohibited involuntary servitude and prescribed liberation to voluntary servants after a certain number of years. Grimké inveighed, "Where, then, I would ask, is the warrant, the justification, or the palliation of American slavery from Hebrew servitude? How many of the southern slaves would now be in bondage according to the laws of Moses; Not one."[29] Stringfellow countered that Grimké's assessment was wrong, because there was no difference between the systems of slavery in the United States and ancient Israel.

At several points Stringfellow's analysis repeated and reinforced earlier proslavery arguments such as the pamphlet from the colonial Massachusetts merchant John Saffin in 1701. Like Saffin, Stringfellow utilized Abraham's slave ownership as proof of divine sanction. He cited the example of Hagar as an enslaved person belonging to Abraham and Sarah in Genesis 16:1–9. The enslavement of Hagar justified several components of American slavery. Hagar's enslaver, Sarah, forced her to have sex with Abraham and bear his child. And when Hagar escaped her enslaver due to Sarah's abusive jealousy, an angel of the Lord appeared to Hagar and commanded her to return to her enslaver. Stringfellow asserted that there was no indication of divine displeasure or wrath toward this unfolding episode of enslavement. The biblical passage did not emphasize the necessity of following the Golden Rule with "a homily upon doing to others," and did not reproach Sarah "as a hypocrite" or Abraham "as a tyrant." Stringfellow added that the angel of the Lord did not take compassion upon Hagar in her plight as a fugitive slave. He did not deny the presence of sexual violence and coercive oppression in the biblical account. Stringfellow rather accentuated the injustices that Hagar suffered as an illustration that her involuntary enslavement comprised many of the "aggravations" that abolitionists charged of American slavery.

There were therefore two possible interpretations. One was to rewrite the Hebrew Bible to incriminate Abraham and Sarah and usurp their positions as holy ancestors responsible for the lineage of Jesus Christ. Stringfellow asserted that the reasoning of the abolitionists would make it so "that Abraham's character must not be transmitted to posterity, with this stain upon it; that Sarah must no longer be allowed to live a stranger to the abhorrence God has for such conduct as she has been guilty of to this poor helpless female [Hagar]." The second interpretation was to acknowledge that Abraham and Sarah were enslavers and that their enslaved persons were "made chattels" in a system that resembled American slavery. Stringfellow cited Genesis 26:13–14 as proof that Abraham and Sarah's son, Isaac, also owned enslaved persons as human property. Stringfellow also interpreted the Tenth Commandment in Exodus 20:17 as a further demonstration that enslaved persons were chattels. Among the possessions that one could not covet from "thy neighbor" were "his man-servant" and "his maid-servant," right next to his house, wife, and animals.[30]

Stringfellow diverged from Saffin on the matter of interpreting Genesis 9:24–27. Even Saffin chafed at the idea that a drunken father's admonition against one of his sons implied that the entire Black race was subject to perpetual slavery. Yet Stringfellow's deployment of this curse illustrated how proslavery Christians emphasized these four scriptural verses in the nineteenth century. Stringfellow asserted that "the first recorded language" on slavery was found in "the inspired language of Noah," which proved two significant scriptural principles. The first insight was that God authorized slavery as an oppressive system in which one person held another person or persons (and their offspring) in the state of involuntary bondage. The second lesson was equally pertinent to American slavery, but it required an interpretive move that Samuel Sewall and other expositors considered illogical. Because the Noahic curse prophesied that the descendants of Japheth and Shem would enslave the descendants of Ham, Stringfellow maintained that Europeans and Asians were the descendants of Noah's sons Japheth and Shem, and that Africans came from the lineage of his son Ham.[31]

Proslavery Christian writers did not meticulously trace how persons of European (or Asian) descent were connected to Japheth and Shem, because they did not have definitive genealogical evidence to do so. But the racial implications of these unproven ethnological associations were too tempting to ignore. They provided a simple explanation for both slavery and anti-Black racism in the United States. In 1857 Frederick A. Ross stated, "When Ham, in his antediluvian recklessness, laughed at his father, God took occasion to give to the world the rule of the superior over the inferior." Without even bothering to provide any scholarly references, Ross went a step further than Stringfellow and definitively connected the white race to Japheth's lineage: "Shem was blessed to rule over Ham. Japheth was blessed to rule over both. God sent Ham to Africa, Shem to Asia, Japheth to Europe."[32] White people enslaved and despised Black persons because the descendants of Noah's older sons were divinely ordained to enslave the descendants of Ham, and these descendants would also be at perpetual odds with one another. According to these Southern pastors, the Noahic curse of Ham, rather than the sinful attitudes and actions of white Christians toward Black people, was the cause of American slavery.

Stringfellow refuted every moral criticism of slavery with scriptural precision. Armed with the word of God, he was a pastor who reckoned with abolitionism in all the wrong ways. He cited Exodus 12:44–45 to illustrate that there were two types of servitude in the Hebrew Bible: Bondservants were enslaved without their consent, whereas hired servants were contractually employed and given wages. Exodus 21:2–4 demonstrated that Hebraic slavery entailed family separation, because the biblical code granted freedom to the husband alone after six years of servitude, with his wife and children remaining with the enslaver. Regulations for ancient Israel in the books of Deuteronomy and Leviticus indicated that God permitted "his chosen people" to "take their money, go into the slave markets of the surrounding nations, (the seven devoted [Canaanite] nations excepted), and purchase men-servants and women-servants, and give them, and their increase, to their children and their children's children, forever." Ephesians 6:5–9 and Colossians 3:22–24 directed enslaved persons to obey their enslavers, and 1 Timothy 6:12 explicitly instructed Christian enslavers. The passages in Ephesians and Colossians linked slavery with the institutions of marriage and family and reified three hierarchical relations: husbands over wives, parents over children, and masters over slaves.

Stringfellow, like Furman, also insisted that the proper application of the Golden Rule was within these hierarchical relations as well as larger social structures. He insisted that the abolitionist attack upon slavery was in fact a call to "level all inequalities in human condition" and overthrow every existing system in their lives, ranging from the nuclear family to antebellum American capitalism. Stringfellow further argued that the New Testament had ushered in radical changes that differentiated Christianity from Judaism, such as the removal of dietary laws and most notably the elimination of circumcision for male believers. He pointed out how the triune God did not abolish slavery at this crucial juncture in world history. When Paul received divine direction to instruct the earliest churches, God was far from silent on slavery. Instead, God inspired Paul to recognize and regulate it in his New Testament epistles.[33]

The briefest section of Stringfellow's article was his elaboration of the claim that slavery was "full of mercy." He stated that enslavement was a better alternative than death in the case of prisoners of war. In the context of American slavery, enslaved persons of African descent were taken from pagan nations and "brought within the range of Gospel influence" in the United States. Stringfellow was careful to note that not every enslaved person converted to

Christianity, but he believed that many of them had more access to Christian worship in North America than in Africa. He also expressed that the Black race was "utterly unprepared for a higher civil state"; therefore enslavement was more beneficial for them than emancipation in a white-dominant society.[34]

Stringfellow's work illumines several insights about him and the world that he inhabited. He was an astute thinker and talented writer who ministered in a society that rewarded pastors and theologians who could intellectually and rhetorically defend slavery as sharply and skillfully as the strongest abolitionists attacked it. Abolitionists such as Garrison and Grimké were formidable foes, and Stringfellow was one of the many white pastors who rose to the task of being their rivals. Stringfellow's proslavery article in 1841 also differed from Furman's work from 1822 in tenor. The former conveyed less nuance and exacted a more ruthless tone on slavery. Whereas Furman ruefully conceded that some enslavers abused their enslaved persons, Stringfellow argued that every injustice within American slavery, including sexual violence and family separation, was explicitly permitted in the Scriptures.

The growth of the abolitionist movement after 1830 provides one explanation for the contrast between the two Baptist pastors. Stringfellow had to grapple with Garrison, the outspoken reformer who refused to retreat even a single inch. He therefore adopted an equally aggressive and hostile temperament in his proslavery advocacy. He did not mention Garrison by name in his article, but Stringfellow surely had Garrison in mind when he assailed the abolitionists as cavalier and haughty individuals who presented themselves as holier than Jesus and more righteous than Abraham, Moses, and Paul combined.[35] Stringfellow ultimately experienced substantial loss in the battle against abolitionism in his own slave ownership. During the Civil War, Union forces occupied his two-thousand-acre plantation and seventy of his enslaved persons seized the opportunity to escape.

Christian Compromises and the Moral Cost "to Keep the Plighted Faith of This Nation"

Mainstream Protestant clergy in the Northern states endeavored to remain neutral in the contest between abolitionism and proslavery Christianity. Even before 1830 it was hard to do so, because both the existence and expansion of slavery were major political issues that gripped the nation. In 1819 the US Congress fiercely debated the possibility of new slaveholding states, and the result was a compromise one year later that annexed two territories, Missouri as a state that permitted slavery and Maine as a state that prohibited slavery, to maintain the same balance of states with and without slavery.

The mainstream denominations were also seeking to preserve a delicate balance between their churches and members in the Northern and Southern states. It was initially difficult because of the antislavery impulse in some of these ecclesial traditions. John Wesley, Thomas Coke, and Francis Asbury were three of the most significant leaders in early American Methodism (Wesley as the founder of the movement in England, and Coke and Asbury as superintendents he dispatched to oversee the movement in the soon-to-be American republic), and they all opposed slavery. When Wesley published the General Rules for the Methodist Church in 1743, he barred "the buying or selling the bodies and souls of men, women, and children, with an intention to enslave them."[36] In 1774, he published a pamphlet outlining his searing criticism of slavery and specifically condemned enslavers in North America as guilty of perpetrating the greatest evils. He challenged enslavers to test their sinful actions before the Christian God, "a wise, powerful, merciful Being, the Creator and Governor of Heaven and Earth," and reckon with their crimes against both God and fellow humans: "You first acted the villain in making them slaves (whether you stole them or bought them). You kept them stupid and wicked, by cutting them off from all opportunities of improving either in knowledge or virtue: And now you assign their want of wisdom and goodness as the reason for using them worse than brute beasts?"[37]

In the United States, Coke and Asbury, as the first two bishops of the Methodist Episcopal Church (MEC), shared Wesley's convictions and desired for their denomination to possess a firm antislavery position. But the two bishops encountered tremendous resistance from its growing membership. As the denomination increased from 15,000 members in 1784 to 58,000 in 1790, it also gained more enslavers and supporters of slavery.[38] In 1785, an angry white mob in Virginia threatened Coke because of his preaching against slavery. Asbury complained of the limits of his leadership in 1798 because white Methodists in Virginia defended slavery with "the highest flights of rapturous piety."[39] Coke and Asbury therefore facilitated compromises on slavery between 1785 to 1812 that suspended some rules, such as the mandate to excommunicate church members who sell enslaved persons, and moved oversight on matters tied to slavery from its national (and highest) legislative body, the General Conference, to its regionally organized annual conferences.[40]

American slavery shaped the mainstream denominations as much as, if not more than, any other doctrinal issue. Regional divisions in the three largest Protestant traditions—Methodists in 1844, Baptists in 1845, and Presbyterians in 1857 and 1861—were the result of ruptures over slavery.[41] But to point to the ecclesial schisms as evidence that the Northern branches of these denominations were staunchly abolitionist overlooks important historical realities. Before the eventual divides, church leaders in each of the denominations actively resisted the implementation of stronger antislavery positions, such as the excommunication of slave-owning church members.

The abolitionist movement gained momentum after 1830, but only a few clergy from these denominations joined their ranks. Many more Methodists, Baptists, and Presbyterians denounced the abolitionists as troublemaking firebrands who set out to destroy the hard-earned regional bonds in both their nation and their denominations. In 1837, the Methodist bishop Beverly Waugh presided over the New England annual conference and refused to allow any antislavery petitions. Waugh chastised the clergy and lay leaders who were seeking to nudge the annual conference toward abolitionism for "agitating those fearfully exciting topics" that would "hazard the unity of the Methodist Episcopal Church."[42]

Because the annual conferences had autonomy to act on slavery, regional bodies in the Southern states leveraged this authority to endorse slavery and assail abolitionism. In 1836 the South Carolina annual conference upheld slavery as "unequivocally" authorized in the Bible and lambasted "the principles and opinions of the abolitionists" as emanating from a "false philosophy" that ran contrary to Christianity.[43] Yet Waugh would not abide any advocacy for Black liberation among Methodists in New England. In addition to his concerns about denominational unity, Waugh feared the political repercussions of abolitionism: "Are you willing to contribute to the destruction of our beautiful and excellent form of civil and political government, after it has cost the labor, treasure and blood of our fathers to establish it?"[44] Some annual conferences, such as in New York and Ohio, expressed stronger antislavery positions. But even after the regional schism of the MEC in 1844, Methodists in the Northern states were careful not to expel slave-owning church members in the border states.[45]

A steadfast contingency of white Christians in the Northern states sought to suppress abolitionism for the sake of ecclesial and national unity. In 1841, the executive committee of the American Baptist Home Mission Society circulated a paper that decried the divisiveness beset upon its churches due to abolitionism. The committee identified the raging debate over slavery as a "secular" matter outside the domain of Christian ministry. It recommended that Baptists from across the nation remain in "a union of hearts, even where there may not be entire union of views." These white Baptists acknowledged a plurality of views on slavery, but their admonition was directed toward abolition stirrings rather than proslavery defenses. They wanted the abolitionists among their fellowship to refrain from speaking out, because the increasing moral and religious condemnations of slavery offended slave-owning Baptist church members.

Although the committee contended that slavery was strictly a civil issue, it conveyed a political rationale to buttress the prioritizing of church unity: "As patriots, we must cherish religious union as one among the strongest, although not the most prominent, of the bonds that hold together the Union of these States."[46] The cautious language that religious unity was not the ultimate bond indicates the persistent tension of white Protestants within the mainstream denominations. At one level they understood that Christian discipleship demanded allegiance to God above nation. Christians had a higher calling to confront evil and reform injustices as God's ambassadors on earth. But at another level they also knew that the United States was founded in a compromise that authorized the legality of Black enslavement. In 1846, Albert Barnes, the white pastor of First Presbyterian Church in Philadelphia, wrote that slavery was embedded in the roots of the entire nation, from its economy to its politics as well as its religion and its education.[47] A white Presbyterian merchant in New York City told an abolitionist that while he believed in his heart that slavery was "a great evil," he nonetheless opposed abolitionism, because he feared the economic consequences of ending slavery, as "the business of the North, as well as the South, has become adjusted to it."[48] At least some white Christians confessed that they willfully compromised their moral convictions and religious commitments to put America (and self-interest) first, but many more did not want to admit, even to themselves, that their fidelity to country was stronger than their devotion to Christ.

Antebellum American Christians were not the first people to grapple with this tension between faith and patriotism. About the year 412, the North African theologian Augustine grappled with faithful Christian citizenship. He began to write the *City of God* as a response to criticism levied against Christians from some Roman citizens after the devastating Gothic invasion of Rome in 410. These detractors impugned Christianity as a subversive religion that undermined public safety and prosperity and accused Christians of being negligent citizens who prioritized their religious obligations over their civic responsibilities. Augustine offered a twofold explanation for why Christians were not to blame. Christians were simultaneously citizens of two cities: the City of Man, the earthly city, and the City of God, the heavenly city. The two cities were distinct, but heavenly teachings motivated Christians to do good in their earthly city. They sought therefore to enhance public flourishing through their personal labor and communal participation.[49]

Another insight from Augustine's work pertains to how Christians may contribute a healthy perspective on nationalism, because their faith in God keeps them attuned to civic idolatry. Christians are equipped to identify the injustices within their earthly city, without succumbing to the prideful excesses of nationalism, and subsequently work toward societal reforms to advance the common good. In their opposition to slavery and racial discrimination, Black and white Christian abolitionists strived to remake the United States in accordance with the spiritual principles of justice and love.

Garrison asserted that the only gospel that he ever proclaimed was Jesus' message of salvation in Matthew 25 and Luke 4 for the "downtrodden and oppressed, whose case he has literally made his own." He insisted that "genuine abolitionism" was "of heaven, not of men," and "called to repentance a guilty nation."[50] Garrison's enactment of faithful citizenship certainly invigorated some Christians, but it found more enemies than allies within the mainstream denominations.

One of Garrison's most prominent critics resided in the same city as the abolitionist. Moses Stuart, the white professor of sacred literature at Andover Theological Seminary, favored the school's restrictions against abolitionist activism on campus and steadfastly refused to classify slavery as a *malum in se* (evil in itself).[51] One of his students, Francis Wayland, the white Baptist pastor who served as president of Brown University from 1827 to 1855, also forbid abolitionist activism on Brown's campus and in 1835 barred its students from even discussing the issue of slavery.[52]

Stuart's sharpest attack against abolitionism is found in his 1850 treatise entitled "Conscience and the Constitution." He was one of the first biblical scholars in the nation—one biographer identifies him as the "father of biblical science in America"—who taught more than fifteen hundred students over nearly four decades at Andover, but he refrained from publishing on slavery for most of his academic career.[53] But the furious debate over the Compromise of 1850 and the Fugitive Slave Act prompted Stuart to defend slavery, the US Constitution, and national unity. Stuart publicly supported Senator Daniel Webster of Massachusetts for his act of political audacity in advocating for the omnibus bill that permitted the extension of slavery in western territories and strengthened statutes on the recapture of enslaved persons who had fled to the Northern states.

Webster's speech in the Senate shocked his colleagues in Washington, DC, and infuriated his constituents at home, and he was forced to resign from office. Stuart agreed with Webster's decision to prioritize national unity and shared his "aim and desire to cherish our Union as inviolable, and to persuade both parties to make all such mutual concessions as they can make, consistently with their consciences, for the sake of peace, of mutual good, and of firm consolidation."[54] As a biblical scholar and Congregational minister, Stuart endeavored to illustrate that American slavery was endorsed in the Scriptures and compatible with the Christian conscience.

Stuart chafed at the abolitionist notion that the United States was a guilty nation because of its compact with slavery. But Stuart's scriptural exposition of American slavery revealed the thorny web of complications and contradictions that were required to soothe the Christian conscience. Stuart found himself on an exegetical tightrope as he desired to avoid association with both proslavery interpreters such as Stringfellow and abolitionists such as Garrison. He ultimately asserted that the Bible offered moral principles that hinted at universal liberty but never explicitly endorsed the abolition of slavery. Stuart acknowledged that the Scriptures regulated a system of slavery that included both violence and involuntary bondage, but he also believed that the human rights abuses recounted in the Bible, such as the unjust practice of forcing enslaved women to have sex with their male enslavers for reproductive purposes, were abrogated with the unfolding illumination of Christian teachings as the religion matured over time.

Stuart maintained that American Christians in the nineteenth century did not permit polygamy and concubinage because "the gospel has given us better light." And he further added that the "Mosaic dispensation," with its regulations on slavery, was "a *preparatory* one, and not a complete, perfect, or permanent one." The ministry of Jesus Christ as recorded in the Gospels of Matthew, Mark, Luke, and John demonstrated "that the Saviour uttered sentiments, which, in their ultimate effects, must abolish—totally and forever abolish—all slavery, except in cases of crime."[55] Stuart, however, concluded that the Bible never condemned slavery as a sin in itself, and he favored the Pauline epistles for their explicit instructions that Christians obey civil authorities, as well as for their detailed regulations for enslavers and enslaved persons who were professing believers. He contended about the biblical books attributed to Paul: "Men, ministers of the gospel, politicians, Christians, are bound to meet it [the Pauline corpus], face to face. If not, then let Paul be abjured. . . . It is hypocrisy, if we profess to acknowledge him as an inspired teacher, and then flout at his doctrines, and ridicule and condemn those who inculcate obedience to him."[56]

Stuart's explication is confounding because, even though he found that so many components of American slavery ran contrary to scriptural principles, he justified it on the grounds that there is no direct biblical command to emancipate all enslaved persons. Stuart went to great lengths to refute what he saw as the overly simplistic biblical literalism of both proslavery and abolitionist Christians. The former wrongly pointed to the account of Abraham, Sarah, and Hagar in Genesis 16 to defend the injustices of sexual exploitation and rape within American slavery, whereas the latter took isolated verses such as Isaiah 58:6 out of context and unrealistically insinuated that the prophetic message to break every yoke directed Christians toward social upheaval and political revolution.

Yet Stuart fell into his own interpretative trap in his reliance on the literal absence of a scriptural reference prohibiting the system of slavery. Earlier abolitionists ridiculed this specific proslavery argument. In 1835 a group of Kentucky Presbyterians compared this facile deployment of biblical literalism with a deathly ill patient who stupidly received the diagnosis that "every limb and organ was diseased" with joy because the doctor never "said in *express terms* that my body is unsound."[57] In John H. Giltner's study of Stuart, the historian assesses this treatise, which was one of Stuart's final works before he died in 1852, as lacking the scholarly integrity displayed within his extensive record of publications and "his most disturbing, for he set forth his mature position [on slavery] and exposed its weaknesses."[58] American slavery had corrupted Stuart's morality and frayed his intellect.

What motivated Stuart to betray the guiding principles that had shaped his long career as a renowned scholar and professor? He had fastidiously avoided taking a public stance on slavery. Stuart gave one unpublished lecture about slavery to his students at Andover in 1835, only because the English abolitionist George Thompson had garnered considerable publicity during a stop in Boston on his lecture tour across the Northern states.[59] Otherwise Stuart remained silent until 1850. The catalyst for Stuart's essay was his patriotism, not his faith. He observed how the cascading influence of the abolitionist movement had hardened positions on slavery in both Northern and Southern states, and he now feared that national unity was hanging on a precipice. Stuart offered a defense of the Constitution that was as vigorous as his affirmation of the Bible. He identified in the Constitution evidence that the American founders employed the impulses of moderation and compromise to enact the higher republican ideals of mutuality and democracy. Stuart believed that many of the founders detested slavery as much as he did, but they did not seek to abolish it, because they honorably (in his view) placed national interests above their own personal convictions.

Stuart positioned the constitutional delegates on nearly the same plane as the biblical authors. He subordinated his own displeasure with slavery to accept the constitutional provenances of states' rights and the requirements for Northern citizens to assist in the return of fugitive slaves. Stuart explained: "'But the states have no right to make men property,' it is said. That may be so, I reply; and considered merely in a Christian light, I believe it to be true.

But what right now has Massachusetts to decide for Virginia, on such a question?" He disagreed with Garrison and other abolitionists who appealed to their consciences over the Constitution. Stuart's most pressing problem with abolitionism was that it necessitated a negative and ultimately destructive view of American history. Abolitionist attacks on the Constitution presented the founders as morally bankrupt leaders "who did not understand even the first rudiments of religion, or of civil freedom and the rights of man."[60]

He also favorably cited a speech, from a Massachusetts senator, Robert C. Winthrop, that assailed the foolhardy arrogance beneath the abolitionist appeal to conscience: "But it is a libel upon the Constitution of the United States—and what is worse, sir, it is a libel upon the great and good men who framed, adopted, and ratified it; it is a libel upon Washington and Franklin, and Hamilton and Madison. . . . [I]t is a libel upon them all, and upon the whole American people of 1789 who sustained them in their noble work."[61] Stuart therefore defended with his scriptural analysis the perpetuation of Black enslavement and the virtue of returning enslaved persons seeking refuge in the Northern states to their Southern enslavers.

On the latter he appealed to the example of how Paul sent back Onesimus, an enslaved man who had escaped to freedom, to his enslaver, Philemon, and Stuart emphasized: "Paul's Christian *conscience* would not permit him to injure the vested rights of Philemon. . . . Paul's conscience, then, like his doctrines, was very different from that of the abolitionists."[62] But Stuart also noted that to disobey the Fugitive Slave Act was "an imputation on the men who framed our government," and he disapproved of how the abolitionists shamed the American founders "as having neither conscience nor humanity."[63] He wanted white Christians in the Northern states to trust the wisdom of both the apostle Paul and the American founders. The Bible, or at least one of the shortest books in the New Testament (Philemon), and the US Constitution determined the morality and legality of the Fugitive Slave Act.

The contest over American slavery involved contrasting biblical interpretations between abolitionist and proslavery Christians, but Stuart's ardent defense of the Constitution reveals the collision of religion and patriotism in the making of American Christianity. Both Stuart and Garrison interpreted American slavery through the spectacles of Christianity and country. But they came to opposite conclusions. Garrison did not hesitate to find fault in his nation's history and criticized the compromises that the American founders made to preserve slavery as immoral, racist, and unjust. He did not advocate for the overthrow of American democracy and a turn to theocratic government, but Garrison believed that the United States would be a nation that more closely exhibited both the teachings of Jesus and the promises of the Declaration of Independence when it abolished slavery.

Stuart refused to reckon with the notion of the American founders as anything less than virtuous leaders. They were not perfect, but the founders wisely compromised to set the nation on a prosperous pathway that respected regional differences. Stuart believed in the American founders with a confidence akin to religious faith, and he supported Daniel Webster for upholding the Constitution. Stuart praised Webster for loving the country more than he hated slavery: "He [Webster] has declared, that bitter as the task may be, to allow of new slavery states, still he must lift up his hand to carry solemn contracts into execution, to keep the plighted faith of this nation. There is—there can be no *repudiating* of such contracts."[64]

One of Stuart's students, a white Congregational pastor, Rufus W. Clark, excoriated in a review essay his former professor's treatise as a nonsensical scriptural exposition that presented a Christian plea for American slavery while outlining its many prevailing sins. Clark further argued that Stuart had omitted how Christians had a clear mandate to disobey unjust civil laws such as the Fugitive Slave Act and seek to undo them. Stuart's former student mourned that "the abominable system of American slavery" had crept into and deformed the thinking of even one of the nation's most venerated biblical scholars.[65]

"The Abolition Spirit Is Undeniably Atheistic": American Slavery and the Remaking of American Christianity

In the Southern states, by 1850 the defense of slavery had come to define and dominate the mainstream Protestant denominations. The mark of a faithful Christian centered on two interlocking tenets: that American slavery was divinely ordained and that abolitionism represented a grave threat to orthodox Christianity. In 1851, the Nashville *Christian Advocate* asserted that abolitionism was "more closely allied to infidelity than is generally supposed," and the movement for Black liberation was especially problematic for Christians because it demanded a recanting of their faith.[66] To abolish slavery was blasphemy and a betrayal against the triune God.

In 1860 Benjamin Morgan Palmer, the white pastor of First Presbyterian Church in New Orleans, proclaimed from his pulpit, "We defend the cause of God and religion. The abolition spirit is undeniably atheistic." Palmer equated American slavery to a "divine trust" that God bestowed as a blessing to both Black and white races. Because of inherent Black racial inferiority and primitive African barbarism, American slavery was the providential means for Black evangelization. God granted white Americans the authority and responsibility to be "the constituted guardians of the slaves" in a racially hierarchical society that exhibited order and mercy. Palmer explained to his white parishioners, "Our lot [as the white population] is not more implicated in theirs [as the enslaved Black population], than is their lot in ours: in our mutual relations we survive or perish together." He believed even white Northerners perceived that what he declared about the Black race was a proven fact: "By nature, the most affectionate and loyal of all races beneath the sun, they are also the most helpless: and no calamity can befall them greater than the loss of that protection they enjoy under this patriarchal system." The "dismal results" of racial integration in the Northern states after emancipation, with many free Black persons residing in impoverished neighborhoods among the destitute classes, demonstrated that the longstanding existence of slavery was morally, politically, and religiously superior to the "experiment" of Black emancipation.[67]

William G. Brownlow, a white Methodist pastor in Tennessee, also advanced the notion of inherent Black racial inferiority in his increasingly strident proslavery advocacy. When Brownlow was an itinerant preacher in the 1830s, he refrained from mentioning slavery on his preaching circuit. But like so many other Southern clergy, in the 1840s and 1850s he developed a strong voice to defend slavery. In 1857, Brownlow published a proslavery address that he had first delivered in Knoxville at the Southern Commercial Convention. He endorsed the declaration in 1835 from the South Carolina governor, George McDuffie, that "slavery is the corner-stone of our republican edifice" and repudiated the abolitionists for their naive use of the mantra that "all men are created equal." Brownlow observed, "God never intended to make the butcher a judge, nor the baker a president, but to protect them according to their claims as butcher and baker." The abolitionists did not need to look any further than among the free Black population in their own cities for irrefutable evidence that persons of African descent could not sustain themselves alongside white people apart from enslavement. Brownlow contended that free Black Americans in the Northern states were "more miserable and destitute as a whole, than the slave population of the South," and the few free Black persons in the Southern states were "the most wretched, indolent, immoral, and dishonest class of persons."[68]

White proslavery Christians such as Palmer and Brownlow incorporated the denigration of the Black race in their defense of American slavery because the system itself was based on race. Religious justifications for slavery required racist ideologies, a terrible and devastating American phenomenon in which religion and racism continually fortified each other. The persistence of racial prejudice long after the end of slavery evinced that this variant form of American Christianity pervaded many white churches, denominations, and traditions for generations, even to the present day.

Brownlow was so confident in the rightness of slavery that he did not expect to see any abolitionists in eternity. He concluded that if he did "find any of the agitators in heaven," they must have fooled the angels, just as they had deceived so many Christians on earth, and only "entered that world of joy, by practicing a gross fraud upon the doorkeeper!"[69] But Brownlow found himself at the receiving end of scorn from his fellow white Southern clergy for his opposition to secession during the Civil War. He was arrested and briefly imprisoned in Knoxville on charges of treason in 1861. He resolutely defended slavery, but he disapproved of the decision to form the Confederate States of America. Ironically, he laid most of the blame for secession on the political preaching from pastors in his own Methodist denomination.[70]

One challenge for the Indigenous, Black, and white Christians who sought to reform the injustices of settler colonialism and slavery was the intentional deflection of their opponents by separating religion and politics. Pequot pastor William Apess and Cherokee preacher David Brown each implored white Christians to integrate their faith commitments with their civic responsibilities to prevent the exploitation and expulsion of Indigenous peoples. The purpose of prayer, worship, and Bible study within the church was to inspire Christians toward righteous action in the world. And the surest way to protect Indigenous rights was to engage in political processes such as voting for legislators who supported just policies and petitioning to remake unfair laws.

Many white Christians simply did not want to practice this kind of publicly oriented faith. Yet to respond with apathy felt unfaithful; so the emergence of a doctrine that emphasized the spiritual identity of the church made for a convenient justification. Preacher after preacher insisted that their churches steered clear of political issues for the sake of peace and purity. They stated that they were seeking to protect their ministries from the corrupting influence of politics, but the overarching reason for their political avoidance was to maintain harmonious relations with and between their congregants.

The evolution of proslavery Christianity illustrates how the doctrine of the church as a strictly spiritual entity was inconsistently applied and ultimately annihilated. White pastors in the Southern states initially did not preach about slavery, because they identified it as a political matter. But the rise of American abolitionism after 1830 demanded a religious counterpunch, and the same clergy soon defended slavery from their pulpits on the grounds that it was a moral issue. During the Civil War, white Southern clergy were among the most vehement supporters of the Confederacy. Ninety-six Confederate pastors, seminary professors, and college presidents representing Baptists, Disciples of Christ, Episcopalians, and Lutherans as well as various Methodist, Presbyterian, and Reformed denominations circulated a letter in 1863 protesting Lincoln's Emancipation Proclamation as "a cruel and shameful device" that violated their new nation's religious and political rights. They declared: "Let it go forth from our lips while we live; let it be recorded of us when we are dead, that we—ministers of our Lord Jesus Christ, and members of His holy Church, with our hands upon the Bible, at once the sacred chart of our liberties and the foundation of faith, call heaven and earth to record, that in the name of Him whose we are, and whom we serve, *we protest!*"[71]

In 1829, William Lloyd Garrison called upon white American churches "to lead in this great enterprise" of Black emancipation. In one of his earliest addresses Garrison desired for the churches to awaken from "their slumbers" and "arm for the holy contest."[72] But he soon realized that the churches had never really been asleep. They were always ready to defend slavery, for a combination of economic, patriotic, political, and social reasons. The mainstream Protestant churches did it with quiet compromises until the abolitionist movement forced them to speak out. The result was no shortage of proslavery articles, books, pamphlets, and sermons. In 1857, William G. Brownlow and Frederick A. Ross disputed with each other about which of their denominations had contributed more to the proslavery cause. Ross offended Brownlow when he wrote that his body of Presbyterians had established "the only defined ground, on the slavery question, in the United States or the world." Brownlow retorted that proslavery Methodists had done more to uphold Black enslavement.[73]

Black abolitionists from the same ecclesial traditions (though in different denominations) as Brownlow and Ross found the pathway for Black liberation in Christianity. In 1846 the African Methodist Episcopal Church pastor and journalist Molliston Madison Clark asserted that "the churches in America ought to use the whole weight of their influence against the practice of slaveholding." Clark believed that the Bible clearly condemned American slavery and that the churches had an obvious mandate to work for its eradication. In doing so, "the Church would be doing *nothing more than acting out her legitimate functions.*"[74] Clark did not ask white churches to be exceptional, just faithful.

The Presbyterian minister James W. C. Pennington contended in 1849 that the gospel of Jesus Christ simultaneously encouraged nationalism and curbed its attendant biases and excesses: "It is a blessing to have a country, and it is a virtue to love it. . . . But this love of country is capable of great abuse." Christians honored God through service to their fellow citizens, but their faith also anchored them in the "immutable justice of God" and constantly reminded them that persons of every nationality shared one common humanity.[75] Pennington's vision of American Christianity readily acknowledged the paradox that patriotism was both a vice and a virtue to faith. American abolitionism was largely a Christian movement that held devotion to God and fidelity to nation together in productive tension. Not every abolitionist was a Christian, and few belonged to the mainstream Protestant denominations, but many believed that their righteous struggle to form a racially just society was the truest enactment of Christianity and democracy.

Near the end of the Civil War in 1865, with Union victory over the Confederacy assured, Garrison made his first visit to Charleston, South Carolina, a city in which his likeness and writings were burned in a public protest thirty years prior. He joined several Union politicians and military officers to celebrate at Zion Presbyterian Church, a congregation with roughly fifteen hundred formerly enslaved Black members. A large crowd gathered to hear Garrison speak. As soon as everyone was seated, one Black man, Samuel Dickerson, approached the pulpit with his two young daughters to give Garrison a wreath of flowers. Dickerson explained, "I have read of you. I have read of the mighty labors you have had for the consummation of this glorious object. Here you see stand before you your handiwork." Dickerson told Garrison of how his enslaver had sold one of his daughters and threatened to sell the other. He then invited Garrison to behold the assembly of newly freed people: "And I tell you it is not this heart alone, but there are mothers, there are fathers, there are sisters, and there are brothers, the pulsations of whose hearts are unimaginable. The greeting that they would give you, sir, it is almost impossible for me to express. . . . We thank you for what you have done for us."[76]

After the crowd cheered, Garrison responded: "My dear friend—I have no language to express the feelings of my heart on listening to your kind and strengthening words, on receiving these beautiful tokens of your gratitude, and on looking into the faces of this vast multitude, now happily liberated from the galling letters of slavery. Let me say at the outset, 'Not unto us, not unto us, but unto God be all the glory' for what has been done in regard to your emancipation." Garrison then shared that he had looked forward to this day for nearly forty years, but he also never imagined meeting Dickerson and so many other emancipated Black people in a Southern state. Garrison continued, "I knew only one thing—all that I wanted to know—that you were a grievously oppressed people; and that, on every consideration of justice, humanity and right, you were entitled to immediate and unconditional freedom."[77]

Garrison, approaching sixty years of age, rejoiced that the task of abolishing slavery was complete. But the gospel paradox would persist. American slavery was vanquished, but it had already shaped and remade American Christianity in its image. There were Christians who continued to push and prod the nation toward fulfilling its promises of racial equality, but a whole lot of other Christians were also armed and ready to oppose them at every turn.

Reckoning

Chapter Eight

The Church That Never Was
(But Still Could Be)

Reckoning with history is not for the faint of heart. The past is powerful but dangerous, because our origin stories reside there. In 1912, German Protestant theologian Ernst Troeltsch asserted that "the understanding of the present is always the final goal of all history."[1] We are interested in history and study the past because we ultimately want to learn more about ourselves and how the world we inhabit came to be. Sometimes our focus is on personal or local histories, as we seek to uncover more about our family, our neighborhood, or our church. At other times we turn our attention to larger histories and pursue the stories that help us better grasp national or religious origins.

Throughout this book I have invited you to reckon with me about the making of American Christianity. I have told the stories of different Indigenous, Black, and white individuals and institutions to explain how settler colonialism and slavery have shaped Christianity in the United States. My heart soars when I think about those moments that exhibit the liberating hope of faith in action as Christians of different races and ethnicities joined together to remake a world that had been broken by the sins of settler colonialism and slavery. Cherokee and white Christians furiously opposed the unjust expulsion of the Cherokee Nation in Georgia. Black and white Christians together built the first autonomous Black church in Philadelphia. On the eve of the American Revolutionary War, the Black poet Phillis Wheatley and the Mohegan pastor Samson Occom exchanged letters. The two friends sought to encourage one another as each strived for justice in their respective racial communities.

Yet my heart also breaks because these very stories entail the tragedies of unrelenting oppression, interminable greed, and ruthless evil. The destructive forces of settler colonialism and slavery overwhelmed American Christianity. White Christians always had a choice. Some chose to seize Indigenous lands and enslave Black persons, over the principles of goodness and righteousness. White Christians who did not violently drive out Indigenous families or hold persons of African descent in bondage as their human property fully understood that they lived in a nation that was formed and sustained through these unjust racial oppressions. They too had a choice. Indigenous and Black Christians as well as their white allies were seeking racial equality and coexistence, not revenge and domination. They grieved the consequences of land dispossession and the transatlantic slave trade, but they also understood that it was impossible to turn back the clock and change the past. They therefore called upon white Christians to engage the injustices before them. Indigenous nations wanted the US federal government to uphold existing treaties and prevent further intrusions from white settlers. Black Americans wanted emancipation from slavery and access to the same opportunities as white persons in education and employment. Neither Indigenous nor Black Christians asked white Americans to give their communities restitution for past sins or preferential treatment in their present day. But the appeal to racial equality was either ignored or denied. Most white Americans chose the nation that was, rather than the nation that could be.

In *The Nation That Never Was: Reconstructing America's Story*, legal scholar Kermit Roosevelt III affirms the emergence of a more honest pursuit of US history today. Roosevelt commends how a growing number of Americans want more than the "standard story," which "told us [white Americans] reassuring things about ourselves—that we were good, that we always succeeded, that our history was a steady progress toward the realization of deep and noble founding ideals."[2] But it is hard for many to let go of this story. For some, the story is ingrained and provides ongoing nourishment and meaning. To revise the story is to uproot foundational understandings of oneself and one's community, and perhaps one's experience of national service in the US armed forces, Peace Corps, and other similar endeavors.

Yet the story needs to change, because it is simply not true. The United States was not founded as a multiracial democracy. Roosevelt observes that the Declaration of Independence expresses the ideal of equal rights, but the legal scholar summons a closer look at the document's origins and maintains that it was composed at a "specific moment" and "for a specific purpose": "to announce that the American colonists were throwing off allegiance to the British Crown and to justify that act."[3] The inclusion of Indigenous nations and Black persons in the document is strictly in reference to complaints against British imperialism. The one reference to Indigenous nations identifies them as "merciless Indian Savages" whom the British seek to marshal as military allies. The passing allusion to Black people is found in a solitary line about the "domestic insurrections amongst us," which is a grievance against the Virginia governor, Lord Dunmore, for his promise of freedom to enslaved persons who enlisted in his army against the rebelling patriots.[4]

Indigenous and Black soldiers fought for both sides in the American Revolutionary War. Veterans of color such as Black abolitionist James Forten battled alongside white patriots for American independence, but the victory they helped to achieve resulted in a democratic nation for white people only. The origins of the United States lie within English colonization, which was undergirded by the systems of settler colonialism and slavery, and these racial oppressions persisted (and in some cases intensified) as the nation developed and expanded in the nineteenth century.

The pursuit of a more honest origin story for American Christianity is also emerging, but I believe it is occurring at a slower pace than the public discourse about US history. Christians in every age have yearned for what Black sociologist W. E. B. Du Bois recognized as the "truer, better thing."[5] These believers were dissatisfied with the partial truths, deliberate omissions, and outright lies that marked the origin stories that they were told. In 1828, a sixty-six-year-old white woman author, Elizabeth Elkins Sanders, published her first work. The Indigenous rights movement to protect the Cherokee Nation from expulsion motivated Sanders to write a more accurate history of settler colonialism, Christianity, and Indigenous peoples. Sanders lived in Massachusetts and argued that the origin story that white New Englanders told themselves about the Puritan colonists failed to address the wicked religious justifications they crafted to oppress Indigenous inhabitants and dispossess them of their territories. Sanders maintained that these colonists willfully misconstrued Christian theology to falsely claim that the Indigenous peoples were "perpetually roaming" and therefore did not own their lands. She also admired the Cherokee preacher David Brown and in her essay cited one of his letters about Cherokee resistance to removal.[6]

Sanders published several other works about white Christian injustices toward Indigenous peoples, writing well into her eighties, and she is an admirable example of the lesson that one is never too old to begin a new vocation. Yet Sanders's life also illustrates that the truer and better origin story was always within grasp. The fullness of history was accessible to white American Christians. Many actively resisted the truth. But they still loved history. So they chose an origin story for white Christian America that presented white believers as intrepid pioneers who shared the message of eternal salvation to primitive Indigenous peoples and enslaved Africans. White Christians made mistakes, but they were primarily portrayed as the heroes trying to fix them. In the first half of the nineteenth century, the ostensibly inherent racial inferiority of Indigenous and Black persons was made the main cause of their demise, expulsion, and enslavement. Racial differences, rather than American racism, were the obstacle to racial equality. This pernicious myth later supported the cruel and unjust systems of racial segregation and American Indian reservations.

The origin story has evolved in recent generations and now omits some of the most overt racist ideologies and theologies. We no longer say that God created Indigenous and Black persons as racially inferior to white people, but racism remains a shadowy evil with no discernible human perpetrators. There is room in this origin story to entertain the notion that a few misguided white Christians did some bad and racist things, but they are treated as outliers. The "standard story" of the nation is powerful precisely because it is reassuring and aspirational. The origin story of American Christianity is even more potent, because it is a welding of how we understand ourselves as Americans and Christians. Both nationalism and faith are simultaneously formidable and fragile. Nothing inspires, provokes, animates, or divides like nationalism or faith. The only force stronger is found at the intersection of the two, most evident in the contest between abolitionism and proslavery Christianity, as each side based their arguments on patriotism and religion. Because the making of American Christianity rests on this intersection, this origin story is harder to revise. Many American Christians do not want to reckon with how the sins of settler colonialism and slavery shaped their country and corrupted their church.

Christianity has always been practiced by humans in specific contexts. As Christians move through the particularities of their time and space, their cultural perspectives and their religious interpretations continually interact with and shape one another. American Christianity was forged in the context of a nation rife with democratic fervor, economic ingenuity, moral compromise, and racial oppression. It is therefore unsurprising that American believers and churches enacted the Christian faith with these same impulses. The American idea that citizens could form their own government and elect their own leaders was a radical departure from life and thought in England and truly a bold political experiment in the late eighteenth century.

Similarly, the notion of a voluntary church comprised a new approach to Christianity. European observers marveled at the growth and strength of church life in the United States. Their churches at home relied upon direct financial support from the government, but American churches exercised an incarnational creativity as they fashioned themselves into institutional forms that resonated with the people living among them.

The outdoor camp meeting in a rural community and the formal worship service in an urban church building differed greatly from one another, but the gatherings shared a common purpose: preachers and worship leaders conveyed spiritual teachings in effective ways to help people know, feel, and commune with God in modes that were familiar and intelligible. Yet one severe limitation in the making of American Christianity is found in the failure of white churches on racial justice. As settler colonialism and slavery expanded in the nation, white American Christians committed a plethora of sins to perpetuate horrible crimes against Indigenous and Black people.

The propagation of racist theology, hollow evangelism, and hypocritical worship entails an abhorrent deviation from Christianity. Frederick Douglass differentiated between "Christianity proper" and American Christianity. The former was "good, pure, and holy," whereas the latter was "bad, corrupt, and wicked." Douglass asserted: "I therefore hate the corrupt, slaveholding, women-whipping, cradle-plundering, partial and hypocritical Christianity of this land."[7]

At one level, it is obvious why Christians today want to emphatically disavow and quickly dismiss the kind of Christianity that participated in settler colonialism and slavery. This history is traumatic and terrible. But at another level, we cannot simply look away from this history. We cannot understand our present without knowing our past.

But the pursuit of a more honest and complete history need not be a fatalistic task that results in hopelessness and despair. Renowned church historian Justo L. González explains how the study of Christian history can be illuminating and liberating: "If we are to break free from an undue bondage to tradition, we must begin by understanding what that tradition is, how we came to be where we are, and how particular elements in our past color our view of the present. It is then that we are free to choose which elements in the past—and in the present—we wish to reject, and which we will affirm."[8]

González never promises that this process of learning and discernment will be easy. It was hard for many American Christians two centuries ago, but some confronted how the past shaped their present and worked to undo the systems of racial oppression they inherited and inhabited. In doing so, they yearned for a church that never was, a church that integrated love and justice to embody a multiracial Christian community that actively participated in constructing a racially just society in the United States. But the church that never was is also the church that still could be. Although this historian does not have all the answers, I offer five insights in this chapter that seek to prompt discussion, aid discernment, and instigate action.

The church is not a strictly spiritual institution.

Christians assemble in churches for many reasons. Certainly two of the primary reasons are communal worship and religious education. But churches also meet social needs. In the antebellum United States, the composition of churches reflected the communities in which they resided and generally consisted of like-minded people sharing the same cultural sensibilities. In some towns and cities, mainstream Protestant churches differentiated themselves by doctrinal (religious) and class (social) distinctions. In 1844, George Lewis, a Presbyterian pastor from Scotland, visited Washington, DC, and it became readily apparent to him that "the wealthier and middle classes attend the Episcopal and Presbyterian churches" and "the poorer whites, and the coloured population, attend the Methodist and Baptist churches."[9] Lewis's specific observation of one city did not universally apply everywhere—not every Episcopalian and Presbyterian was wealthy and not every Methodist and Baptist was impoverished—but it does indicate that people joined churches for a combination of reasons. And one reason was the church's role as a hub of social belonging.

Churches therefore adhered to social customs and hierarchies. In colonial New England, persons of higher social rank were given priority during communion and received the elements first. On some occasions, ministers and lay leaders who were responsible for distributing the elements struggled to discern where to go with the bread and cup that represented the body and blood of Jesus Christ. In a colonial Massachusetts church, a deacon once deeply offended Samuel Sewall, a prominent and wealthy worshiper, when he offered the cup to another nearby worshiper before him. Churches in the North American colonies and the United States also practiced racial segregation in their sanctuaries. Worshipers of color sat in a designated section apart from white worshipers, and they also received the communion elements after white worshipers. Absalom Jones, Richard Allen, and several other Black worshipers angrily left a Methodist church in Philadelphia due to its enforcement of racial segregation. A few white worshipers also protested the racism within their churches, but many more accepted the discriminatory practices, because they resembled their white-dominant societies. In one Presbyterian church in New York City, a group of white worshipers in 1834 irately opposed the action of one of its members, the white abolitionist Arthur Tappan, when he invited Samuel Eli Cornish, his Black friend and colleague in the American Anti-Slavery Society, to sit next to him during worship. The pastor tried to reason with the enraged white members by noting that Jesus was a man of color, but he failed to persuade them to choose spiritual principles over social norms.[10]

The social aspects of church life are inescapable, and some components bear their own complexities. The tradition of adorning fancy apparel to worship, to look one's "Sunday best," has both religious and social motivations. A worshiper wants to dress finely to honor God and to impress fellow worshipers. For worshipers in the middling classes, Sunday worship provided the only time of the week in which one could wear their finest clothes, and the act of dressing up for church attendance was a means to restore dignity and celebrate self-worth. But some slave-owning church members clothed their enslaved persons in elegant churchgoing attire for the selfish purpose of flaunting in public their own kindness and generosity.

One pitfall for American churches is found in the overt and subtle ways that unjust social norms such as racial prejudice permeate the ministry and worship of a congregation. Churches must resemble the specific cultural contexts they inhabit, but the regnant social patterns should not determine the direction of their ministries. More than a few church members may resist the necessary imposition of the gospel, but there is no change without confrontation, no progress without protest, and no discipleship without dissent.

The church must equip people of faith for civic participation.

Many American Christians have struggled to discern how to negotiate the relationship between religion and politics. One reason is the centrality of politics in the United States. Political elections, especially presidential ones, dominate public discourse in this country, because it was founded as a democracy. It is not surprising that Americans care deeply about whom they vote for, since what first set the United States apart was the radical idea that a nation works best when its citizens choose their own leaders.

English Wesleyan Methodist pastor Frederick J. Jobson was one of many European observers who highlighted the passion, fury, and divisiveness of American politics. In 1857 Jobson expressed astonishment at how Americans viewed the politicians vying for their votes. Candidates were spoken of in either reverential or caustic tones, depending on whom one supported, and voters transformed the candidates into projections of their own intelligence and morality. English traveler and author Frances Trollope was also bewildered by how Americans identified themselves by the presidential candidate they preferred. One person exclaimed "Jackson forever" and another shouted "Clay forever," as both distinguished themselves by their political support for Andrew Jackson and Henry Clay, respectively.[11]

Politics have always mattered a great deal to Americans, because voting is a crucial component to civic participation. But American churches find themselves on a tightrope in seeking to fulfill their spiritual mission within this political context. Churches err when they elevate presidential politics to the highest priority of their ministry. But churches also stumble when they forgo the imperative to reform social injustices because they want to escape the intensity and rancor of presidential politics.

The extent to which the contentious political debate over slavery shaped American churches is evident in the ecclesiology of James Henley Thornwell. In 1851 the white South Carolinian proslavery theologian joined other Christian thinkers in his advocacy of the position that churches should refrain from participating in the abolition movement, because slavery was a political matter outside the spiritual jurisdiction of church governance. But Thornwell stretched the notion of an apolitical ecclesiology to an extreme measure and insisted that the church was not "a moral institute of universal good, whose business it is to wage war upon every form of human ill, whether social, civil, political or moral." He further argued that the Bible did not instruct churches "to construct society afresh" or "to adjust its elements in different proportions."[12]

In order to uphold the evil system of slavery, Thornwell stripped the American church bare and remade it into little more than a self-interested religious club. But proslavery Christians such as Thornwell never retreated from civic participation. They fervently defended slavery and actively opposed abolitionism. Churches applied this doctrine of the spirituality of the church selectively. It became a convenient tool to maintain a comfortable and easy approach to civic participation. Churches chose what social issues to engage in accordance with the interests of their congregants. After the Civil War, many white churches deemed racial prejudice and poverty as political matters beyond the scope of their spiritual ministries. But the same churches interpreted their mobilizing efforts to maintain segregationist laws (and establish their own private schools after integration) as within the bounds of appropriate and faithful civic participation.

American churches must acknowledge that the roots of our contemporary struggle to balance evangelism, worship, and social justice lie in proslavery Christianity. Equipping people of faith for civic participation is a long, hard, and worthy endeavor. Shirley Chisholm, the first Black woman to be elected to the US House of Representatives, challenged American churches in 1973 to incorporate civic participation within its spiritual mission: "Quite often the church gives the distinct impression that it is concerned exclusively with its own self-preservation, but the clergy must assume a strong role in preparing young men and women to function meaningfully as religiously oriented citizens who are able to cope with the economic, social, religious and political problems of the day."[13] The ministry of equipping religiously engaged citizens does not belong exclusively to any single denomination, tradition, theological viewpoint, or political party.

The task includes discussion and education about how biblical, ethical, and theological perspectives inform one's voting determinations, but it also extends beyond the ballot to discernment regarding how both individual congregants and the congregation itself can embody and enact the principles of love and justice locally, regionally, nationally, and globally. Every church across the spectrum of conservative, evangelical, mainline, and progressive Christianity has this mandate to educate, inform, pray, and act toward addressing the most pressing social injustices.

I am a seminary professor, and some of my students come from ecclesial traditions that emphasize the doctrine of the spirituality of the church. Our conversations therefore often engage the strong feeling of suspicion, or even outright antipathy, toward social justice that exists among more than a few Christians. I share my own parable to elucidate how Christian discipleship intersects with civic participation: One day, a pastor purchases a loaf of bread from a local bakery. While walking home, the pastor encounters a person who is hungry and impoverished. The pastor prays, "God, what are you calling me to do?" and decides to offer the loaf of bread to this person. But in addition to this act of charity, the gospel inspires the pastor to ask another question: "Why doesn't this person have bread in the first place?"

Christian ministry must be simultaneously devoted to pursuing worship that honors God in the church and to seeking liberation for persons facing oppression in the world. Since every person is a beloved child of God, created in God's image, Christians must work toward constructing a society in which every person has freedom, dignity, and fair structural access to education, employment, food, clean water, worship, and other necessities of life. In 1843, John Jay II, a lawyer and active member of the Episcopal Church, implored white Christians to confront "caste and slavery in the American church." Jay marked the complicity among white Christians toward racial oppression as a betrayal of scriptural teachings. He was also dismayed at how these Christians expended all their energy and piety to build magnificent sanctuaries and prove the religious superiority of their distinctive doctrines. Jay surmised, "Are we given to make arbitrary bodies for ourselves, parties, little sects, selfish distinctions, churches with the Church? Our hearts, then, are not large enough."[14] My challenge for churches to equip persons of faith for civic participation is ultimately a test of the heart. I am not criticizing churches for caring about their worship spaces and doctrinal distinctives, because I agree that these are important components of Christian ministry. But I want to amplify Jay's insight and ask whether our hearts are large enough to also enact justice, love, mercy, and righteousness in the world that we inhabit.

The church often mistakes congregational activity for civic action.

Churches can be busy places. Christians frequently point to the number of congregational activities as an indicator of ministry success. At one level, the presence of an array of worship services, youth group outings, Bible study meetings, short-term mission trips, reading groups, and committees is a sign of a vibrant congregation. But at another level, churches working toward racial justice fall short when they equate their congregational activities with concrete civic action. The racial justice ministries of some churches focus on two activities: reading groups and multicultural worship services. Reading groups select several books, ranging from fiction novels by authors of color to history and theology books about racism, and discuss them together. Committees plan occasional multicultural worship services that integrate liturgies, prayers, and songs from diverse racial and ethnic sources, and sometimes invite special choirs and preachers representing various communities of color. Both endeavors often invigorate a congregation. But these two activities alone do not amount to effective action if the goal is to participate in constructing a more racially just society. One way that churches can assess their ministries for racial justice is to examine how their congregational activities have resulted in civic actions. For example, how did our reading groups and multicultural worship services transform the lives and actions of individual church members? How is our church working to advance the common good in our local community?

I recognize that people across many organizations, including Christians in churches, enjoy activities. Activities are fun and meaningful ways to establish and fortify bonds as a group of different individuals collaboratively work toward achieving a common goal. But I also heed the warning from the Indigenous rights activist Jeremiah Evarts in 1827. Evarts recounted in his diary that his efforts to mobilize white churches toward racial justice were sometimes stymied by insufficient activity, not outright resistance. During one such visit to a church, Evarts found that its members heartily expressed interest in his work, but their immediate response was to form a committee that would recommend a plan for future involvement to the congregation.

Evarts remarked, "I do not flatter myself with the expectation of any great results." He outlined two significant obstacles to his work. One involved hostility as some antagonistic church members were easily offended when he sought to persuade them of his position. The other was equally insidious: "You are in danger of making people contented with themselves, when they do not give one fiftieth part as much as they ought to give."[15] The lure of making congregational activity the ends, rather than the means, of a church's racial justice ministry is strong. But church leaders must lovingly and firmly direct their congregations toward tangible civic action.

History informs our congregational activity and our civic action. But history, like biblical interpretation, is not an impartial discipline. People interpret the past in accordance with their perspectives, sources, and moral sensibilities. One obstacle for American Christians is that the study of church history has often fallen into the highlight reel trap. In Sunday school and seminary classrooms, church history is taught for the primary purpose of imitable inspiration. This approach therefore necessitates a presentation of historical actors that spurs believers toward love and good deeds. There is little room for depth and nuance, and the educational experience is akin to watching a highlight reel of isolated Christian moments devoid of context and light on content. Some approaches to church history intentionally distort the past to falsely bolster Christian triumphalism, but even the approaches that do not propagate this spurious agenda have left Christians unprepared to draw clear lessons and cogent applications from the fullness of history.

Randy Woodley, a Cherokee theologian, compares the superficiality of reconciliation gestures and services toward Indigenous peoples within white churches to the German theologian Dietrich Bonhoeffer's admonition against "cheap grace." Woodley explains why he and his spouse, Edith Woodley, an Eastern Shoshone tribal member, decline the many invitations they receive to assist in reconciliation activities. They believe that reconciliation "does not occur in a 'service' but must be wrought through working together on tough issues with Native American (or other) people in the midst of committed relationships."

Woodley identifies the historical ignorance of white Christians as a significant challenge to building such interracial partnerships. Too many white Christians do not know that the US government betrayed and oppressed Indigenous peoples. And Woodley finds that some mistakenly believe that their ecclesial traditions opposed these injustices. Woodley summarizes his response to this untrue assertion: "In almost every action of the government against America's host people the American church either actively participated (such as in boarding schools) or passively sat by and watched while unthinkable atrocities occurred."[16] Robert Tracy McKenzie, a history professor at Wheaton College, advises church historians to exercise care when teaching in local congregations. McKenzie acknowledges that part of the task requires speaking hard truths, but the historian warns against "employing a sledgehammer" when a "scalpel" will be more effective.[17] Yet it is difficult for church historians to implement this counsel on the histories and consequences of settler colonialism and slavery when every scalpel feels like a sledgehammer, because of the woeful miseducation in American Christianity.

The church should prioritize responsibility and repair over guilt and privilege.

Pequot pastor Willam Apess delivered a lecture before white audiences in 1835 and 1836 that differentiated between responsibility and guilt. He specifically stated that Indigenous peoples and white Americans were not guilty of their ancestors' crimes. But Apess also believed that past mistakes shaped present injustices in the world that everyone living in the 1830s inhabited. White American Christians therefore had a responsibility to repair the nation and church that they inherited. Roxanne Dunbar-Ortiz concludes her seminal work, *An Indigenous Peoples' History of the United States*, with an emphasis on Americans accepting responsibility "for the society they live in, which is a product of that past," because "assuming this responsibility provides a means of survival and liberation."[18] A clearer and fuller understanding of history is a crucial step toward accepting responsibility and enacting repair, because we need to precisely comprehend the consequences of settler colonialism and slavery in our neighborhoods, communities, churches, and nation.

One challenge that has emerged in recent years as we strive toward racial justice is the confusion between responsibility and guilt. I have participated in diversity, equity, and inclusion (DEI) workshops that intentionally and unintentionally accentuated guilt and privilege over responsibility and repair. The historical facts presented were accurate and therefore revealed an ugly, racist, and brutal past. But the objective in some cases was to induce guilt and shame from participants who were white or non-Indigenous and non-Black people of color. In other instances, facilitators moved the group from charting a timeline of past sins to ranking hierarchies of privilege in the present. Inherent and unearned privilege across race, gender, and class certainly exists in American society today, and privilege is a historically constructed phenomenon, but I find that racial privilege is often overemphasized and oversimplified. The task of understanding racial privilege is helpful when the exercise is directed toward responsibility and repair. It is important to recognize that some people, simply on the basis of skin color, have more access to flourishing than other people, and that people of color endure the harsh pains of racism in the arenas of education and employment as well as in the everyday rhythms of life. But I find that discussions of racial privilege quickly devolve into heated debates about how to incorporate gender, class, sexuality, and other considerations. I appreciate the attention to intersectionality, but I am discouraged when dialogues about privilege focus less on building diverse coalitions and more on determining who embodies the least privilege and who bears the most guilt.

I find that discussions of racial privilege also frequently conflate the histories of settler colonialism, slavery, and other racial oppressions in ways that obscure the unique histories of different communities of color. The descendants of Indigenous nations and the descendants of Black enslavement share a common history, but each community also has their own distinctive stories of courage, tragedy, joy, and subjugation. Other communities of color, such as Asian Americans, Hispanic Americans, and Latino/a Americans, have their own particular stories of hope, travail, resilience, and oppression.

Throughout this book I tell the stories of different Indigenous, Black, and white Christians. In doing so, I feature the witness of white Indigenous rights activists such as Harriett Ruggles Gold Boudinot and white abolitionists such as William Lloyd Garrison. Because Gold Boudinot and Garrison do not represent how most white Christians lived, it would be wrong to present them as counterpoints that disprove the failures of white Christianity. But their stories give us blueprints to learn from in our contemporary ministries of racial justice. One lesson is the necessity for white Christians to confront and rebuke the racist attitudes and actions of other white Christians, especially within their own churches and denominations. Church unity is one goal of Christian ministry, but we fall into grave sin and idolatry when we make church unity the only goal. We want to learn one another's stories to honor one another and more effectively work toward substantive repair that simultaneously addresses the consequences of specific historic sins and constructs a more just and inclusive society for people of all races, ethnicities, genders, classes, sexual orientations, and abilities.

Black theologian and ethicist Scott C. Williamson offers two insights that aid us in our journey of responsibility and repair. The first is that "character and circumstance render each other," meaning that our lives are "shaped by moral systems even as we lend shape to them." The second is that "we inherit and edit a moral world," or put in another way, we edit what we inherit.[19] In the age of settler colonialism and slavery, the racially unjust circumstances of these devastating realities shaped the life and faith of every American. Some persons displayed good character, many more exhibited bad character, and all of them together edited their moral world. In the same way that Americans then could not transcend the systems and structures of settler colonialism and slavery, we too cannot escape the nation that we have inherited. We rejoice in the reforms that have transpired and the progress that has been made, but we must also continue to repair the social injustices in our world today.

We do not need American churches to be exceptional, just faithful. The circumstances of voluntarism have shaped the character of American churches. As voluntary organizations, churches in this country have always exercised authenticity and imagination to meet the needs and wants of Christians across diverse social contexts. At their best, churches constantly integrate the pastoral and prophetic components of Christian ministry, such that their ministries provide comfort for the afflicted, meaningful opportunities for worship and fellowship, and spiritual instruction that leads to individual growth and social transformation. At their worst, churches succumb to larger cultural, economic, and social forces and promote a false gospel of self-interest and self-delusion with scriptural interpretations that justify the perpetuation of horrible sins. This is a hard but necessary truth we must acknowledge as editors of our moral world.

> *The church must be deeply hopeful and deeply honest*
> *about our past, present, and future.*

Just as the fullness of history inspires and infuriates us, so too does the complexity of our world today. There exist beauty and brokenness as well as abundance and scarcity all around us. Many Christians survey the ongoing contradictions and compromises within American Christianity and want to overturn desecrated tables just as Jesus did. Yet these same Christians are also thankful for the churches that have nurtured them, and they affirm the churches today that are enacting love and justice in their communities. John H. Leith, a white theologian, observes that "the church has never found it easy to balance gratitude with critical judgment."[20] The easier pathway is to set gratitude and critical judgment against one another in a winner-takes-all contest. And the church's struggle is also the nation's, as Americans grapple with practicing a patriotism that holds the successes, failures, ideals, and injustices of the United States in productive tension.

One irony is that churches have the resources to foster healthy and productive dialogues among persons with diverse cultural and political perspectives that enable mutual understanding and growth in balancing gratitude with critical judgment. Churches are voluntary associations that require foundational bonds of relational trust. Church members do not always agree on every issue, but they usually trust one another. Good pastors also develop strong relationships with church members over time and through accompaniment in hardship. But too many churches refrain from hosting difficult, urgent, and edifying conversations.

The notion of the "purple church" is recent in terms of nomenclature but as old as the church itself in US history. The common definition of the purple church today is a congregation in which persons who vote for (red) Republican Party candidates and persons who vote for (blue) Democratic Party candidates worship together. Other articulations extend the metaphor beyond political polarization to encompass a congregation with Christians who disagree on a variety of social and theological issues. The promises and perils within purple churches have therefore existed throughout the history of American Christianity, most notably on the struggle to end Black enslavement. Abolitionists directed their energy toward mobilizing churches because of the vital role that churches occupied in their society. But mainstream Protestant churches chose to avoid communal discussion and discernment on the greatest human rights violation of their day.

The possibilities of conflict and departure continue to temper the potential for deep and sustained engagement about our most pressing matters, such as how to honor military veterans and police officers while also dealing with the problems of excessive militarism and police brutality and how to support securing our nation's borders without demeaning refugees and vilifying immigrants. My challenge to purple churches is to continually examine the motivations for and outcomes of ministry. Civility and harmony are worthy virtues for a church to embody, but these principles need to be weighed alongside a church's mission of spiritual discipleship, religious education, and civic participation.

Churches can and have done great things that exemplify the love and justice of God. But churches also can do and have done terrible deeds in the name of the same God. Robert Allen Warrior, an Osage literary scholar, offers a new interpretation of the book of Exodus. Warrior observes that Christians across the Americas have drawn inspiration and insight from the stories of deliverance and migration regarding ancient Israel. European colonists understood their transatlantic journeys and settlements through the narrative lens of Exodus as they found hope, resolve, and justification for land theft and violence toward Indigenous peoples. Enslaved Black persons identified with the ancient Israelites and drew strength from their liberation from bondage and oppression. In the face of corrupt proslavery doctrines about providential Black racial inferiority and the promise of eternity as the only means of Black deliverance, these enslaved Christians believed that the Exodus story revealed a God who was truly on their side.

Warrior maintains that both theological interpretations overlook the Canaanite part of the Exodus narrative: "The obvious characters in the story for Native Americans to identify with are the Canaanites, the people who already lived in the promised land. . . . [T]he Canaanites should be at the center of Christian theological reflection and political action. They are the last remaining ignored voice in the text, except perhaps for the land itself."[21] To read a familiar scriptural text anew is inherently a risky undertaking because a multiplicity of interpretive possibilities awaits. Some pathways lead to profundity and inspiration, whereas others lead to perplexity and doubt. Similarly, there is simply no way to sterilize a reckoning with history and make it a fully safe endeavor. To study the making of American Christianity is to confront the facts of conquest and domination alongside testimonies of courage and protest. It is a story of dreams denied, dreams deferred, and dreams come true. Perhaps what C. S. Lewis wrote about love is also true of faith: "To love at all is to be vulnerable. Love anything, and your heart will certainly be wrung and possibly be broken."[22] Heartbreak need not mark the end of the journey, but it is a step toward a more honest faith and a more resilient hope.

One common thread across the stories of the Indigenous Christians, Black Christians, and white Indigenous rights activists and abolitionists featured in this book is that they all wrestled with disappointment. Their love for God and neighbor was steadfast, but they had to reconcile their faith in God with the apathy and opposition they encountered in many American churches. Not every church was bad, but not enough of them were good. One century after Lincoln's Emancipation Proclamation, a young Black Baptist minister was imprisoned in Birmingham, Alabama, for helping to organize a nonviolent demonstration against racial segregation. As Martin Luther King Jr. sat in a prison cell in 1963, he composed a letter reflecting on the resistance to racial justice that abounded in many white churches. King saw majestic churches filled with busy worshipers participating in a plethora of congregational activities and wondered, "What kind of people worship here? Who is their God?" He divulged that these questions swirled in his mind and caused him to weep. But King wrote that his tears were "tears of love": "There can be no deep disappointment where there is not deep love."[23]

In addition to teaching in my seminary classroom, I am grateful for the opportunities I have had to share my research in churches and church-related institutions. It is invigorating to meet people of faith and reckon with history together. Their insights and questions have challenged, deepened, and sharpened my analysis. On one occasion, a person asked me about this book project. After hearing my answer, the person exclaimed, "Oh my, you are writing the kind of book that is going to make people lose their faith." I concede that this is one possibility. But there is another outcome. Perhaps readers will not lose their faith but *find* it in the pages of this book.

Notes

Chapter 1: The Church with the Soul of a Nation

1. Ebenezer Davies, *American Scenes, and Christian Slavery: A Recent Tour of Four Thousand Miles in the United States* (London: John Snow, 1849), iii. English primary sources from the fifteenth to nineteenth centuries sometimes employed a style of capitalization that is unlike our contemporary age. Several words, in addition to proper nouns, in any given sentence begin in upper case form. Historians and scholars have made different decisions regarding quotations from these sources. Some retained the original, whereas others, as early as the nineteenth century, made revisions in accordance with the upper and lower cases familiar to us today. Existing anthologies and sourcebooks also differ on this editorial matter. My decision throughout the book is to revise capitalization while otherwise retaining the original spelling and grammar of cited primary sources unless specifically noted.

2. Davies, *American Scenes, and Christian Slavery*, 26.

3. Edwin Scott Gaustad, *Historical Atlas of Religion in America* (New York: Harper & Row, 1962), 43.

4. *The American Almanac and Repository of Useful Knowledge, for the Year 1850* (Boston: Charles C. Little & James Brown, 1849), 208.

5. C. C. Goen, *Broken Church, Broken Nation: Denominational Schisms and the Coming of the American Civil War* (Macon, GA: Mercer University Press, 1985), 54. Goen lists 5,536 Methodist churches (45.3%), 4,495 Baptist churches (36.8%), 1,423 Presbyterian churches (11.7%), and 762 churches from all other traditions (6.2%).

6. Davies, *American Scenes, and Christian Slavery*, 26–27, and Frances Trollope, *Domestic Manners of the Americans*, 4th ed. (London: Whittaker, Treacher, & Co., 1832), 189.

7. Davies, *American Scenes, and Christian Slavery*, 27 and 29. I revise "West India eyes" to "West Indian eyes."

8. Davies, *American Scenes, and Christian Slavery*, 64 and 71–72.

9. E. Wyn James, "'Blessèd Jubil!': Slavery, Mission and the Millennial Dawn in the Work of William Williams of Pantycelyn," in *Cultures of Radicalism in Britain and Ireland*, ed. John Kirk, Michael Brown, and Andrew Noble (London: Pickering & Chatto, 2013), 95–112. The verses to "O'er the Gloomy Hills of Darkness" are found on pages 101–2. I retain all capitalizations within the original.

209

10. James, "'Blessèd Jubil!,'" 109.

11. Davies, *American Scenes, and Christian Slavery,* 150. I revise "Slave-holders" to "Slaveholders."

12. "James McCune Smith to Gerrit Smith, December 28–31, 1846," in *The Works of James McCune Smith: Black Intellectual and Abolitionist,* ed. John Stauffer (New York: Oxford University Press, 2006), 303–4.

13. Gerrit Smith, *Three Discourses on the Religion of Reason* (New York: Ross & Tousey, 1859), 8. Smith originally delivered this discourse on February 21, 1858.

14. Gerrit Smith, *Letter of Gerrit Smith to Rev. James Smylie of the State of Mississippi* (New York: R. G. Williams, 1837), 62.

15. Smith, *Three Discourses on the Religion of Reason,* 9.

16. Smith, *Three Discourses,* 16–17. I revise "wide-spread" to "widespread."

17. Smith, *Three Discourses,* 17.

18. Harriet Martineau, *Society in America,* vol. 1 (Paris: Baudry's European Library, 1842), 71. The work was initially published as three volumes in 1837. This edition includes all content in two volumes.

19. Martineau, *Society in America,* vol. 1, 65.

20. Martineau, *Society in America,* vol. 1, 68–72.

21. Colin G. Calloway, *The Indian World of George Washington: The First President, the First Americans, and the Birth of the Nation* (New York: Oxford University Press, 2018), 4.

22. Martineau, *Society in America,* vol. 2 (Paris: Baudry's European Library, 1842), 219.

23. Philip Schaff, *America: A Sketch of the Political, Social, and Religious Character of the United States of North America, in Two Lectures, Delivered at Berlin, with a Report Read before the German Church Diet at Frankfort-on-the-Maine, September 1854* (New York: C. Scribner, 1855), 87–88.

24. Martineau, *Society in America,* vol. 2, 242–43.

25. Martineau, *Society in America,* vol. 2, 244.

26. Sidney E. Mead, *The Nation with the Soul of a Church* (New York: Harper & Row, 1975), 4.

27. Robert N. Bellah, "Civil Religion in America," *Daedalus* 96, no. 1 (Winter 1967): 4.

28. Mead, *Nation with the Soul of a Church,* 125.

29. Mead, *Nation with the Soul of a Church,* 48.

30. Mead, *Nation with the Soul of a Church,* 56–57.

31. Lyman Beecher, *The Memory of Our Fathers, a Sermon Delivered at Plymouth, on the Twenty-Second of December, 1827* (Boston: T. R. Marvin, 1828), 13–14. Mead cites this part of Beecher's sermon, without the connection to Forefathers' Day, as an illustration of the merging between Protestantism and American exceptionalism. See Mead, *Nation with the Soul of a Church,* 71–72.

32. Alexis de Tocqueville, *Democracy in America,* vol. 1, trans. Henry Reeve, Francis Bowen, and Phillips Bradley (New York: Alfred A. Knopf, 1960), 67 and 242. This work was first published in 1835.

33. Gustave de Beaumont, *Marie, or Slavery in the United States: A Novel of Jacksonian America,* trans. Barbara Chapman (Stanford, CA: Stanford University Press, 1958), 37–38. This work was first published in 1835.

34. Frederick J. Jobson, *America, and American Methodism* (New York: Virtue, Emmins, 1857), 80.

35. Jobson, *America, and American Methodism,* 30.

36. Tocqueville, *Democracy in America,* 244.

37. Tocqueville, *Democracy in America,* 12–13, 231, 339–42.

38. Beaumont, *Marie,* 46.

39. Jobson, *America, and American Methodism,* 284–85.

40. Jobson, *America, and American Methodism*, 285–86.
41. Jobson, *America, and American Methodism*, 86.
42. Jobson, *America, and American Methodism*, 88.
43. Jobson, *America, and American Methodism*, 393.
44. Beaumont, *Marie*, 34.
45. Beaumont, *Marie*, 73–74, and 81–84.
46. Jane Louise Mesick, *The English Traveller in America, 1785–1835* (New York: Columbia University Press, 1922), 27.
47. Vincent Carretta, *Phillis Wheatley: Biography of a Genius in Bondage* (Athens: University of Georgia Press, 2011), 46.
48. Phillis Wheatley, *Memoir and Poems of Phillis Wheatley, a Native African and a Slave* (Boston: Geo. W. Light, 1834), 9–10. Margaretta Matilda Odell, a relative of Susanna Wheatley, composed a brief biographical introduction of Wheatley in this volume.
49. Carretta, *Phillis Wheatley*, 4–7.
50. Wheatley, *Memoir and Poems*, 9.
51. "Phillis Wheatley to Rev. Samson Occom, February 11, 1774," in *Letters from Black America: Intimate Portraits of the African American Experience*, ed. Pamela Newkirk (Boston: Beacon, 2009), 91.
52. "Phillis Wheatley to Rev. Samson Occom, February 11, 1774," in Newkirk, *Letters from Black America*, 92. See also James P. Byrd and James Hudnut-Beumler, *The Story of Religion in America: An Introduction* (Louisville, KY: Westminster John Knox, 2021), 124.
53. "Benjamin Banneker to Secretary of State Thomas Jefferson, August 19, 1791," in Newkirk, *Letters from Black America*, 93.
54. "Phillis Wheatley to Rev. Samson Occom, February 11, 1774," in Newkirk, *Letters from Black America*, 92.
55. Samson Occom, "Thou Shalt Love Thy Neighbor as Thyself," in *The Collected Writings of Samson Occom, Mohegan: Leadership and Literature in Eighteenth-Century Native America*, ed. Joanna Brooks (New York: Oxford University Press, 2006), 199. According to Occom's diary, he preached this sermon on May 13, 1787.
56. Occom, "Thou Shalt Love Thy Neighbor as Thyself," 206. I revise "Slaves too," to "slaves too?"
57. Occom, "To the Oneida Tribe," in *The Collected Writings of Samson Occom, Mohegan: Leadership and Literature in Eighteenth-Century Native America*, 112. I revise "Peace Maker" to "peacemaker" and "quarrils" to "quarrels."
58. Thomas S. Kidd, *The Great Awakening: The Roots of Evangelical Christianity in Colonial America* (New Haven, CT: Yale University Press, 2007), 305.
59. Occom, "Thou Shalt Love Thy Neighbor as Thyself," 201 and 204. I revise "showd" to "showed" and "dispisd" to "despised."
60. "Declaration of Independence: A Transcription, July 4, 1776," The US National Archives and Records Administration, https://www.archives.gov/founding-docs/declaration-transcript. I retain all capitalizations within the original.
61. Thomas Jefferson, *Notes on the State of Virginia* (Boston: Lilly & Wait, 1832), 144 and 146.
62. Jefferson, *Notes on the State of Virginia*, 146–47.
63. Jefferson, *Notes on the State of Virginia*, 144–45.
64. "From Thomas Jefferson to Chastellux, June 7, 1785," in *The Papers of Thomas Jefferson*, vol. 8, *February 1785 to October 1785*, ed. Julian P. Boyd (Princeton, NJ: Princeton University Press, 1953), 184.

65. Jefferson, *Notes on the State of Virginia*, 169–70.

66. Jefferson, *Notes on the State of Virginia*, 170.

67. Jefferson, *Notes on the State of Virginia*, 147 and 171. I revise "almighty" to "Almighty." See also Byrd and Hudnut-Beumler, 108–9.

68. Francis Le Jau, *The Carolina Chronicle of Dr. Francis Le Jau, 1706–1717*, ed. Frank J. Klingberg (Berkeley and Los Angeles: University of California Press, 1956), 16 and 28–30.

69. Le Jau, *The Carolina Chronicle*, 24. I revise "appearance, their in reality" to "appearances, theirs in reality."

70. Le Jau, *The Carolina Chronicle*, 50. I revise "Whispers & Conduct" to "whispers and conduct" and "wou'd" to "would."

71. Absalom Jones and Richard Allen, "A Narrative of the Proceedings of the Black People, during the Late Awful Calamity in Philadelphia, in the Year, 1793," in *Negro Protest Pamphlets*, ed. Dorothy Porter (New York: Arno Press, 1969), 5.

72. Jones and Allen, "A Narrative of the Proceedings," 20–21.

73. Joel W. Martin, introduction, in *Native Americans, Christianity, and the Reshaping of the American Religious Landscape*, ed. Joel W. Martin and Mark A. Nicholas (Chapel Hill: University of North Carolina Press, 2010), 1.

74. "Address of Dewi Brown, a Cherokee Indian," in *Proceedings of the Massachusetts Historical Society*, vol. 12, *1871–1873*, 30–31. I revise "catastrophies" to "catastrophes." Several newspapers published extracts from Brown's address in 1823 and following. One white woman from Salem, Elizabeth Manning Peabody, copied the entire original manuscript, and the Massachusetts Historical Society published her version as "Address of Dewi Brown, a Cherokee Indian" in February 1871. See Joel W. Martin, "Crisscrossing Projects of Sovereignty and Conversion: Cherokee Christians and New England Missionaries During the 1820s," in Martin and Nicholas, *Native Americans, Christianity, and the Reshaping of the American Religious Landscape*, 86.

75. "Address of Dewi Brown, a Cherokee Indian," 35–37.

76. E. Brooks Holifield, "On Teaching the History of Christianity: Traditions and Presuppositions," *Church History* 72, no. 2 (June 2003): 238.

77. Holifield, "On Teaching the History," 239.

78. Samuel H. Moffett, *A History of Christianity in Asia*, vol. 2, *1500–1900* (Maryknoll, NY: Orbis, 2005), xiii.

79. Charles Augustus Briggs further criticized the doctrine of biblical inerrancy on the grounds that it was a modern invention that biblical scholars and theologians devised in response to the rise of historical criticism: "The Bible itself nowhere makes this claim [of inerrancy]. The creeds of the Church nowhere sanction it. It is the ghost of modern evangelicalism to frighten children." See Charles Augustus Briggs, *The Authority of Holy Scripture: An Inaugural Address*, 2nd ed., *with Preface and Appendix Containing Additional Notes and Explanations* (New York: Charles Scribner's Sons, 1891), 35.

80. Briggs, *The Authority of Holy Scripture*, 29.

81. Le Jau, *The Carolina Chronicle*, 102.

82. John Fletcher, *Studies on Slavery: In Easy Lessons* (Natchez, MS: Jackson Warner, 1852), 407–8, and Elizabeth Fox-Genovese and Eugene D. Genovese, *The Mind of the Master Class: History and Faith in the Southern Slaveholders' Worldview* (Cambridge and New York: Cambridge University Press, 2005), 558.

83. Isaac McCoy, *Remarks on the Practicability of Indian Reform, Embracing Their Colonization* (Boston: Lincoln & Edmands, 1827), 13, and Isaac McCoy, *Address to the Philanthropists in the*

United States, Generally, and to Christians in Particular, on the Condition and Prospects of the American Indians (n.p., 1831), 7. I revise "favoured" to "favored."

Chapter 2: "What Right Have I to Go Live in the Heathens' Country?"

1. Lisa Brooks and Kelly Wisecup, "Plymouth in Patuxet: A Reorientation," in *Plymouth Colony: Narratives of English Settlement and Native Resistance from the Mayflower to King Philip's War*, ed. Lisa Brooks and Kelly Wisecup (New York: Library of America, 2022), xv.
2. John G. Turner, *They Knew They Were Pilgrims: Plymouth Colony and the Contest for American Liberty* (New Haven, CT: Yale University Press, 2020), 7–8.
3. Turner, *They Knew They Were Pilgrims*, 40–41.
4. Turner, *They Knew They Were Pilgrims*, 86.
5. Robert Cushman, "Reasons and Considerations Touching the Lawfulness of Removing out of England into the Parts of America," in *A Journal of the Pilgrims at Plymouth*, ed. Dwight B. Heath (New York: Corinth Books, 1963), 91.
6. Cushman, "Reasons and Considerations," 89.
7. A. R. Michell, "The European Fisheries in Early Modern History," in *The Cambridge Economic History of Europe*, vol. 5, *The Economic Organization of Early Modern Europe*, ed. E. E. Rich and C. H. Wilson (Cambridge: Cambridge University Press, 1977), 155 and 158.
8. Cushman, "Reasons and Considerations," 91.
9. Eric Williams, *Capitalism and Slavery* (London: Andre Deutsch, 1964), 4. This work was first published in 1944.
10. David J. Silverman, *This Land Is Their Land: The Wampanoag Indians, Plymouth Colony, and the Troubled History of Thanksgiving* (New York: Bloomsbury, 2019), 26–27.
11. Cushman, "Reasons and Considerations," 91–93. I revise "Gen. 13:6" to "Genesis 13:6."
12. Lawrence A. Clayton and David M. Lantigua, introduction, in *Bartolomé de las Casas and the Defense of Amerindian Rights: A Brief History with Documents*, ed. Lawrence A. Clayton and David M. Lantigua (Tuscaloosa: University of Alabama Press, 2020), 6–7.
13. Bartolomé de las Casas, "History of the Indies, ca. 1503–1509," in Clayton and Lantigua, *Bartolomé de las Casas*, 41.
14. Luke Glanville, David Lupher, and Maya Feile Tomes, introduction, in *Sepúlveda on the Spanish Invasion of the Americas: Defending Empire, Debating Las Casas*, ed. Luke Glanville, David Lupher, and Maya Feile Tomes (New York: Oxford University Press, 2023), 35.
15. Glanville, Lupher, and Tomes, *Sepúlveda on the Spanish Invasion*, 18–20.
16. Glanville, Lupher, and Tomes, *Sepúlveda on the Spanish Invasion*, 13.
17. Christopher Columbus, *The Log of Christopher Columbus*, trans. Robert H. Fuson (Camden, ME: International Marine Publishing, 1987), 76–77.
18. Clayton and Lantigua, *Bartolomé de las Casas*, 6.
19. Gustavo Gutiérrez, *Las Casas: In Search of the Poor of Jesus Christ*, trans. Robert R. Barr (Maryknoll, NY: Orbis, 1993), 436–41.
20. Glanville, Lupher, and Tomes, *Sepúlveda on the Spanish Invasion*, 35–51, and Clayton and Lantigua, *Bartolomé de las Casas*, 19.
21. Bartolomé de las Casas, "The Only Way of Attracting All Peoples to the True Religion, ca. 1534," in Clayton and Lantigua, *Bartolomé de las Casas*, 75.
22. Bartolomé de las Casas, "In Defense of the Indians, ca. 1550–1552," in Clayton and Lantigua, *Bartolomé de las Casas*, 80.
23. Glanville, Lupher, and Tomes, *Sepúlveda on the Spanish Invasion*, 48.

24. This is a slightly abbreviated title of this translated edition of Bartolomé de las Casas's *Brevísima relación de la destrucción de las Indias*. See *The Tears of the Indians: Being an Historical and True Account of the Cruel Massacres and Slaughters of Above Twenty Millions of Innocent People Committed by the Spaniards in the Islands of Hispaniola, Cuba, Jamaica, Etc. As Also in the Continent of Mexico, Peru, and Other Places of the West Indies, to the Total Destruction of Those Countries*, ed. John Phillips (London: J. C., 1656).

25. Kristina Bross, *Dry Bones and Indian Sermons: Praying Indians in Colonial America* (Ithaca, NY: Cornell University Press, 2004), 15. I retain the original spelling of the English title to *Historia natural y moral de las Indias*.

26. José de Acosta, *Natural and Moral History of the Indies*, trans. Frances M. López-Morillas (Durham, NC: Duke University Press, 2002), 44–45. This work was first published in 1590.

27. Gutiérrez, *Las Casas*, 427 and 617. Gutiérrez examines multiple editions of José de Acosta's *De procuranda Indorum salute* and notes how the Biblioteca de Autores Católicos edition shortens a passage in which Acosta sharply criticizes the greed of Spanish colonization.

28. Edmund S. Morgan, *American Slavery, American Freedom: The Ordeal of Colonial Virginia* (New York: W. W. Norton, 2003), 8. This work was first published in 1975. I retain the original spelling of John Ponet's title.

29. Morgan, *American Slavery, American Freedom*, 25–35.

30. Thomas Hariot, *A Briefe and True Report of the New Found Land of Virginia* (New York: J. Sabin, 1871), 24. This work was first published in 1588. I revise "Deere" to "deer"; "feare" to "fear"; "inhabite" to "inhabit."

31. Hariot, *A Briefe and True Report*, 25–27.

32. Morgan, *American Slavery, American Freedom*, 38–39.

33. Morgan, *American Slavery, American Freedom*, 37. I revise "to confesse a truthe" to "To confess a truth:" and "quietter" to "quieter."

34. "Letters Patent to Sir Thomas Gates, Sir George Somers, and Others, for Two Several Colonies and Plantations, to Be Made in Virginia, and Other Parts and Territories of America," in *The Statutes at Large; Being a Collection of All the Laws of Virginia from the First Session of the Legislature, in the Year 1619*, vol. 1, ed. William Waller Hening (New York: R. & W. & G. Bartow, 1823), 57. I revise "licence" to "license."

35. "Letters Patent to Sir Thomas Gates," 57–58.

36. Edward W. Said, *Culture and Imperialism* (New York: Vintage, 1994), 9.

37. D. K. Fieldhouse, *Colonialism, 1870–1945: An Introduction* (New York: St. Martin's Press, 1981), 7.

38. Walter L. Hixson, *American Settler Colonialism: A History* (New York: Palgrave Macmillan, 2013), 4.

39. Patrick Wolfe, "Settler Colonialism and the Elimination of the Native," *Journal of Genocide Research* 8, no. 4 (2006): 387–409.

40. Deborah Bird Rose, *Hidden Histories: Black Stories from Victoria Rover Downs, Humbert River and Wave Hill Stations* (Canberra: Aboriginal Studies Press, 1991), 46.

41. Powhatan's proper name was Wahunsenacawh. He was the *weroance* (commander) of a confederacy comprising six tribes: Appamattuck, Arrohateck, Mattaponi, Pamunkey, Powhatan, and Youghtanund. Several scholars have used "Powhatans" or "Powhatan Indians" when referring to Indigenous peoples belonging to this confederacy. See Helen C. Rountree, *Pocahontas, Powhatan, Opechancanough: Three Indian Lives Changed by Jamestown* (Charlottesville: University of Virginia Press, 2005), 16–29.

42. Karen Ordahl Kupperman, *The Jamestown Project* (Cambridge, MA: Harvard University Press, 2008), 222. I revise "monarchicall" to "monarchical" and "civill" to "civil."

43. Kupperman, *Jamestown Project*, 150. I revise "Soile" to "soil" and "Spaniards" to "Spaniard."

44. Kupperman, *Jamestown Project*, 227.

45. Morgan, *American Slavery, American Freedom*, 83–84.

46. James Axtell, *The Invasion Within: The Contest of Cultures in Colonial North America* (New York: Oxford University Press, 1985), 30.

47. Kupperman, *Jamestown Project*, 192.

48. Kupperman, *Jamestown Project*, 242–43. Adjustments to 2023 US dollars here and following come from MeasuringWorth.com, a website founded by Samuel H. Williamson, emeritus professor of economics at Miami University.

49. William Symonds, *Virginia: A Sermon Preached at White-Chapel, in the Presence of Many, Honourable and Worshipfull, the Adventurers and Planters for Virginia, 25 April 1609* (London: Edgar & Welby, 1609), 1, 6, 8, 10, and 15. I revise "countrey" to "country"; "rule, and governe it in their owne right" to "rule and govern it in their own right"; "equitie" to "equity"; "bloudy" to "bloody"; "Gospell" to "gospel"; "Virgine to Christ" to "virgin to Christ."

50. Robert Gray, *A Good Speed to Virginia* (London: Welby, 1609), no page numbers. I revise "generall residencie" to "general residence" and "downe the Countrey" to "down the country."

51. William Crashaw, *A Sermon Preached in London before the Right Honorable the Lord Lavvarre, Lord Governour and Captaine General of Virginia, and Others of His Majesties Counsell for That Kingdome, and the Rest of the Adventurers in That Plantation* (London: Welby, 1609), no page numbers. I revise "faire and lawfull" to "fair and lawful" and "cover their soules" to "cover their souls."

52. Russell Bourne, *Gods of War, Gods of Peace: How the Meeting of Native and Colonial Religions Shaped Early America* (New York: Harcourt, 2002), 33, and Jerome J. McGann, *Culture and Language at Crossed Purposes: The Unsettled Records of American Settlement* (Chicago: University of Chicago Press, 2022), 25–26. Massasoit's proper name was Ousamequin, and he is referred to as either Massasoit or Ousamequin. Massasoit means "great sachem" in Wampanoag.

53. Axtell, *Invasion Within*, 158.

54. Bourne, *Gods of War*, 33.

55. Lisa Brooks and Kelly Wisecup, "James Rosier: A True Relation—The Editors' Comment," in Brooks and Wisecup, *Plymouth Colony*, 34.

56. James Rosier, "A True Relation of the Most Prosperous Voyage Made This Presente Yeare 1605," in Brooks and Wisecup, *Plymouth Colony*, 26. I revise "travellers" to "travelers."

57. Rosier, "True Relation," 23. I revise "harbours" to "harbors" and "itselfe from God and nature affoordeth as much diversitie" to "itself from God and nature affordeth as much diversity."

58. Rosier, "True Relation," 13 and 28. I revise "kinde civility" to "kind civility" and "true zeale of promulgating Gods holy Church" to "true zeal of promulgating God's holy Church."

59. Kirkpatrick Sale, *Christopher Columbus and the Conquest of Paradise* (London: Tauris Parke, 2006), 98. This work was first published in 1990.

60. Charles C. Mann, *1491: New Revelations of the Americas before Columbus*, 2nd ed. (New York: Vintage, 2011), 31.

61. Mann, *1491*, 99–105.

62. Mann, *1491*, 62, and Silverman, *This Land Is Their Land*, 95–103.

63. Thomas Morton, *The New English Canaan* (Boston: Prince Society, 1883), 132–33. This work was first published in 1637. I revise "died on heapes" to "died in heaps"; "severall" to "several"; "new found Golgotha" to "newfound Golgotha."

64. Richard W. Pointer, *Encounters of the Spirit: Native Americans and European Colonial Religion* (Bloomington and Indianapolis: Indiana University Press, 2007), 165. I revise "small Pox" to "smallpox."

65. Edward Winslow, "Good News from New England," in *Good News from New England by Edward Winslow: A Scholarly Edition*, ed. Kelly Wisecup (Amherst: University of Massachusetts Press, 2014), 114. This work was first published in 1624.

66. John Winthrop, "A Model of Christian Charity," in *The Puritans in America: A Narrative Anthology*, ed. Alan Heimert and Andrew Delbanco (Cambridge, MA: Harvard University Press, 1985), 83.

67. Winthrop, "Model of Christian Charity," 91.

68. John Winthrop, "Reasons to Be Considered," in *Proceedings of the Massachusetts Historical Society*, vol. 8, *1864–1865* (Boston: Wiggin & Lunt, 1866), 422–23. This work was first written in 1629. I revise "soweing, and feeding" to "sowing and feeding"; "inclose noe land" to "enclose no land"; "setled" to "settled"; "& soe have noe other but a naturall right to those countries" to "and so have no other but a natural right to those countries."

69. Winthrop, "Reasons to be Considered," 423. I revise "more then" to "more than."

70. William Cronon, *Changes in the Land: Indians, Colonists, and the Ecology of New England* (New York: Hill & Wang, 1983), 57. I revise "Countrey" to "country" and "yeare" to "year."

71. Edwin S. Gaustad, *Liberty of Conscience: Roger Williams in America* (Grand Rapids: Eerdmans, 1991), 35.

72. John M. Barry, *Roger Williams and the Creation of the American Soul* (New York: Viking, 2012), 205–7.

73. Edwin S. Gaustad, *Roger Williams: Prophet of Liberty* (New York: Oxford University Press, 2001), 37–38.

74. Roger Williams, *A Key into the Language of America: Or, an Help to the Language of the Natives in That Part of America, Called New-England* (London: Gregory Dexter, 1643), 16 and 53. I revise "finde" to "find."

75. William Kellaway, *The New England Company, 1649–1776: Missionary Society to the American Indians* (New York: Barnes & Noble, 1962), 4. I revise "possesse" to "possess" and "gaine" to "gain."

76. Gaustad, *Roger Williams: Prophet*, 48–49.

77. Cushman, "Reasons and Considerations," 91.

78. William Wood, *New England's Prospect* (London: Bellamie, 1634), 56. I revise "in relation to the Indians, is divided" to "in relation to the Indians is divided" and "severall division being swayde by a severall king" to "several division being swayed by a several king."

79. Wolfe, "Settler Colonialism," 390.

Chapter 3: "If the People of the United States Will Imitate the Ruler Who Coveted Naboth's Vineyard"

1. E. C. Tracy, *Memoir of the Life of Jeremiah Evarts, Esq.* (Boston: Crocker & Brewster, 1845), 10. See also John A. Andrew III, *From Revivals to Removal: Jeremiah Evarts, the Cherokee Nation, and the Search for the Soul of America* (Athens: University of Georgia Press, 2007), 10–11. This work was first published in 1992.

2. Tracy, *Memoir of the Life of Jeremiah Evarts,* 12.

3. Andrew, *From Revivals to Removal,* 18.

4. Joseph Tracy, *History of the American Board of Foreign Commissioners for Foreign Missions* (Worcester, MA: Spooner & Howland, 1840), 345.

5. Jeremiah Evarts, "Essays on the Present Crisis in the Condition of the American Indians (1829)," in Jeremiah Evarts, *Cherokee Removal: The "William Penn" Essays and Other Writings,* ed. Francis Paul Prucha (Knoxville: University of Tennessee Press, 1981), 50.

6. "Barack Obama: Al-Arabiya Television Interview with Hisham Melhem, January 26, 2009," https://www.americanrhetoric.com/speeches/barackobama/barackobamaal -arabiya.htm. See also Mahmood Mamdani, *Neither Settler nor Native: The Making and Unmaking of Permanent Minorities* (Cambridge, MA: Harvard University Press, 2020), 37. Mamdani provides cogent analysis of Obama's remarks but mistakenly attributes them to Obama's first inaugural address on January 20, 2009, instead of a television interview six days later.

7. Martin Luther King Jr., *Why We Can't Wait* (New York: Harper & Row, 1964), 130–31.

8. Mamdani, *Neither Settler nor Native,* 37.

9. Mamdani, *Neither Settler nor Native,* 38.

10. Randall Kennedy, "The Limits of Exceptionalism," *Time,* January 28, 2013.

11. Theresa Stewart-Ambo and K. Wayne Yang, "Beyond Land Acknowledgment in Settler Institutions," *Social Text* 39, no. 1 (March 2021): 23.

12. Stewart-Ambo and Yang, "Beyond Land Acknowledgment," 26. I revise "kinship and alliance" to "kinship, and alliance."

13. Francis Jennings, *The Invasion of America: Indians, Colonialism, and the Cant of Conquest* (New York: W. W. Norton, 1975), 15.

14. Increase Mather, *An Earnest Exhortation to the Inhabitants of New England* (Boston: John Foster, 1676), 9.

15. Mather, *Earnest Exhortation,* 12. Italics in original.

16. Mather, *Earnest Exhortation,* 12. I revise "profess themselves Christians, have forsaken Churches, and Ordinances" to "profess themselves Christians have forsaken churches and ordinances." On William Bradford's failed experiment in communal farming at Plymouth, see Neal Salisbury, *Manitou and Providence: Indians, Europeans, and the Making of New England, 1500–1643* (New York: Oxford University Press, 1984), 141–44.

17. Jennings, *Invasion of America,* 105–45, and Joanna Brooks, "Petitions and Tribal Documents," in *The Collected Writings of Samson Occom, Mohegan: Leadership and Literature in Eighteenth-Century Native America,* ed. Joanna Brooks (New York: Oxford University Press, 2006), 143.

18. David E. Wilkins, *Hollow Justice: A History of Indigenous Claims in the United States* (New Haven, CT: Yale University Press, 2013), 5.

19. Jedidiah Morse, *A Report to the Secretary of War of the United States, on Indian Affairs, Comprising a Narrative of a Tour Performed in the Summer of 1820* (New Haven, CT: S. Converse, 1822), 15 and 94.

20. Jill Lepore, *These Truths: A History of the United States* (New York: W. W. Norton, 2019), 16–17. This work was first published in 2018.

21. Francis Higginson, *New England's Plantation, or, A Short and True Description of the Commodities and Discommodities of That Country* (London: Michael Sparke, 1630), no page numbers. I revise "aboundance of Sea-Fish are" to "abundance of sea fish is"; "beleeving" and "beleeved" to "believing" and "believed"; "seene it with mine owne" to "seen it with my own"; "poore" to

"poor"; "possesse" to "possess"; "Timber & Fire" to "timber and fire"; "yeelds" to "yields"; "then many Noble men" to "than many noblemen"; "plentie" to "plenty."

22. Higginson, *New England's Plantation,* no page numbers.

23. William Cronon, *Changes in the Land: Indians, Colonists, and the Ecology of New England* (New York: Hill & Wang, 1983), 33.

24. Colin G. Calloway, *New Worlds for All: Indians, Europeans, and the Remaking of Early America* (Baltimore, MD: Johns Hopkins University Press, 1998), 15.

25. Calloway, *New Worlds for All,* 15.

26. Carolyn Merchant, *Ecological Revolutions: Nature, Gender, and Science in New England,* 2nd ed. (Chapel Hill: University of North Carolina Press, 2010), 66–67.

27. Cronon, *Changes in the Land,* 80.

28. James Axtell, *The Invasion Within: The Contest of Cultures in Colonial North America* (New York: Oxford University Press, 1985), 36–39.

29. Everett Emerson, foreword, in *Letters from New England: The Massachusetts Bay Colony, 1629–1638,* ed. Everett Emerson (Amherst: University of Massachusetts Press, 1976), xiii.

30. Salisbury, *Manitou and Providence,* 216.

31. Russell R. Menard, "British Migration to the Chesapeake Colonies in the Seventeenth Century," in *Colonial Chesapeake Society,* ed. Lois Green Carr, Philip D. Morgan, and Jean B. Russo (Chapel Hill: University of North Carolina Press, 1988), 102.

32. "Leift Lion Gardener His Relation of the Pequot Warres," in *Collections of the Massachusetts Historical Society,* 3rd series, vol. 3 (Cambridge, MA: E. W. Metcalf, 1833), 154. I revise "turkies" to "turkeys."

33. "Leift Lion Gardener," 154.

34. Barbara Arneil, *John Locke and America: The Defence of English Colonialism* (Oxford: Oxford University Press, 1996), 76.

35. Arneil, *John Locke and America,* 75.

36. Richard Eburne, *A Plain Pathway to Plantations,* ed. Louis B. Wright (Ithaca, NY: Cornell University Press, 1962), 7. This work was first published in 1624.

37. Eburne, *Plain Pathway,* 8.

38. Eburne, *Plain Pathway,* 7 and 13.

39. Eburne, *Plain Pathway,* 11.

40. Eburne, *Plain Pathway,* 12 and 44–45.

41. Christopher Levett, "A Voyage into New England," in *Christopher Levett of York: The Pioneer Colonist in Casco Bay,* ed. James Phinney Baxter (Portland, ME: Gorges Society, 1893), 119. I revise "doe" to "do"; "more then" to "more than"; "corne fields" to "cornfields"; "corne" to "corn"; "Deare" to "deer"; "leape" to "leap."

42. Eburne, *Plain Pathway,* 60.

43. John Donne, *A Sermon Preached to the Honourable Company of the Virginian Plantation* (London: Thomas Jones, 1622), 2 and 11.

44. "George Thorpe to Sir Edwin Sandys, 15 May 1621," in *The Records of the Virginia Company of London,* vol. 3, ed. Susan Myra Kingsbury (Washington, DC: United States Government Printing Office, 1933), 446. I revise "amongest us that doth soe much as afforde" to "amongst us that doth so much as afford"; "hart" to "heart"; "theire mouthes" to "their mouths"; "nothinge" to "nothing."

45. "George Thorpe to Sir Edwin Sandys," 446. I revise "bee" to "be"; "wronge" to "wrong"; "soe" to "so"; "beinge" to "being"; "espetiallye" to "especially"; "peaceable & vertuous" to "peaceable and virtuous."

46. Edmund S. Morgan, *American Slavery, American Freedom: The Ordeal of Colonial Virginia* (New York: W. W. Norton, 2003), 98–99.

47. Morgan, *American Slavery, American Freedom*, 100.

48. Morgan, *American Slavery, American Freedom*, 100.

49. Francis Wyatt, "Letter of Sir Francis Wyatt, Governor of Virginia, 1621–1626," *William and Mary Quarterly* 6, no. 2 (April 1926): 114–21.

50. Alfred A. Cave, *The Pequot War* (Amherst: University of Massachusetts Press, 1996), 151.

51. Cave, *Pequot War*, 151.

52. John Underhill, *Newes from America; Or, A New and Experimentall Discoverie of New England: Containing, A True Relation of Their War-Like Proceedings These Two Yeares Last Past, with a Figure of the Indian Fort, or Palizado* (London: Peter Cole, 1638), 36. I revise "some-time the case alters" to "sometimes the case alters."

53. Underhill, *Newes from America*, 38. I revise "slaies" to "slays." Italics in original.

54. Cave, *Pequot War*, 2 and 158–59.

55. Jack Brubaker, *Massacre of the Conestogas: On the Trail of the Paxton Boys in Lancaster County* (Charleston, SC: History Press, 2010), 23.

56. Brubaker, *Massacre of the Conestogas*, 114.

57. Robert Proud, *The History of Pennsylvania in North America*, vol. 2 (Philadelphia: Zachariah Poulson Jr., 1798), 326–27.

58. Proud, *History of Pennsylvania*, 328, and Brubaker, *Massacre of the Conestogas*, 69–74.

59. Colin G. Calloway, *The Scratch of a Pen: 1763 and the Transformation of North America* (New York: Oxford University Press, 2006), 78–79.

60. Karen Ordahl Kupperman, *The Jamestown Project* (Cambridge, MA: Harvard University Press, 2008), 230. I revise "availl" to "avail"; "food." to "food?"; "warre" to "war."

61. Theda Perdue, introduction, in *Cherokee Editor: The Writings of Elias Boudinot*, ed. Theda Perdue (Athens: University of Georgia Press, 1996), 7.

62. Theresa Strouth Gaul, introduction, in *To Marry an Indian: The Marriage of Harriett Gold and Elias Boudinot in Letters, 1823–1839*, ed. Theresa Strouth Gaul (Chapel Hill: University of North Carolina Press, 2005), 4.

63. "Foreign Mission School: Letter to the Editor, from a Minister of the Gospel from the South, on a Visit to the East," *Religious Remembrancer*, June 9, 1821. Italics in original.

64. Perdue, introduction, in *Cherokee Editor*, 7–8.

65. Gaul, introduction, in *To Marry an Indian*, 8–9. I revise "heart rending pan" to "heart-rending pang." Italics in original. The surname "Northrup" was also spelled "Northrop."

66. Andrew, *From Revivals to Removal*, 135–36.

67. "Cornelius Everest to Stephen Gold, 2 July 1825," in Gaul, *To Marry an Indian*, 103–4. I revise "& neighboring" to "and neighboring."

68. Gaul, *To Marry an Indian*, 14.

69. Gaul, *To Marry an Indian*, 17. I revise "to us & a desire" to "to us and a desire"; "They can not suppose" to "They cannot suppose"; "If they loved us how could they treat us in this manner." to "If they loved us, how could they treat us in this manner?"; "Baptists, Methodist & Presbeterian churches" to "Baptist, Methodist, and Presbyterian churches."

70. Gaul, *To Marry an Indian*, 18. I revise "dear br. Boudinot" to "dear brother Boudinot." Emphases in original.

71. Andrew, *From Revivals to Removal*, 136.

72. Theda Perdue, "Georgia Policy," in *The Cherokee Removal: A Brief History with Documents*, 3rd ed., ed. Theda Perdue and Michael D. Green (Boston and New York: Bedford/St. Martin's, 2016), 72–73.

73. See *A Map of That Part of Georgia Occupied by the Cherokee Indians, Taken from an Actual Survey Made during the Present Year 1831, in Pursuance of an Act of the General Assembly of the State* (Milledgeville, GA: John Bethune, 1831).

74. Claudio Saunt, *Unworthy Republic: The Dispossession of Native Americans and the Road to Indian Territory* (New York: W. W. Norton, 2020), xiii–xiv. Saunt cites the Massachusetts representative Edward Everett for the phrase "soft word," as Everett himself criticized "removal" as a "soft word" when opposing the Indian Removal Act on the floor of the US House of Representatives in 1830.

75. "Elias and Harriett Gold Boudinot to Herman and Flora Gold Vaill, 1 July 1831," in Gaul, *To Marry an Indian*, 177. I revise "work & the sufferings" to "work and the sufferings."

76. Elias Boudinot, *An Address to the Whites: Delivered in the First Presbyterian Church, on the 26th of May, 1826* (Philadelphia: William F. Geddes, 1826), 3 and 16. Italics in original.

77. John Ridge, "Letter to Albert Gallatin, February 27, 1826," in Perdue and Green, *Cherokee Removal*, 34–35. I revise "Half breeds and full Indians" to "[biracial] and full Indians."

78. Boudinot, *An Address to the Whites*, 15.

79. Andrew, *From Revivals to Removal*, 179–80 and 222–34.

80. Evarts, "Essays on the Present Crisis in the Condition of the American Indians (1829)," 175 and 177. I revise "neither savages, nor criminals" to "neither savages nor criminals" and "fellow-citizens" to "fellow citizens."

81. Evarts, "Essays on the Present Crisis," 195.

82. Andrew, *From Revivals to Removal*, 225. I revise "an humble missionary" to "a humble missionary."

83. Catharine E. Beecher, *Educational Reminiscences and Suggestions* (New York: J. B. Ford, 1874), 62.

84. Saunt, *Unworthy Republic*, 65.

85. "Harriett Gold Boudinot to Herman and Flora Gold Vaill, 29 March 1832," in Gaul, *To Marry an Indian*, 180. I revise "usual, & that" to "usual, and that"; "E learns" to "Eleanor learns"; "Indeed I" to "Indeed, I"; "families, & how" to "families, and how." Emphases in original.

86. William G. McLoughlin, *Cherokees and Missionaries, 1789–1839* (New Haven, CT: Yale University Press, 1984), 35–36.

87. "Elias Boudinot to Benjamin and Eleanor Gold, 16 August 1836," in Gaul, *To Marry an Indian*, 185.

88. Jeremiah Evarts, "Contingent Prospects of Our Country," *The Spirit of the Pilgrims*, April 1831, 181 and 185. I revise "dependant" to "dependent." Italics in original

Chapter 4: "And the Mantle of Prejudice Torn from Every American Heart"

1. Virginia Bernhard, *Slaves and Slaveholders in Bermuda, 1616–1782* (Columbia: University of Missouri Press, 1999), 56.

2. Drew Lopenzina, *Through an Indian's Looking Glass: A Cultural Biography of William Apess, Pequot* (Amherst: University of Massachusetts Press, 2017), 35.

3. John Mason, "A Brief History of Pequot War," in Charles Orr, *History of the Pequot War: The Contemporary Accounts of Mason, Underhill, Vincent, and Gardener*, ed. Charles Orr (Cleveland: Helman-Taylor, 1897), 35.

4. Barry O'Connell, introduction, in *On Our Own Ground: The Complete Writings of William Apess, a Pequot*, ed. Barry O'Connell (Amherst: University of Massachusetts Press, 1992), xxv. I revise "Amalech" to "Amalek."

5. William Apess, *A Son of the Forest: The Experience of William Apes, A Native of the Forest, Comprising a Notice of the Pequod Tribe of Indians* (New York: William Apess, 1829), 7.

6. Philip D. Gura, *The Life of William Apess, Pequot* (Chapel Hill: University of North Carolina Press, 2015), xv.

7. William Apess, "Indian Nullification of the Unconstitutional Laws of Massachusetts Relative to the Marshpee Tribe; or, The Pretended Riot Explained (1835)," in O'Connell, *On Our Own Ground*, 210–11. This document is a compilation of articles and essays that Apess initially wrote in 1833 and 1834.

8. Apess, "Indian Nullification of the Unconstitutional Laws," 211.

9. Apess, *Son of the Forest*, 14–15.

10. Apess, *Son of the Forest*, 16. See also Gura, *Life of William Apess*, 9–12, and Lopenzina, *Through an Indian's Looking Glass*, 62–63.

11. Apess, *Son of the Forest*, 25.

12. Apess, *Son of the Forest*, 27.

13. Apess, *Son of the Forest*, 40–41.

14. William Apess, "The Indians—The Ten Lost Tribes," *The Monthly Repository and Library of Entertaining Knowledge* 1, no. 3 (August 1830): 64. See also Lopenzina, *Through an Indian's Looking Glass*, 178.

15. William Apess, "The Experiences of Five Christian Indians of the Pequot Tribe (1833)," in O'Connell, *On Our Own Ground*, 157.

16. Apess, "Experiences of Five Christian Indians," 160–61.

17. Michael C. Coleman, *Presbyterian Missionary Attitudes toward American Indians* (Jackson: University Press of Mississippi, 1985), 181.

18. John C. Lowrie, *Missionary Papers* (New York: Robert Carter & Brothers, 1882), 102–4.

19. Samuel Kirkland, "A Journal of the Rev. Samuel Kirkland, April 7, 1765," in *The Journals of Samuel Kirkland: 18th-Century Missionary to the Iroquois, Government Agent, Father of Hamilton College*, ed. Walter Pilkington (Clinton, NY: Hamilton College, 1980), 23–24. I revise "nation & revere" to "nation and revere"; "customs & practices" to "customs and practices"; "white peoples Book" to "white people's Book." See also Carla Cevasco, *Violent Appetites: Hunger in the Early Northeast* (New Haven, CT: Yale University Press, 2022), 54–55.

20. "Red-Jacket—Speech to a Missionary," in Samuel G. Drake, *The Book of the Indians; or, Biography and History of the Indians of North America, from Its First Discovery to the Year 1841, Book V* (Boston: Antiquarian Bookstore, 1841), 98–100. I revise "a religion which was given" to "a religion, which was given."

21. Anonymous [Thomas Shepard?], "The Day-Breaking, If Not the Sun-Rising of the Gospell with the Indians in New England (1647)," in *The Eliot Tracts: With Letters from John Eliot to Thomas Thorowgood and Richard Baxter*, ed. Michael P. Clark (Westport, CT: Praeger, 2003), 93. Richard W. Cogley maintains that Thomas Shepard is the author of this document as well as another document, "The Clear Sun-Shine of the Gospel Breaking Forth upon the Indians in New-England (1648)," in which Shepard's authorship is certain. See Michael P. Clark, introduction, *The Eliot Tracts*, 31 and 46.

22. Anonymous [Thomas Shepard?], "Day-Breaking," 93.

23. Kristina Bross, *Dry Bones and Indian Sermons: Praying Indians in Colonial America* (Ithaca, NY: Cornell University Press, 2004), 22–23.

24. Anonymous [Thomas Shepard?], "Day-Breaking," 97–98.

25. Henry W. Bowden and James P. Ronda, introduction, in *John Eliot's Indian Dialogues: A Study in Cultural Interaction*, ed. Henry W. Bowden and James P. Ronda (Westport, CT: Greenwood Press, 1980), 40.

26. Jean M. O'Brien, *Dispossession by Degrees: Indian Land and Identity in Natick, Massachusetts, 1650–1790* (Cambridge and New York: Cambridge University Press, 1997), 52.

27. O'Brien, *Dispossession by Degrees*, 52–53.

28. Bross, *Dry Bones and Indian Sermons*, 153.

29. O'Brien, *Dispossession by Degrees*, 12.

30. O'Brien, *Dispossession by Degrees*, 33.

31. Rachel Wheeler, *To Live upon Hope: Mohicans and Missionaries in the Eighteenth-Century Northeast* (Ithaca, NY: Cornell University Press, 2008), 32.

32. William Kellaway, *The New England Company, 1649–1776: Missionary Society to the American Indians* (New York: Barnes & Noble, 1962), 269. I revise "Incouragement" to "Encouragement."

33. Wheeler, *To Live upon Hope*, 35–36 and 56–57. I revise "appear'd" to "appeared" and "liv'd" to "lived."

34. Jonathan Edwards, "To the Reverend Isaac Hollis, Summer 1751," in *The Works of Jonathan Edwards*, vol. 16, *Letters and Personal Writings*, ed. George S. Claghorn (New Haven, CT: Yale University Press, 1998), 389.

35. In his farewell sermon to the congregation in Northampton, Jonathan Edwards imagined a scene in which he and the congregation were reunited before the throne of God on the judgment day. While Edwards could confidently testify to his indefatigable preaching, teaching, and spiritual care of souls, he wondered aloud what God would think of the congregation's harsh treatment (in Edwards's estimation) of its pastor. See George M. Marsden, *Jonathan Edwards: A Life* (New Haven, CT: Yale University Press, 2003), 362.

36. Wilson H. Kimnach, Kenneth P. Minkema, and Douglas A. Sweeney, editors' introduction, in *The Sermons of Jonathan Edwards: A Reader* (New Haven, CT: Yale University Press, 1999), xxxv, and Marsden, *Jonathan Edwards: A Life*, 392–93.

37. Wheeler, *To Live upon Hope*, 214–15.

38. Wheeler, *To Live upon Hope*, 216.

39. Wheeler, *To Live upon Hope*, 216–17.

40. Jonathan Edwards, "He That Believeth Shall Be Saved (1751)," in Kimnach, Minkema, and Sweeney, *The Sermons of Jonathan Edwards*, 112–13.

41. Edwards, "He That Believeth Shall Be Saved," 114.

42. William B. Hart, *"For the Good of Their Souls": Performing Christianity in Eighteenth-Century Mohawk Country* (Amherst and Boston: University of Massachusetts Press, 2020), 28. I revise "& establish Traffick" to "and establish traffic" and "coat & not" to "coat and not."

43. Edwards, "To the Mohawks at the Treaty, August 16, 1751," in Kimnach, Minkema, and Sweeney, *Sermons of Jonathan Edwards*, 107–8.

44. Edwards, "To Joseph Paice, February 24, 1751/2," in Claghorn, *Letters and Personal Writings*, 436–37. Between 1582 and 1752, two different calendars were in use in Europe. One calendar, known as the Julian calendar, observed the first day of a new year on March 25. Another calendar, known as the Gregorian calendar, established January 1 as the first day of a new year. English persons at home and abroad therefore included both calendar years with a slash mark for dates falling between January 1 and March 25. Edwards therefore wrote February 24, 1751/2 in this letter.

45. Edwards, "To the Reverend William McCulloch, April 10, 1756," in Claghorn, *Letters and Personal Writings*, 686.
46. Kirkland, "A Journal of the Rev. Samuel Kirkland, June 10, 1774," 94. I revise "prudent & necessary" to "prudent and necessary" and "condesind" to "condescend."
47. Peter Kalm, *The America of 1750: Peter Kalm's Travels in North America, the English Version of 1770*, vol. 2, ed. Adolph B. Benson (New York: Dover Publications, 1966), 347. This work was first published in 1753. The author is known as Pehr Kalm and Peter Kalm.
48. Richard White, *The Middle Ground: Indians, Empires, and Republics in the Great Lakes Region, 1650–1815*, 2nd ed. (Cambridge and New York: Cambridge University Press, 2010), 50 and 52.
49. White, *Middle Ground*, 60.
50. White, *Middle Ground*, 256. I revise "presents, & pay" to "presents, and pay."
51. White, *Middle Ground*, 257–58.
52. White, *Middle Ground*, 268. I revise "Cloathing" to "clothing" and "uneasey" to "uneasy."
53. Tracy Neal Leavelle, "The Catholic Rosary, Gendered Practice, and Female Power in French-Indian Spiritual Encounters," in *Native Americans, Christianity, and the Reshaping of the American Religious Landscape*, ed. Joel W. Martin and Mark A. Nicholas (Chapel Hill: University of North Carolina Press, 2010), 159–61.
54. Leavelle, "Catholic Rosary," 170–71.
55. Jill Lepore, *In the Name of War: King Philip's War and the Origins of American Identity* (New York: Vintage Books, 1999), 28–36.
56. Drew Lopenzina, *Red Ink: Native Americans Picking Up the Pen in the Colonial Period* (Albany: State University of New York Press, 2012), 174, and David J. Silverman, *This Land Is Their Land: The Wampanoag Indians, Plymouth Colony, and the Troubled History of Thanksgiving* (New York: Bloomsbury, 2019), 324.
57. Heather Miyano Kopelson, *Faithful Bodies: Performing Religion and Race in the Puritan Atlantic* (New York: New York University Press, 2014), 57–59.
58. Kopelson, *Faithful Bodies*, 79.
59. Samuel Sewall, "Samuel Sewall to Sir William Ashhurst, May 3, 1700," in *Collections of the Massachusetts Historical Society*, 6th series, vol. 1 (Boston: Massachusetts Historical Society, 1886), 232–33. I revise "crouded" to "crowded."
60. Robert Dale Parker, "Introduction: The World and Writings of Jane Johnston Schoolcraft," in *The Sound the Stars Make Rushing through the Sky: The Writings of Jane Johnston Schoolcraft*, ed. Robert Dale Parker (Philadelphia: University of Pennsylvania Press, 2007), 1–6.
61. Jane Johnston Schoolcraft, "The Contrast, a Splenetic Effusion, March 1823," and "The Contrast," in Parker, *The Sound the Stars Make*, 116–18. See also Parker, "Introduction: The World and Writings of Jane Johnston Schoolcraft," 52–54.
62. Jane Johnston Schoolcraft, "Lines Written at Castle Island, Lake Superior," in Parker, *The Sound the Stars Make*, 92.
63. Helen Hunt Jackson, *A Century of Dishonor: A Sketch of the United States Government's Dealings with Some of the Indian Tribes* (New York: Harper & Brothers, 1881), 341–42.
64. Colin G. Calloway, *The Scratch of a Pen: 1763 and the Transformation of North America* (New York: Oxford University Press, 2006), 92–93.
65. Wayland F. Dunaway, *The Scotch-Irish of Colonial Pennsylvania* (Hamden and London: Archon Books, 1962), 75.
66. Dunaway, *Scotch-Irish of Colonial Pennsylvania*, 144.

67. William H. Egle, *An Illustrated History of the Commonwealth of Pennsylvania, Civil, Political, and Military* (Harrisburg, PA: De Witt C. Goodrich, 1876), 794. See also Dunaway, *The Scotch-Irish of Colonial Pennsylvania*, 85–88.

68. White, *Middle Ground*, 340.

69. John Styles, *The Life of David Brainerd, Missionary to the Indians, with an Abridgment of His Diary and Journal*, 2nd ed. (London: F. Westley, 1820), 65 and 122.

70. Pilkington, "Biographical Note," in Pilkington, *The Journals of Samuel Kirkland*, 120–22, and Samantha Seeley, *Race, Removal, and the Right to Remain: Migration and the Making of the United States* (Williamsburg, VA: Omohundro Institute of Early American History and Culture and Chapel Hill: University of North Carolina Press, 2021), 74–76.

71. Mark Puls, *Henry Knox: Visionary General of the American Revolution* (New York: Palgrave Macmillan, 2008), 1–2.

72. White, *Middle Ground*, 416.

73. Henry Knox, "Enclosure: Report on Indian Affairs, 29 December 1794," *Founders Online*, National Archives, https://founders.archives.gov/documents/Washington/05-17-02 -0223-0002.

74. Emer de Vattel, *Le Droit des Gens, ou Principes de la Loi Naturelle, Appliqués à la Conduite et aux Affaires des Nations et des Souverains*, vol. 1 (Washington: Carnegie Institution, 1916), 79. This work is a reproduction of the original French version from 1758. An English translation was first published in 1760. See also Gustavo Gozzi, *Rights and Civilizations: A History and Philosophy of International Law*, trans. Filippo Valente (Cambridge and New York: Cambridge University Press, 2019), 70.

75. Puls, *Henry Knox*, 206–9, and White, *Middle Ground*, 416–17.

76. White, *Middle Ground*, 384.

77. Henry Knox, "Enclosure: Report on Indian Affairs, 29 December 1794," *Founders Online*, National Archives.

78. Solomon Stoddard, *Question: Whether God Is Not Angry with the Country for Doing So Little towards the Conversion of the Indians?* (Boston: B. Green, 1723), 9–10.

79. Coleman, *Presbyterian Missionary Attitudes*, 43.

80. William G. McLoughlin, *Cherokees and Missionaries, 1789–1839* (New Haven, CT: Yale University Press, 1984), 319–27.

81. George A. Schultz, *An Indian Canaan: Isaac McCoy and the Vision of an Indian State* (Norman: University of Oklahoma Press, 1972), 4.

82. William G. McLoughlin, *Champions of the Cherokees: Evan and John B. Jones* (Princeton, NJ: Princeton University Press, 1990), 95.

83. McLoughlin, *Champions of the Cherokees*, 123–34.

84. Schultz, *Indian Canaan*, 64.

85. Isaac McCoy, *Remarks on the Practicability of Indian Reform* (Boston: Lincoln & Edmands, 1827), 4.

86. McCoy, *Remarks on the Practicability of Indian Reform*, 10. Italics in original.

87. McCoy, *Remarks on the Practicability of Indian Reform*, 11. Italics in original.

88. McCoy, *Remarks on the Practicability of Indian Reform*, 46.

89. Wilson Lumpkin, *The Removal of the Cherokee Indians from Georgia*, vol. 1 (New York: Dodd, Mead, & Company, 1907), 64–66.

90. Schultz, *Indian Canaan*, 194.

91. Isaac McCoy, *History of Baptist Indian Missions: Embracing Remarks on the Former and Present Condition of the Aboriginal Tribes; Their Settlement within the Indian Territory, and Their Future Prospects* (Washington: William M. Morrison, 1840), 582.

92. Schultz, *Indian Canaan*, 195.

93. *A Vindication of the Cherokee Claims, Addressed to the Town Meeting in Philadelphia, on the 11th of January, 1830* (n.p.), 8.

94. Lopenzina, *Through an Indian's Looking Glass*, 253.

95. William Apess, "Indian Nullification of the Unconstitutional Laws of Massachusetts Relative to the Marshpee Tribe; or, The Pretended Riot Explained (1835)," in O'Connell, *On Our Own Ground*, 205. I revise "Marshpee" to "Mashpee."

96. William Apess, "Eulogy on King Philip, as Pronounced at the Odeon, in Federal Street, Boston (1836)," in O'Connell, *On Our Own Ground*, 287 and 310.

Chapter 5: "Churches Dreaded Abolitionism"

1. William C. Beecher, Samuel Scoville, and Eunice White Beecher, *A Biography of Rev. Henry Ward Beecher* (New York: Charles L. Webster, 1888), 268.

2. Clifford E. Clark Jr., *Henry Ward Beecher: Spokesman for a Middle-Class America* (Urbana and Chicago: University of Illinois Press, 1978), 39.

3. Clark, *Henry Ward Beecher*, 40.

4. Paxton Hibben, *Henry Ward Beecher: An American Portrait* (New York: Press of the Readers Club, 1942), 67 and 79. This work was first published in 1927. Hibben disputes Eunice White Beecher's accounts of Henry Ward Beecher's annual salaries of $300 at First Presbyterian Church in Lawrenceburg and $600 at Second Presbyterian Church in Indianapolis.

5. John R. Howard, "Review of Mr. Beecher's Personality and Political Influence," in Henry Ward Beecher, *Patriotic Addresses in America and England, from 1850 to 1885, on Slavery, the Civil War, and the Development of Civil Liberty in the United States*, ed. John R. Howard (New York: Fords, Howard, & Hulbert, 1891), 47.

6. Leon F. Litwack, *North of Slavery: The Negro in the Free States, 1790–1860* (Chicago: University of Chicago Press, 1961), 70.

7. *Report of the Debates and Proceedings of the Convention for the Revision of the Constitution of the State of Indiana, 1850* (Indianapolis: A. H. Brown, 1850), 573. Italics in original.

8. Howard, "Review of Mr. Beecher's Personality," 49.

9. Clark, *Henry Ward Beecher*, 77.

10. Henry Ward Beecher, "American Slavery," in Howard, *Patriotic Addresses*, 179.

11. Beecher, "American Slavery," 180.

12. Beecher, Scoville, and Beecher, *A Biography of Rev. Henry Ward Beecher*, 247–48.

13. *Sixth Annual Report of the Executive Committee of the American Anti-Slavery Society, with the Speeches Delivered at the Anniversary Meeting Held in the City of New-York, on the 7th of May, 1839* (New York: William S. Dorr, 1839), 11.

14. Alvan Stewart, "Extracts from Speech before the General Assembly of the Presbyterian Church, Philadelphia, 1839," in *Writings and Speeches of Alvan Stewart on Slavery*, ed. Luther Rawson Marsh (New York: A. B. Burdick, 1860), 188. I revise "defence" to "defense."

15. David Hackett Fischer, *African Founders: How Enslaved People Expanded American Ideals* (New York: Simon & Schuster, 2022), 37–39, and Lorenzo Johnston Greene, *The Negro in Colonial New England* (New York: Atheneum, 1969), 16–17. Greene's work was first published in 1942.

16. John Josselyn, *John Josselyn, Colonial Traveler: A Critical Edition of Two Voyages to New-England*, ed. Paul J. Lindholdt (Hanover: University Press of New England, 1988), 24. I revise "perswasions" to "persuasions."

17. Josselyn, *John Josselyn*, 99. I revise "Christianitie" to "Christianity."

18. Fischer, *African Founders*, 38.

19. William H. Sumner, *A History of East Boston* (Boston: J. E. Tilton, 1858), 97.

20. Francis J. Bremer, *The Puritan Experiment: New England Society from Bradford to Edwards*, rev. ed. (Hanover: University Press of New England, 1995), 207.

21. Richard Baxter, *Baxter's Directions to Slave-holders Revived, First Printed in London, in the Year 1673, To Which Is Subjoined, A Letter from the Worthy Anthony Benezet* (Philadelphia: Francis Bailey, 1785), 6–7.

22. Fischer, *African Founders*, 53.

23. Sean M. Kelley, *American Slavers: Merchants, Mariners, and the Transatlantic Commerce in Captives, 1644–1865* (New Haven, CT: Yale University Press, 2023), 31.

24. Bremer, *The Puritan Experiment*, 207.

25. Samuel Sewall, *The Selling of Joseph: A Memorial* (Boston: Green & Allen, 1700), 1.

26. Sewall, *Selling of Joseph*, 1–3.

27. John Saffin, "A Brief and Candid Answer to a Late Printed Sheet, Entitled, The Selling of Joseph," in George H. Moore, *Notes on the History of Slavery in Massachusetts* (New York: D. Appleton, 1866), 253. This work was first published in 1701.

28. Sewall, *Selling of Joseph*, 2.

29. Saffin, "Brief and Candid Answer," 254.

30. Sewall, *Selling of Joseph*, 2. I revise "Color, & Hair" to "color, and hair."

31. Saffin, "Brief and Candid Answer," 252–53. I revise "Re imbursed out of the Publick Treasury" to "reimbursed out of the public treasury."

32. Saffin, "Brief and Candid Answer," 256. I revise "the Negroes character" to "the Negroes' character."

33. Zachary McLeod Hutchins, *Before Equiano: A Prehistory of the North American Slave Narrative* (Chapel Hill: University of North Carolina Press, 2022), 32–33.

34. Hutchins, *Before Equiano*, 36.

35. Greene, *Negro in Colonial New England*, 108.

36. Kelley, *American Slavers*, 119–20.

37. "Receipt for Slave Venus (1731)," in *A Jonathan Edwards Reader*, ed. John E. Smith, Harry S. Stout, and Kenneth P. Minkema (New Haven, CT: Yale University Press, 1995), 296.

38. Kenneth P. Minkema, "Jonathan Edwards's Defense of Slavery," *Massachusetts Historical Review* 4 (2002): 28 and 51.

39. George M. Marsden, *Jonathan Edwards: A Life* (New Haven, CT: Yale University Press, 2003), 1 and 255–58, and John Saillant, "Ministry to the Bound and Enslaved," in *The Oxford Handbook of Jonathan Edwards*, ed. Douglas A. Sweeney and Jan Stievermann (Oxford: Oxford University Press, 2021), 439–43.

40. David W. Kling and Douglas A. Sweeney, eds., *Jonathan Edwards at Home and Abroad: Historical Memories, Cultural Movements, Global Horizons* (Columbia: University of South Carolina Press, 2003), 325–30.

41. Charles E. Hambrick-Stowe, "All Things Were New and Astonishing: Edwardsian Piety, the New Divinity, and Race," in Kling and Sweeney, *Jonathan Edwards at Home and Abroad*, 122.

42. Jonathan Edwards, "Draft Letter on Slavery," in *The Works of Jonathan Edwards*, vol. 16, *Letters and Personal Writings*, ed. George S. Claghorn (New Haven, CT: Yale University Press, 1998), 72, and Kenneth P. Minkema, "Jonathan Edwards on Slavery and the Slave Trade," *The William and Mary Quarterly* 54, no. 4 (October 1997): 826.

43. Edwards, "Draft Letter on Slavery," 75, and Minkema, "Jonathan Edwards on Slavery and the Slave Trade," 827. I revise "winking at" to "winked at."

44. Minkema, "Jonathan Edwards's Defense of Slavery," 42.

45. Minkema, "Jonathan Edwards's Defense of Slavery," 42.

46. Sheryl A. Kujawa, "'The Path of Duty Plain': Samuel Hopkins, Sarah Osborn, and Revolutionary Newport," *Rhode Island History* 58, no. 3 (August 2000): 80. The author's current name is Sheryl A. Kujawa-Holbrook.

47. Joseph Conforti, "Samuel Hopkins and the Revolutionary Antislavery Movement," *Rhode Island History* 38, no. 2 (May 1979): 40.

48. Samuel Hopkins, "A Dialogue Concerning the Slavery of the Africans," in *The Works of Samuel Hopkins, D.D.*, vol. 2 (Boston: Doctrinal Tract and Book Society, 1852), 549.

49. Hopkins, "Dialogue Concerning the Slavery of the Africans," 551.

50. Hopkins, "Dialogue Concerning the Slavery of the Africans," 553–54.

51. Christy Clark-Pujara, *Dark Work: The Business of Slavery in Rhode Island* (New York: New York University Press, 2016), 4 and 19–21. In addition to sixty-two African captives, the *Adventure* obtained gold dust, palm oil, pepper, and rice.

52. Hopkins, "Dialogue Concerning the Slavery of the Africans," 554.

53. William Fox, *An Address to the People of Great Britain, Proving the Necessity of Refraining from Sugar and Rum, in Order to Abolish the African Slave Trade*, 3rd ed. (London: Phillips & Gurney, 1791), 9.

54. *Considerations; Addressed to Professors of Christianity, of Every Denomination, on the Impropriety of Consuming West-India Sugar & Rum, as Produced by the Oppressive Labour of Slaves*, 3rd ed. (Manchester: Wheeler, 1792), 2–4.

55. *No Rum! No Sugar! Or, The Voice of Blood, Being Half an Hour's Conversation between a Negro and an English Gentleman, Shewing the Horrible Nature of the Slave Trade, and Pointing Out an Easy and Effectual Method of Terminating It* (London: Wayland, 1792), 22.

56. Clark-Pujara, *Dark Work*, 19.

57. Samuel Hopkins, "The Slave Trade and Slavery," in *Works of Samuel Hopkins, D.D.*, vol. 2, 615.

58. Hopkins, "Dialogue Concerning the Slavery of the Africans," 571.

59. James MacSparran, *A Letter Book and Abstract of Our Services*, ed. Daniel Goodwin (Boston: Merrymount Press, 1899), 52. I revise "eno'" to "enough."

60. MacSparran, *Letter Book and Abstract*, 54–55.

61. MacSparran, *Letter Book and Abstract*, 78. Italics in original.

62. MacSparran, *Letter Book and Abstract*, 78–79.

63. "Rhode Island Heritage Hall of Fame: Rev. James MacSparran, Inducted 1998, Civil Leaders, Religion & Churches," https://riheritagehalloffame.com/rev-james-macsparran/.

64. "Sarah Osborn to Samuel Hopkins, July 29, 1769," in *Sarah Osborn's Collected Writings*, ed. Catherine A. Brekus (New Haven, CT: Yale University Press, 2017), 301. Hopkins was inducted into the Rhode Island Heritage Hall of Fame one year after James MacSparran in 1999. Osborn is not in the Rhode Island Heritage Hall of Fame.

65. Sarah Osborn, "The Employment and Society of Heaven," in Brekus, *Sarah Osborn's Collected Writings*, 328.

66. Hopkins, "Dialogue Concerning the Slavery of the Africans," 556.

67. Hopkins, "Dialogue Concerning the Slavery of the Africans," 556.

68. Hopkins, "Dialogue Concerning the Slavery of the Africans," 557.

69. Samuel Hopkins, "A Discourse upon the Slave Trade and the Slavery of the Africans," in *Works of Samuel Hopkins, D.D.*, vol. 2, 603.

70. Sarah Osborn, "April 14, 1767, Tuesday Morning," in Brekus, *Sarah Osborn's Collected Writings*, 283. I revise "O thou guide" to "O, thou guide."

71. Edwards A. Park, *Memoir of the Life and Character of Samuel Hopkins, D.D.*, 2nd ed. (Boston: Doctrinal Tract and Book Society, 1854), 157.

72. Conforti, "Samuel Hopkins and the Revolutionary Antislavery Movement," 40.

73. Kujawa, "'Path of Duty Plain,'" 85.

74. Saillant, "Ministry to the Bound and Enslaved," 440–43.

75. Hopkins, "Dialogue Concerning the Slavery of the Africans," 562.

76. Hopkins, "Dialogue Concerning the Slavery of the Africans," 562. I revise "every one else" to "everyone else."

77. Hopkins, "Dialogue Concerning the Slavery of the Africans," 567.

78. William Yoo, *What Kind of Christianity: A History of Slavery and Anti-Black Racism in the Presbyterian Church* (Louisville, KY: Westminster John Knox, 2022), 41.

79. Hopkins, "Dialogue Concerning the Slavery of the Africans," 567.

80. Helen MacLam, "Black Puritan on the Northern Frontier: The Vermont Ministry of Lemuel Haynes," in *Black Preacher to White America: The Collected Writings of Lemuel Haynes, 1774–1833*, ed. Richard Newman (Brooklyn, NY: Carlson, 1990), xix.

81. Timothy Mather Cooley, *Sketches of the Life and Character of the Rev. Lemuel Haynes* (New York: Harper & Brothers, 1837), 28. I revise "New-England" to "New England."

82. Cooley, *Sketches of the Life and Character*, 30.

83. Cooley, *Sketches of the Life and Character*, 48, and MacLam, "Black Puritan on the Northern Frontier," xx.

84. Lemuel Haynes, "Liberty Further Extended," in Newman, *Black Preacher to White America*, 17–21 and 23–24. I revise "Essencially" to "essentially"; "Lamantable" to "lamentable"; "vicious practises of those upon whome" to "vicious practices of those upon whom."

85. James P. Byrd and James Hudnut-Beumler, *The Story of Religion in America: An Introduction* (Louisville, KY: Westminster John Knox, 2021), 125.

86. Haynes, "The Character and Work of a Spiritual Watchman Described," in Newman, *Black Preacher to White America*, 49–50.

87. Haynes, "Dissimulation Illustrated," in Newman, *Black Preacher to White America*, 164–66. I revise "authority," to "authority?"

88. Samuel Hopkins, "Letter to Moses Brown, October 22, 1787," in *The Works of Samuel Hopkins, D.D.*, vol. 1 (Boston: Doctrinal Tract and Book Society, 1852), 158.

89. Samuel Hopkins, "The Slave Trade and Slavery," in *Works of Samuel Hopkins, D.D.*, vol. 2, 617–18.

90. Hopkins, "Dialogue Concerning the Slavery of the Africans," 573.

91. MacLam, "Black Puritan on the Northern Frontier," xxiii and xxxi–xxxiv.

92. MacLam, "Black Puritan on the Northern Frontier," xxxiv. Italics in original.

Chapter 6: "These Things Have Fired My Soul with a Holy Indignation"

1. Oliver Johnson, *William Lloyd Garrison and His Times; or, Sketches of the Anti-Slavery Movement in America, and of the Man Who Was Its Founder and Moral Leader* (Boston: B. B. Russell, 1879), 51–52.

2. William Lloyd Garrison, "To the Public," *The Liberator*, January 1, 1831.

3. Marilyn Richardson, introduction, in *Maria W. Stewart: America's First Black Woman Political Writer*, ed. Marilyn Richardson (Bloomington: Indiana University Press, 1987), 10–11.

4. Kristin Waters, *Maria W. Stewart and the Roots of Black Political Thought* (Jackson: University Press of Mississippi, 2022), 20.
5. Maria W. Stewart, "Religion and the Pure Principles of Morality, the Sure Foundation on Which We Must Build," in Richardson, *Maria W. Stewart: America's First Black Woman Political Writer*, 28.
6. Waters, *Maria W. Stewart and the Roots of Black Political Thought*, 45 and 49.
7. Stewart, "Lecture Delivered at the Franklin Hall," in Richardson, *Maria W. Stewart: America's First Black Woman Political Writer*, 46.
8. Maria W. Stewart, *Meditations from the Pen of Maria W. Stewart* (Washington: Maria W. Stewart, 1879), 36. This work was first published by William Lloyd Garrison and Isaac Knapp in 1832. In 1879, after receiving the long-delayed pension of her deceased husband, James W. Stewart, for his naval service, Maria W. Stewart immediately published a revised edition.
9. Stewart, *Meditations*, 41. I revise "whited sepulchres" to "whited sepulchers."
10. Stewart, *Meditations*, 36.
11. William Lloyd Garrison and Isaac Knapp, "For Sale at This Office," *The Liberator*, October 8, 1831.
12. Stewart, "Religion and the Pure Principles of Morality," 34–35.
13. Stephen Kendrick and Paul Kendrick, *Sarah's Long Walk: The Free Blacks of Boston and How Their Struggle for Equality Changed America* (Boston: Beacon, 2004), 21–22.
14. Stewart, "Religion and the Pure Principles of Morality," 39.
15. Stewart, "Cause for Encouragement," in Richardson, *Maria W. Stewart: America's First Black Woman Political Writer*, 43.
16. Stewart, "Religion and the Pure Principles of Morality," 29.
17. Richardson, preface, in Richardson, *Maria W. Stewart: America's First Black Woman Political Writer*, xiii–xiv, and Waters, *Maria W. Stewart and the Roots of Black Political Thought*, 227–28. Richardson contends that Stewart's lecture in Boston's Franklin Hall was the first political speech from a woman in US history. Waters maintains that it was one of the earliest rather than the very first of its kind.
18. Stewart, "Lecture Delivered at the Franklin Hall," in Richardson, *Maria W. Stewart: America's First Black Woman Political Writer*, 46–47.
19. Stewart, "An Address Delivered at the African Masonic Hall," in Richardson, *Maria W. Stewart: America's First Black Woman Political Writer*, 57.
20. Frederick Douglass, "American Slavery, American Religion, and the Free Church of Scotland: An Address Delivered in London, England, 22 May 1846," in *The Speeches of Frederick Douglass: A Critical Edition*, ed. John R. McKivigan, Julie Husband, and Heather L. Kaufman (New Haven, CT: Yale University Press, 2018), 19–23.
21. Stewart, "Lecture Delivered at the Franklin Hall," 45–47.
22. Stewart, "Address Delivered at the African Masonic Hall," 63.
23. Stewart, "Lecture Delivered at the Franklin Hall," 45.
24. Frederick Douglass, *Narrative of the Life of Frederick Douglass, an American Slave* (Boston: Anti-Slavery Office, 1845), 45. See also Daina Ramey Berry, *The Price for Their Pound of Flesh: The Value of the Enslaved, from Womb to Grave, in the Building of a Nation* (Boston: Beacon, 2017), 84–85.
25. Douglass, *Narrative*, 63.
26. Steve Luxenberg, *Separate: The Story of Plessy v. Ferguson, and America's Journey from Slavery to Segregation* (New York: W. W. Norton, 2019), 3 and 12–14.

27. Frederick Douglass, "A Nation in the Midst of a Nation: An Address Delivered in New York, New York, 11 May 1853," in McKivigan, Husband, and Kaufman, *Speeches of Frederick Douglass*, 98–100. I revise "them that are bound" to "them who are bound."

28. Richard Newman, Patrick Rael, and Philip Lapsansky, "James Forten," in *Pamphlets of Protest: An Anthology of Early African American Protest Literature, 1790–1860*, ed. Richard Newman, Patrick Rael, and Philip Lapsansky (New York: Routledge, 2001), 66, and Julie Winch, "'Onward, Onward, Is Indeed the Watchword': James Forten's Reflections on Revolutions and Liberty," in *Prophets of Protest: Reconsidering the History of American Abolitionism*, ed. Timothy Patrick McCarthy and John Stauffer (New York: New Press, 2006), 81–82.

29. Winch, "'Onward, Onward, Is Indeed the Watchword,'" 83.

30. James Forten, "Series of Letters by a Man of Colour," in Newman, Rael, and Lapsansky, *Pamphlets of Protest: An Anthology of Early African American Protest Literature*, 71–72.

31. Forten, "Series of Letters," 67–68. I revise "different species." to "different species?" and "same means." to "same means?"

32. Forten, "Series of Letters," 68–69. I revise "tyranize" to "tyrannize."

33. Forten, "Series of Letters," 68.

34. Gary B. Nash and Jean R. Soderlund, *Freedom by Degrees: Emancipation in Pennsylvania and Its Aftermath* (New York: Oxford University Press, 1991), 100–106. George Bryan worked with George Clymer, Robert Knox, and William Lewis to write the initial abolition bill.

35. Nash and Soderlund, *Freedom by Degrees*, 133.

36. Nash and Soderlund, *Freedom by Degrees*, 137.

37. "Germantown Friends' Protest against Slavery, 1688," in *Am I Not a Man and a Brother: The Antislavery Crusade of Revolutionary America, 1688–1788*, ed. Roger Bruns (New York: Chelsea House, 1983), 3–4. I revise "that we shall doe to all men" to "that we shall do to all men" and "that ye Quakers doe here handel men as they handel there ye cattle" to "that ye Quakers do here handle men as they handle there ye cattle."

38. Kathleen M. Brown, *Undoing Slavery: Bodies, Race, and Rights in the Age of Abolition* (Philadelphia: University of Pennsylvania Press, 2023), 22.

39. Forten, "Series of Letters," 69–70.

40. Luxenberg, *Separate: The Story of Plessy v. Ferguson*, 4.

41. Matthew Rebhorn, *Pioneer Performances: Staging the Frontier* (New York: Oxford University Press, 2012), 72.

42. Patrick Rael, *Black Identity and Black Protest in the Antebellum North* (Chapel Hill: University of North Carolina Press, 2001), 86.

43. Thomas Paine, "African Slavery in America," in *Life and Works of Thomas Paine*, vol. 2, ed. William M. Van der Weyde (New Rochelle, NY: Thomas Paine National Historical Association, 1925), 8.

44. Gary B. Nash, *Forging Freedom: The Formation of Philadelphia's Black Community, 1720–1840* (Cambridge, MA: Harvard University Press, 1988), 42.

45. Nash, *Forging Freedom*, 45.

46. Ira Berlin, *Generations of Captivity: A History of African-American Slaves* (Cambridge, MA: Harvard University Press, 2003), 105.

47. Berlin, *Generations of Captivity*, 106.

48. Nash, *Forging Freedom*, 85–86.

49. Leonard L. Richards, *"Gentlemen of Property and Standing": Anti-Abolition Mobs in Jacksonian America* (New York: Oxford University Press, 1970), 5.

50. Nash, *Forging Freedom*, 213.
51. Nash, *Forging Freedom*, 145.
52. Richard Allen, *The Life, Experience, and Gospel Labors of the Rt. Rev. Richard Allen* (Philadelphia: Ford & Riply, 1880), 14–15. This work was first published in 1833. I revise "in a body" to "as a body."
53. Richard S. Newman, *Freedom's Prophet: Bishop Richard Allen, the AME Church, and the Black Founding Fathers* (New York: New York University Press, 2008), 58–63.
54. Allen, *Life, Experience, and Gospel Labors*, 16.
55. Nash, *Forging Freedom*, 116.
56. Newman, *Freedom's Prophet*, 59.
57. Benjamin Rush, "To Jeremy Belknap, 21 June 1792," in *Letters of Benjamin Rush*, vol. 1, *1761–1792*, ed. L. H. Butterfield (Princeton, NJ: Princeton University Press, 1951), 620.
58. Nash, *Forging Freedom*, 119.
59. Rush, "To Jeremy Belknap," 620–21.
60. Samuel Hopkins, "A Dialogue Concerning the Slavery of the Africans," in *The Works of Samuel Hopkins, D.D.*, vol. 2 (Boston: Doctrinal Tract and Book Society, 1852), 594.
61. Raphael G. Warnock, *The Divided Mind of the Black Church: Theology, Piety, and Public Witness* (New York: New York University Press, 2013), 13.
62. Allen, *Life, Experience, and Gospel Labors*, 17–18.
63. Allen, *Life, Experience, and Gospel Labors*, 18 and 31.
64. Richard Allen, "Eulogy for Washington, December 29, 1799," in *Lift Every Voice: African American Oratory, 1787–1900*, ed. Philip S. Foner and Robert James Branham (Tuscaloosa: University of Alabama Press, 1998), 58.
65. Benjamin Rush, "To Mrs. Julia Rush, 22 August 1793," in *Letters of Benjamin Rush*, vol. 2, *1793–1813*, ed. L. H. Butterfield (Princeton, NJ: Princeton University Press, 1951), 639.
66. Rush, "To Mrs. Julia Rush," 639–40.
67. Nash, *Forging Freedom*, 177.
68. Nash, *Forging Freedom*, 6.
69. Archibald Alexander, *A History of Colonization on the Western Coast of Africa* (Philadelphia: William S. Martien, 1846), 20.
70. Samuel Eli Cornish and John Brown Russwurm, "Continued from No. 3," in *Freedom's Journal*, April 13, 1827.
71. David E. Swift, "Black Presbyterian Attacks on Racism: Samuel Cornish, Theodore Wright and Their Contemporaries," *Journal of Presbyterian History* 51, no. 4 (Winter 1973): 445–46.
72. Theodore S. Wright, "Rev. Theodore S. Wright, of New York," in *Proceedings of the New England Anti-Slavery Convention, Held in Boston, May 24, 25, 26, 1836* (Boston: Isaac Knapp, 1836), 48.
73. Wright, "Rev. Theodore S. Wright, of New York," 48–49.
74. Rael, *Black Identity and Black Protest*, 283.
75. Wright, "Rev. Theodore S. Wright, of New York," 49.
76. Rael, *Black Identity and Black Protest*, 283.
77. Richardson, introduction, in Richardson, *Maria W. Stewart: America's First Black Woman Political Writer*, 26–27.
78. Swift, "Black Presbyterian Attacks on Racism," 458.

Chapter 7: "It Is a Gospel Paradox"

1. William Lloyd Garrison, *An Address, Delivered before the Free People of Color, in Philadelphia, New-York and Other Cities, during the Month of June, 1831*, 3rd ed. (Boston: Stephen Foster, 1831), 3.
2. William E. Cain, "Introduction: William Lloyd Garrison and the Fight against Slavery," in *William Lloyd Garrison and the Fight against Slavery: Selections from* The Liberator, ed. William E. Cain (Boston and New York: Bedford, 1995), 7.
3. William Lloyd Garrison, *The "Infidelity" of Abolitionism* (New York: American Anti-Slavery Society, 1860), 4–7.
4. William Lloyd Garrison, "Remarks upon Mr. Ladd's Letters," *The Liberator*, November 23, 1838.
5. Garrison, *"Infidelity" of Abolitionism*, 3–4. I revise "social, political and religious" to "social, political, and religious."
6. William Lloyd Garrison, "The War—Its Cause and Cure," in Cain, *William Lloyd Garrison and the Fight against Slavery*, 164–67.
7. William Lee Miller, *Arguing about Slavery: The Great Battle in the United States Congress* (New York: Alfred A. Knopf, 1996), 10. The Abraham Lincoln Papers held at the Library of Congress include Lincoln's copies of William Lloyd Garrison's newspaper, *The Liberator*, from 1864. See List of Images for more information.
8. Miller, *Arguing about Slavery*, 9–10.
9. William Lloyd Garrison, *Thoughts on African Colonization* (Boston: Garrison & Knapp, 1832), 128–29.
10. Garrison, *"Infidelity" of Abolitionism*, 6.
11. Cain, *William Lloyd Garrison and the Fight against Slavery*, 36.
12. David Rice, *A Kentucky Protest against Slavery: Slavery Inconsistent with Justice and Good Policy* (New York: Samuel Wood, 1812), 3.
13. Frederick A. Ross, *Position of the Southern Church in Relation to Slavery* (New York: John A. Gray, 1857), 10–11.
14. Mitchell Snay, *Gospel of Disunion: Religion and Separation in the Antebellum South* (Chapel Hill: University of North Carolina Press, 1997), 63.
15. Snay, *Gospel of Disunion*, 61.
16. Richard Furman, *Rev. Dr. Furman's Exposition of the Views of the Baptists, Relative to the Coloured Population of the United States, in a Communication to the Governor of South-Carolina* (Charleston, SC: A. E. Miller, 1823), 9–10.
17. Furman, *Rev. Dr. Furman's Exposition*, 12.
18. James A. Rogers, *Richard Furman: Life and Legacy* (Macon, GA: Mercer University Press, 1985), 222.
19. Larry E. Tise, *Proslavery: A History of the Defense of Slavery in America, 1701–1840* (Athens: University of Georgia Press, 1987), 302.
20. Tise, *Proslavery*, 305. Italics in original.
21. Tise, *Proslavery*, xvii.
22. William Lloyd Garrison, "To the Public," *The Liberator*, January 1, 1831.
23. E. Brooks Holifield, *The Gentlemen Theologians: American Theology in Southern Culture* (Durham, NC: Duke University Press, 1978), 12.
24. Benjamin Drew, *The Refugee: Or the Narratives of Fugitive Slaves in Canada, Related by Themselves, with an Account of the History and Condition of the Colored Population of Upper Canada* (Boston: John P. Jewett, 1856), 30.

25. Drew Gilpin Faust, "Introduction to Thornton Stringfellow," in *Ideology of Slavery: Proslavery Thought in the Antebellum South, 1830–1860*, ed. Drew Gilpin Faust (Baton Rouge: Louisiana State University Press, 1981), 136–37.

26. Thornton Stringfellow, "A Brief Examination of Scripture Testimony on the Institution of Slavery," in Faust, *Ideology of Slavery*, 138–39.

27. James Henley Thornwell, "Relation of the Church to Slavery," in *The Collected Writings of James Henley Thornwell*, vol. 4, ed. John B. Adger and John L. Girardeau (Richmond, VA: Presbyterian Committee of Publication, 1873), 385.

28. Stringfellow, "A Brief Examination of Scripture Testimony," 139, 149, and 165.

29. Angelina Emily Grimké, "Appeal to the Christian Women of the South," in *The Public Years of Sarah and Angelina Grimké: Selected Writings, 1835–1839*, ed. Larry Ceplair (New York: Columbia University Press, 1989), 47–48.

30. Stringfellow, "Brief Examination of Scripture Testimony," 142–44.

31. Stringfellow, "Brief Examination of Scripture Testimony," 140.

32. Frederick A. Ross, *Slavery Ordained of God* (Philadelphia: J. B. Lippincott, 1857), 50.

33. Stringfellow, "Brief Examination of Scripture Testimony," 145, 150–55, and 164–65.

34. Stringfellow, "Brief Examination of Scripture Testimony," 165–66.

35. Stringfellow, "Brief Examination of Scripture Testimony," 162–64.

36. Donald G. Mathews, *Slavery and Methodism: A Chapter in American Morality, 1780–1845* (Princeton, NJ: Princeton University Press, 1965), 5–6.

37. John Wesley, *Thoughts upon Slavery*, 3rd ed. (London: Hawes, 1774), 18.

38. Mathews, *Slavery and Methodism*, 13.

39. Albert Raboteau, *Slave Religion: The "Invisible Institution" in the Antebellum South* (New York: Oxford University Press, 1978), 144.

40. Mathews, *Slavery and Methodism*, 23–29 and 302.

41. Methodists divided into regional denominations in 1844 after delegates at the General Conference refused to approve an enslaver as a bishop. Baptists from the Southern states separated in 1845 after a decision at the National Triennial Convention one year prior to deny the appointment of enslavers as missionaries. Presbyterians in their second largest denomination, the Presbyterian Church in the United States of America (New School), divided into regional ecclesial bodies over slavery in 1857. Presbyterians in their largest denomination, the Presbyterian Church in the United States of America (Old School), separated in 1861.

42. John Nelson Norwood, *The Schism in the Methodist Episcopal Church, 1844: A Study of Slavery and Ecclesiastical Politics* (Alfred, NY: Alfred Press, 1923), 35. See also C. C. Goen, *Broken Church, Broken Nation: Denominational Schisms and the Coming of the American Civil War* (Macon, GA: Mercer University Press, 1985), 80–81.

43. William Capers, "Report of the South Carolina Conference Missionary Society (1836)," in *The Methodist Experience in America: A Sourcebook*, vol. 2, ed. Russell E. Richey, Kenneth E. Rowe, and Jean Miller Schmidt (Nashville: Abingdon, 2000), 240.

44. Norwood, *Schism in the Methodist Episcopal Church*, 35–36.

45. John R. McKivigan and Mitchell Snay, "Introduction: Religion and the Problem of Slavery in Antebellum America," in *Religion and the Antebellum Debate over Slavery*, ed. John R. McKivigan and Mitchell Snay (Athens: University of Georgia Press, 1998), 12.

46. Goen, *Broken Church, Broken Nation*, 93, and McKivigan and Snay, *Religion and the Antebellum Debate over Slavery*, 12.

47. Albert Barnes, *An Inquiry into the Scriptural Views of Slavery* (Philadelphia: Perkins & Purves, 1846), 19–20.

48. Samuel J. May, *Some Recollections of Our Antislavery Conflict* (Boston: Fields, Osgood, 1869), 127.

49. Gerard O'Daly, *Augustine's* City of God, *A Reader's Guide,* 2nd ed. (Oxford: Oxford University Press, 2020), 28–56, and James Wetzel, introduction, in *Augustine's* City of God, *A Critical Guide,* ed. James Wetzel (New York: Cambridge University Press, 2012), 1–3.

50. Garrison, *The "Infidelity" of Abolitionism,* 10–11. I revise "down-trodden" to "downtrodden."

51. Moses Stuart, *Conscience and the Constitution, with Remarks on the Recent Speech of the Hon. Daniel Webster in the Senate of the United States on the Subject of Slavery* (Boston: Crocker & Brewster, 1850), 22.

52. Deborah Bingham Van Broekhoven, "Suffering with Slaveholders: The Limits of Francis Wayland's Antislavery Witness," in McKivigan and Snay, *Religion and the Antebellum Debate over Slavery,* 196–97.

53. John H. Giltner, *Moses Stuart: The Father of Biblical Science in America* (Atlanta: Scholars Press, 1988), 1–7 and 124–26. See also W. Andrew Hoffecker, "Stuart, Moses," in *American National Biography,* vol. 21, ed. John A. Garraty and Mark C. Carnes (New York: Oxford University Press, 1999), 79–80.

54. Stuart, *Conscience and the Constitution,* 7–8.

55. Stuart, *Conscience and the Constitution,* 25, 36, and 45. Italics in original.

56. Stuart, *Conscience and the Constitution,* 48.

57. *An Address to the Presbyterians of Kentucky, Proposing a Plan for the Instruction and Emancipation of Their Slaves, by a Committee of the Synod of Kentucky* (Newburyport, MA: Charles Whipple, 1836), 23–24. Italics in original.

58. Giltner, *Moses Stuart,* 126.

59. Giltner, *Moses Stuart,* 124.

60. Stuart, *Conscience and the Constitution,* 59 and 62.

61. Stuart, *Conscience and the Constitution,* 72.

62. Stuart, *Conscience and the Constitution,* 61. Italics in original.

63. Stuart, *Conscience and the Constitution,* 71.

64. Stuart, *Conscience and the Constitution,* 81. Italics in original.

65. Rufus W. Clark, *A Review of the Rev. Moses Stuart's Pamphlet on Slavery, Entitled Conscience and the Constitution* (Boston: C. C. P. Moody, 1850), 9–10 and 46–49.

66. Edward R. Crowther, "'Religion Has Something . . . to Do with Politics': Southern Evangelicals and the North, 1845–1860," in McKivigan and Snay, *Religion and the Antebellum Debate over Slavery,* 332.

67. Benjamin Morgan Palmer, *Slavery, a Divine Trust: The Duty of the South to Preserve and Perpetuate the Institution as It Now Exists* (New York: George F. Nesbitt, 1861), 9–11.

68. William G. Brownlow, *A Sermon on Slavery; A Vindication of the Methodist Church, South* (Knoxville, TN: Kinsloe & Rice, 1857), 14–15.

69. William G. Brownlow and Abram Pryne, *Ought American Slavery to Be Perpetuated?* (Philadelphia: J. P. Lippincott, 1858), 41. I revise "practising" to "practicing" and "door-keeper" to "doorkeeper."

70. David B. Chesebrough, *Clergy Dissent in the Old South, 1830–1865* (Carbondale and Edwardsville: Southern Illinois University Press, 1996), 54–56.

71. *Address to Christians throughout the World by the Clergy of the Confederate States of America* (London: James Nisbet, 1863), 11. Italics in original. Signatories include faculty and administrators from Columbia Theological Seminary (John B. Adger, George Howe, A. W. Leland, and James Woodrow), Davidson College (John L. Kirkpatrick), Duke University (Braxton

Craven), Erskine College (E. L. Patton), Hampden-Sydney College (John M. P. Atkinson), Mercer University (N. M. Crawford), Oglethorpe University (Samuel K. Talmage), Randolph-Macon College (William A. Smith), Roanoke College (David F. Bittle), Southern Baptist Theological Seminary (James P. Boyce, John A. Broadus, Basil Manly Jr., and William Williams), Union Theological Seminary in Virginia (Robert L. Dabney, Thomas E. Peck, and Benjamin M. Smith), and Wofford College (Albert M. Shipp).

72. William Lloyd Garrison, "Address to the American Colonization Society, July 4, 1829," in Cain, *William Lloyd Garrison and the Fight against Slavery*, 69.

73. Brownlow, *Sermon on Slavery; A Vindication of the Methodist Church, South*, 23–24.

74. Molliston Madison Clark, "M. M. Clark to Editor, London Patriot, 9 October 1846," in *The Black Abolitionist Papers*, vol. 1, *The British Isles, 1830–1865*, ed. C. Peter Ripley (Chapel Hill: University of North Carolina Press, 1985), 139. Italics in original.

75. James W. C. Pennington, "Speech by J. W. C. Pennington, Delivered at Salle de La Sainte Cecile, Paris, France, 24 August 1849," in *Black Abolitionist Papers*, vol. 1, *The British Isles, 1830–1865*, 157–59.

76. "Another Great Rejoicing," *The Liberator*, May 5, 1865.

77. "Another Great Rejoicing," *The Liberator*, May 5, 1865.

Chapter 8: The Church That Never Was (But Still Could Be)

1. Ernst Troeltsch, *Protestantism and Progress: A Historical Study of the Relation of Protestantism to the Modern World*, trans. W. Montgomery (New York: G. P. Putnam's Sons, 1912), 3.

2. Kermit Roosevelt III, *The Nation That Never Was: Reconstructing America's Story* (Chicago: University of Chicago Press, 2022), 8.

3. Roosevelt, *Nation That Never Was*, 35.

4. "Declaration of Independence: A Transcription, July 4, 1776," The US National Archives and Records Administration, https://www.archives.gov/founding-docs/declaration-transcript.

5. W. E. B. Du Bois, *Prayers for Dark People*, ed. Herbert Aptheker (Amherst: University of Massachusetts Press, 1980), 38.

6. Elizabeth Elkins Sanders, *Conversations Principally on the Aborigines of North America* (Salem, MA: W. & S. B. Ives, 1828), 83 and 140–45.

7. Frederick Douglass, *Narrative of the Life of Frederick Douglass, an American Slave* (Boston: Anti-Slavery Office, 1845), 118.

8. Justo L. González, *The Story of Christianity*, vol. 1, *The Early Church to the Dawn of Reformation*, rev. and updated (New York: HarperOne, 2010), 3.

9. George Lewis, *Impressions of America and the American Churches* (Edinburgh: W. P. Kennedy, 1845), 100.

10. William Yoo, *What Kind of Christianity: A History of Slavery and Anti-Black Racism in the Presbyterian Church* (Louisville, KY: Westminster John Knox, 2022), 147.

11. Frances Trollope, *Domestic Manners of the Americans*, 4th ed. (London: Whittaker, Treacher, & Co., 1832), 207. I revise "for ever" to "forever."

12. James Henley Thornwell, "Relation of the Church to Slavery," in *The Collected Writings of James Henley Thornwell*, vol. 4, ed. John B. Adger and John L. Girardeau (Richmond, VA: Presbyterian Committee of Publication, 1873), 382–83.

13. Shirley Chisholm, "The Relationship between Religion and Today's Social Issues," in *Can I Get a Witness? Prophetic Religious Voices of African American Women: An Anthology*, ed. Marcia Y. Riggs (Maryknoll, NY: Orbis, 1997), 185.

14. John Jay II, *Caste and Slavery in the American Church* (New York: Wiley & Putnam, 1843), 21.
15. E. C. Tracy, *Memoir of the Life of Jeremiah Evarts, Esq.* (Boston: Crocker & Brewster, 1845), 273.
16. Randy Woodley, *When Going to Church Is Sin: And Other Essays on Native American Christian Missions* (Scotland, PA: Healing the Land Publishers, 2007), 65–66 and 72.
17. Robert Tracy McKenzie, "Don't Forget the Church: Reflections on the Forgotten Dimension of Our Dual Calling," in *Confessing History: Explorations in Christian Faith and the Historian's Vocation*, ed. John Fea, Jay Green, and Eric Miller (Notre Dame, IN: University of Notre Dame Press, 2010), 294.
18. Roxanne Dunbar-Ortiz, *An Indigenous Peoples' History of the United States* (Boston: Beacon, 2014), 235.
19. Scott C. Williamson, *The Narrative Life: The Moral and Religious Thought of Frederick Douglass* (Macon, GA: Mercer University Press, 2002), x.
20. John H. Leith, *An Introduction to the Reformed Tradition: A Way of Being the Christian Community*, rev. ed. (Atlanta: John Knox, 1978), 7.
21. Robert Allen Warrior, "Canaanites, Cowboys, and Indians: Deliverance, Conquest, and Liberation Theology Today," *Christianity and Crisis*, September 11, 1989, 262 and 264.
22. C. S. Lewis, *The Four Loves* (London: Geoffrey Bles, 1960), 138.
23. Martin Luther King Jr., "Letter from Birmingham City Jail," in *American Religions: A Documentary History*, ed. R. Marie Griffith (New York: Oxford University Press, 2008), 511.

Index

www.ingramcontent.com/pod-product-compliance
Lightning Source LLC
Chambersburg PA
CBHW020826150125
20335CB00003B/8